Rachel Harrison

G•L•O•R•I•A

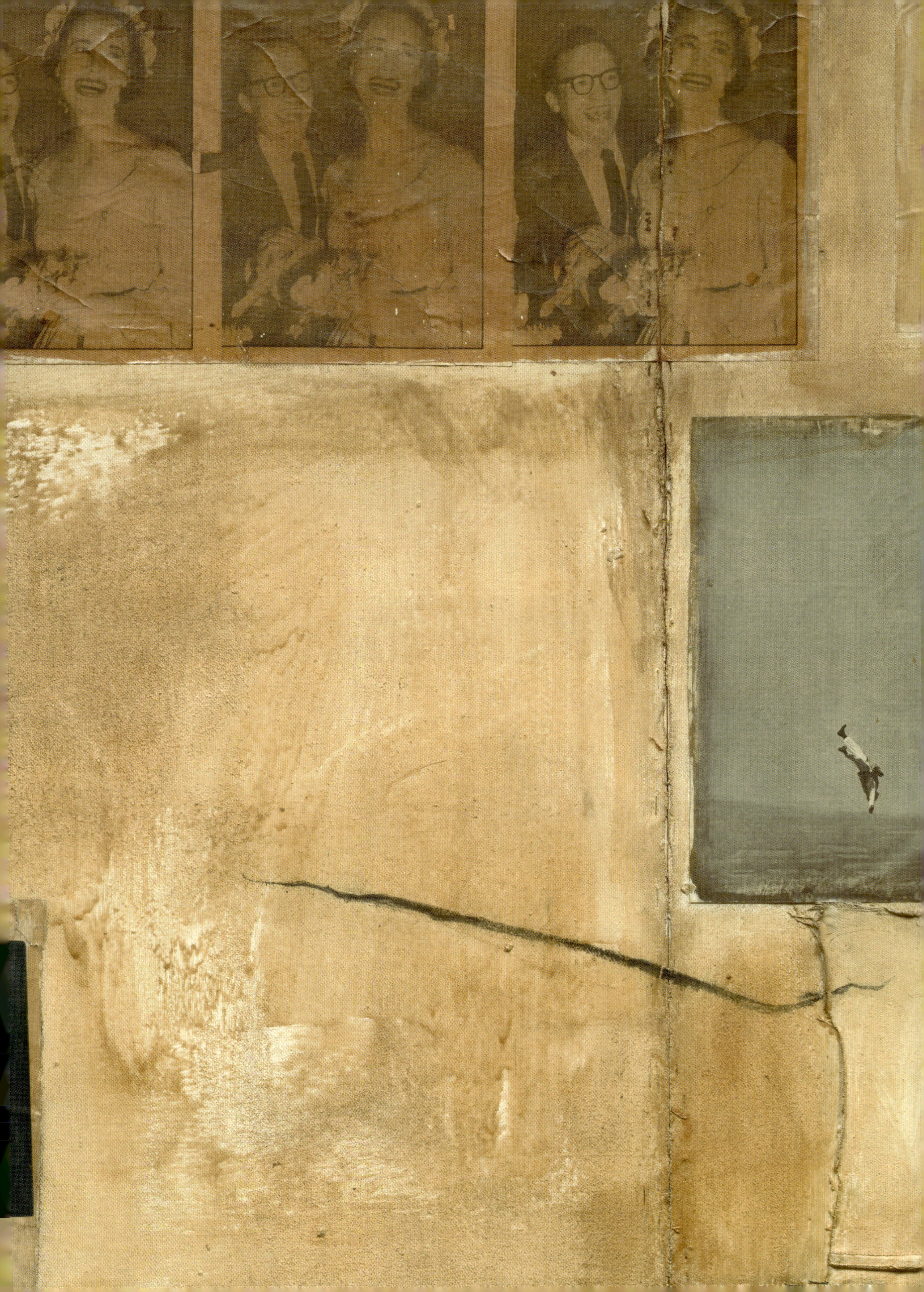

Rachel Harrison

G•L•O•R•I•A

The Cleveland Museum of Art
Distributed by Yale University Press, New Haven and London

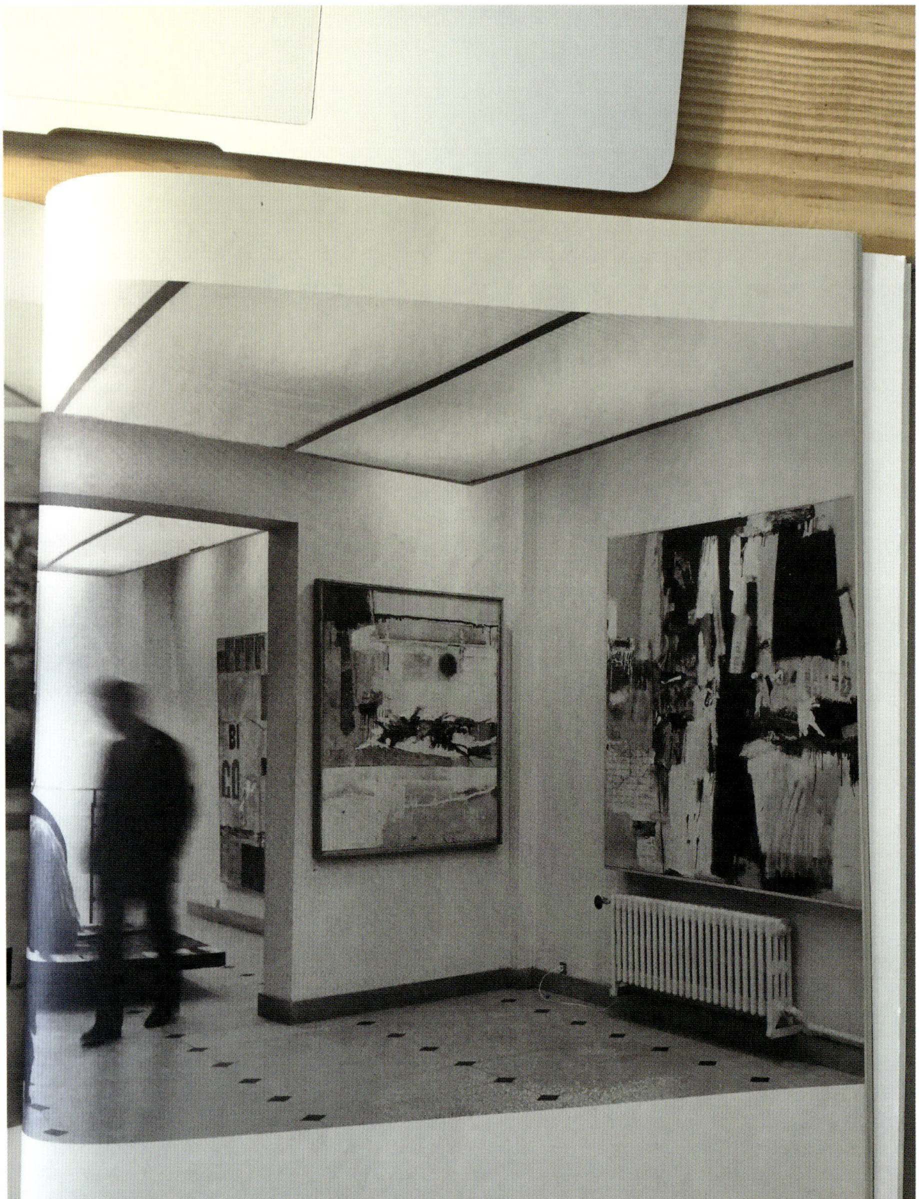

Contents

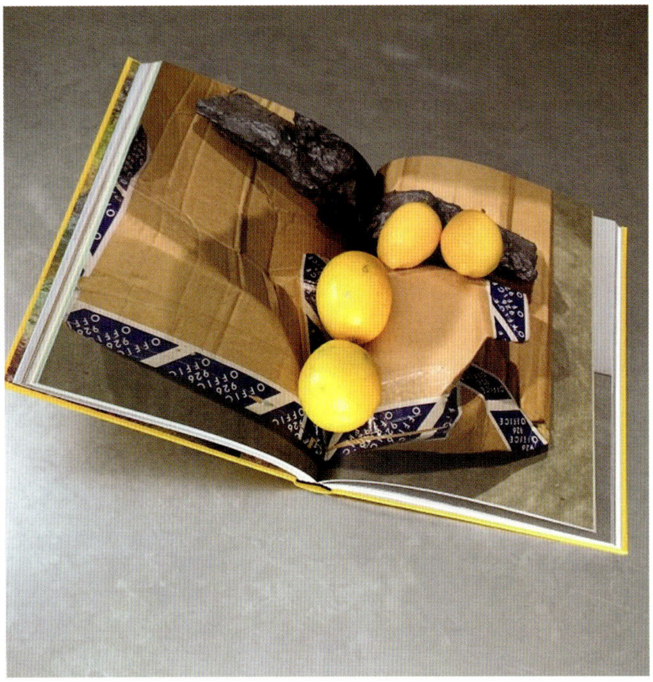

Adriana Farmiga (American, b. 1974). *Still Life w/ Rachel Harrison and Meyer Lemons (redux)*, 2013. Instagram photograph.

Foreword

The Cleveland Museum of Art opened its doors in 1916, and it soon became internationally renowned for the strength and quality of its acquisitions. While we are always looking forward, both in our programming and in our acquisitions, many of the objects in our collection originated long ago and have accrued new meanings over time. By approaching our historical holdings from a contemporary vantage point, we not only refresh and enhance an artwork's signification and importance, but also create new connections between the past, present, and future.

While the exhibition *Gloria: Robert Rauschenberg & Rachel Harrison* does just this, it also reflects the museum's newly invigorated commitment to contemporary art. This innovative project pairs the work of Robert Rauschenberg, one of the most influential American artists of the twentieth century, with that of Rachel Harrison, who has become known for an original practice that at once addresses and analyzes the conventions of artistic and mass culture. The exhibition takes its name from one of the highlights of the museum's collection, Rauschenberg's compelling *Gloria* (1956), a Combine that was featured in many of the artist's solo shows during the 1950s and 1960s. In 1966 the museum presciently acquired this masterpiece from the legendary New York gallerist Leo Castelli.

Beginning in the 1990s, Harrison earned international acclaim for her artwork, which takes on the chaos that is inseparable from existence in the twenty-first century. Harrison's keen attentiveness to the experiences of being alive and thinking about what it means to create art at this moment makes her an apt companion for Rauschenberg, who famously aimed to work within "the gap between art and life." The project of this exhibition, which is the first to compare these artists, is given added breadth and depth in this striking catalogue, *Rachel Harrison G·L·O·R·I·A*. Here, Assistant Curator of Contemporary Art Beau Rutland thoughtfully explores both the origins of *Gloria* and Harrison's relationship to Rauschenberg. Johanna Burton, the New Museum's Keith Haring Director and Curator of Education and Public Engagement, offers a lively and ingenious text that limns the role of symbiosis within Harrison's work. Amy Adler, the Emily Kempin Professor of Law at New York University School of Law, proves to be a deft interlocutor in her conversation with Harrison. We are especially thrilled with Harrison's unique contribution to this undertaking, which includes new digital collages that provide unprecedented insight into her creative process. In the section titled *Heir Fresheners*, she creatively documents the process of researching and preparing for a historical exhibition of this kind while also reckoning with her own creative output. It is immensely rewarding for the museum to work with a contemporary artist in this way, and I am most grateful for her time and effort. I would also like to acknowledge the Robert Rauschenberg Foundation, which offered vital support for this publication from its inception; Carol Greene and the staff of Greene Naftali, New York, for their support and unyielding assistance; and all those who generously lent works from their collections: Albright-Knox Art Gallery, Buffalo; Sascha S. Bauer; Agnes Gund and the Museum of Modern Art, New York; Scott J. Lorinsky; Susan and Michael Hort; and those who would like to remain anonymous. I hope readers and visitors enjoy the publication and exhibition, and I look forward to similarly thoughtful and highly collaborative undertakings in the future.

William M. Griswold
Sarah S. and Alexander M. Cutler Director
The Cleveland Museum of Art

Introduction

When I happened upon *Gloria*, a 1956 Combine by Robert Rauschenberg, shortly after arriving at the Cleveland Museum of Art, I was stunned. *Gloria* doesn't look or act its age. Despite its sixty years, it remains surprisingly striking because of the many ways it resonates with artwork being made today. Full of Rauschenberg's wry humor and sharp intellect, *Gloria* needed to be reintroduced to contemporary audiences. Its cultural references—including large images of millionairess Gloria Vanderbilt on her wedding day—range from the piquant to the open-ended and exist alongside completely self-aware brushstrokes; stuttering, repeated imagery; and a central void that reveals the wall that *Gloria* hangs upon. Given the work's unusual presence, it seemed that it would only be appropriate for its reemergence to be aided by a guide with an acute sensitivity to the twenty-first century. To my mind, Rachel Harrison, an acclaimed contemporary artist whose practice also blurs the boundaries of painting and sculpture, was that ideal navigator.

While a curious assortment of artists, ranging from Isa Genzken to David Hammons, comes to mind when considering how Rauschenberg's line of thought has been extended into the twenty-first century, his characteristic mélange of specificity and ambiguity is rarely approximated. Indeed, few today are as close to approaching the wit, criticality, and innovation of Rauschenberg's 1950s work as Harrison. Throughout her career, she has employed her medium-defiant artwork to explore life itself in every aspect, from pop and consumer culture to societal norms, religion, art history, and the amorphous nature of art. This exhibition attempts to view Rauschenberg's 1950s output through Harrison's eyes—or at least those of her abstract objects. The two have been brought together here for the first time.

The exhibition features *Gloria* as well as two other outstanding examples from the middle period of the Combine series, which Rauschenberg began around 1953 and ended in 1964. These are *Rhyme* (1956; Museum of Modern Art, New York), which in an early state was paired with the famed taxidermy goat of *Monogram* (1955–59; Moderna Museet, Stockholm), and *Painting with Red Letter S* (1957; Albright-Knox Gallery, Buffalo), whose square format, isolated painterly daubs, and matter-of-fact title mirror those of *Gloria*. The artist Jasper Johns once explained Rauschenberg's Combines not as a combination of painting and sculpture, but specifically as "painting playing the game of sculpture."[1] The inverse would aptly describe many of Harrison's works. Four of her sculptures are included in this exhibition, each of them exemplifying different aspects of her wide-ranging practice. Additionally, a small pairing of Rauschenberg's early photographs with drawings by Harrison reveals these artists' facility across media.

After I approached Harrison to see if she would be interested in working on a project using *Gloria* as a starting point, she mentioned that *that* Patti Smith song kept popping up in her mind. Though perhaps coincidental, such cultural references are also weightier than they originally appear in both Harrison and Rauschenberg's work. The mid-1970s punk-rock anthem is notable not only for launching Smith's music career, but also—and more significantly—for rattling the heteronormative foundations of the song that it triumphantly appropriates. The original recording of "Gloria" by Them, featuring a young Van Morrison, is a 1960s Brit-rock classic. In it, the singer-narrator offers a rather gritless rehashing of a sexual dalliance with a woman named Gloria, and as he climaxes—not quite in sync with the tempo—he calls her name with an orgasmic bellow. Gloria herself appears to be speechless, perhaps because she isn't given any voice. In Smith's retelling, she casts herself as the lead, a swoon-worthy lothario.[2] Despite the ironic machismo in Smith's reworking of the song, which she infiltrated with her poem "Oath," her narrator gives Gloria agency and identity when she whispers her name, the song's iconic refrain. Her name is G·L·O·R·I·A.

Smith's lyrics ("AND I GOTTA TELL THE WORLD THAT I MAKE HER MINE MAKE HER MINE MAKE HER MINE MAKE HER MINE") sprawled across the planning and research stages of this exhibition. This publication, *Rachel Harrison G·L·O·R·I·A*, offers a unique opportunity: it presents itself as a traditional museum catalogue, yet square in the middle is *Heir Fresheners*, an artist's project created for this occasion. With Harrison's mining of so much content relating to Rauschenberg's practice and her own, we could ask, who is she trying to make hers? Rauschenberg? Gloria Vanderbilt? *Gloria*? Patti Smith? And what about that goat that keeps popping up? Throughout *Heir Fresheners*, Harrison does not seek to change or compete with Rauschenberg's art but rather uses his work to broaden our understanding of both her practice and his. Like Smith before her, Harrison is giving voice to "Gloria" the punk-rock anthem, but she is also speaking for *Gloria* the Combine and Gloria the socialite—and along the way, a serial-killer nurse, a handful of politicians, an assortment of pop stars, and Willem de Kooning's *Woman*.

In *Heir Fresheners*, Harrison offers a meditation on the history, folklore, and meanings surrounding Rauschenberg and his oeuvre that bravely enmeshes the two artists' lives and work, registering the gap between his art and hers. Within these pages, one can also find individual illustrations of the artworks included in the exhibition. Here, Harrisons and Rauschenbergs fade into and out of each other. On the opening page, Harrison has heightened a detail of a particularly drippy Combine with Photoshop drips and a faintly visible image of Amy Winehouse rendered in colored pencil. Elsewhere, canned air fresheners give lift to the painterly bald eagle in the iconic *Canyon* (1959; Museum of Modern Art, New York). Non-Rauschenbergian sources appear as well—instances of everyday life, if you will. Among these are a buildup of leftover frosting on a particularly artful dessert plate that recalls the surface of Harrison's sculptures. In 1953 Rauschenberg famously requested a *Woman* drawing from Willem de Kooning in order to make an artwork through its erasure. In the spirit of this generative act, Harrison attempts to re-create de Kooning's original gestures as revealed in a digitally enhanced infrared scan of *Erased de Kooning Drawing* published by its current owner, the San Francisco Museum of Modern Art (2010).[3] In other instances, she has erased images of Rauschenbergs to reveal slivers of her art lurking below. After sorting through this catalogue, it's easy to see that Harrison's dutiful recycling of gestures actively keeps the past present.

Beau Rutland
Assistant Curator of Contemporary Art
The Cleveland Museum of Art

NOTES

1. Calvin Tomkins, "Everything in Sight: Robert Rauschenberg's New Life," *New Yorker*, May 23, 2005, 76.
2. See Patti Smith, *Just Kids* (New York: Ecco, 2010), 246–47.
3. For this scan, see Sarah Roberts, "Erased de Kooning Drawing," Rauschenberg Research Project, July 2013. San Francisco Museum of Modern Art, http://www.sfmoma.org/explore/collection/artwork/25846/essay/erased_de_kooning_drawing, fig. 8.

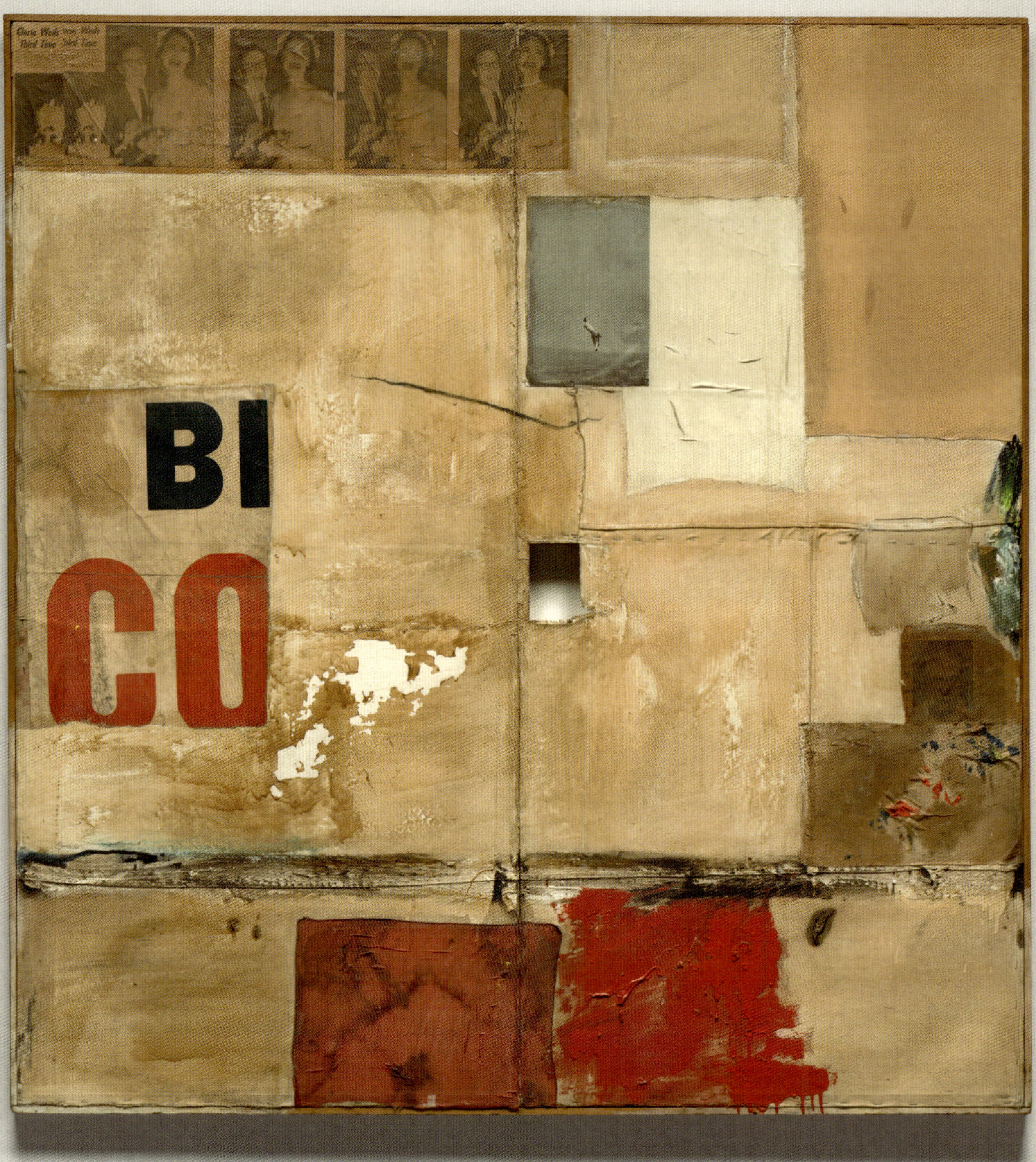
Gloria Weds
Third Time
BI
CO

Make Her Mine

Beau Rutland

Jesus died for somebody's sins, but not mine.

The smallest things can ruin an otherwise perfect day. On August 27, 1956, Gloria Vanderbilt, a "wan, wistful heiress, summer-stock actress, painter and poetess"—and a media darling since her scandalized childhood—got married in a surprise ceremony.[1] This was her third time walking down the aisle (the first was at age seventeen), and it was not long after the finalization of her divorce to conductor Leopold Stokowski (she was twenty-one when they married, he sixty-three). This time around, her partner in sickness and in health was Sidney Lumet, a TV hotshot who would go on to become an iconic Hollywood director.

The next day, their celebrity union made the front page of newspapers across the country from the *Pasadena Independent* to the *Chicago Daily Tribune* and the widely circulated, Hearst-owned *New York Daily Mirror*. For the *Mirror*'s morning edition, the front page was split between Vanderbilt's announcement, "GLORIA TAKES A THIRD MATE," and the investigation of a violent acid attack on a journalist.[2] The late edition, marked down to four cents, featured Vanderbilt and Lumet splashed across the front page. Other articles lauded the bride for finally finding an appropriate husband: "Gloria Weds Again, to Man Her Own Age."[3] The media's frequent use of her Christian name suggests an intimate familiarity with Vanderbilt and a widespread fascination with her story.

Unfortunately, the honeymoon, so to speak, was cut short: another woman rained on Gloria's third big day with an eye-catching article on the same page headlined "POLICE NAB NURSE IN 3 BABY DEATHS." Editors of newspapers across the country interrupted Gloria's wedding chatter—perhaps gleefully—with the tale of the "serial killer nurse" Virginia B. Jaspers, who was arrested for murdering three infants. The crimes of Jaspers, the daughter of a railroad executive and former state senator, were a grim discovery leading to the first diagnosis of Shaken Baby Syndrome. Attempting to make sense of her brutality, one *Newsweek* writer plunged headfirst into a pseudoscientific reading of her physiognomy: "The brutal and tragic career of nurse Virginia Jaspers is tied to her massive physical traits. Now 33, she is an ungainly 6 feet, weighs 220 pounds, has a 52-inch waist. Police concluded that she probably had no idea of the strength in her cruelly big arms and hands."[4] Jaspers's reply to investigators, "Children sometimes get on my nerves," is perhaps the most beguiling and unbelievable aspect of the case.[5] Any number of Americans would have read the news that day, perhaps rolling their eyes at the absurdity and elitism of a front-page article about a socialite marrying a Hollywood guy, again. And then turning the page, one imagines readers gasping at the cruelty of this plain-looking woman in horn-rimmed glasses. *Gloria* is Latin for "glory," and both Vanderbilt and Jaspers achieved a twisted version of it that Tuesday.

These juxtaposed images, persons, stories, and symbols caught the eye of artist Robert Rauschenberg that August night—he was intrigued enough to buy at least five copies of the paper and bring them back to his studio on Pearl Street in lower Manhattan. Images from the *New York Daily Mirror* appear multiple times in his 1956 Combine *Gloria* along with scraps of fabric, various kinds of paper, and infrequent yet gestural applications of paint. Five clippings of the wedding were applied to the work's top left corner, but Rauschenberg overlapped each cutout so that the couple is only seen in four. Appearing just across the canvas from the happy couple is Jaspers. When assembling *Gloria*, the artist trimmed her mug shot irregularly, leaving a small margin that includes partial excerpts from the article about her arrest as well as florid descriptions of Vanderbilt's wedding; he veiled the caption running below the photograph with a piece of cloth so that Jaspers's identity is masked. One can assume that her name itself may have made Rauschenberg look twice, as it resembles that of Jasper Johns, his close friend, collaborator, and at that time, lover.[6]

Couplings aside, what are we to think of the stark void piercing the center of *Gloria*? Around this time, several other artists were attempting to, as Paul Schimmel has framed it, "destroy the picture" by tormenting canvas rather than simply painting it. Yet both the precise geometry of *Gloria*'s rectangular cutout and its shellacked edges, which were presumably treated to keep them from further fraying, suggest that Rauschenberg intended viewers to

Robert Rauschenberg (American, 1925–2008). *Gloria*, 1956.

not just perceive emptiness, but to view the supporting wall itself, a work of architecture built with enforced codes, design strictures, and so on.[7] Although created more than a decade earlier, *Gloria* anticipates philosopher Henri Lefebvre's critique of the built environment in his book *The Production of Space* as well as the first wave of institutional critique by practitioners such as Daniel Buren and Michael Asher, whose work encompasses every aspect of art's display, purchase, and preservation.

Much of the academic discourse surrounding *Gloria* concerns itself with issues of duplication and separation, whether in respect to formal composition or a relationship between two individuals. In the final image of the wedding montage, Vanderbilt and Lumet are split in half by a vertical fissure that divides the work in two, perhaps foretelling their inevitable divorce. Other unions include two red squares in the lower half, one made of cloth and the other of enamel paint; a large piece of paper cut so that it only contains the prefixes *BI* in blue and *CO* in red, which imply doubling themselves; a horizontal crease between these terms that further halves them; and an echo of red and blue oil paint underneath the photograph of Jaspers.

Gloria in many ways seems like a distinctly modern, distinctly American work of art. Pictured plainly on the canvas is a nurse who murdered children wrapped in a rapturous report of a celebrity wedding—"Gloria wore a crownlet of orchids in her hair and a 19th century French period dress in beige silk."[8] Until recently Jaspers went completely unrecognized—the discovery of her fascinating and repellant story and the shared *Daily Mirror* source material has never been claimed.[9] The introduction of Jaspers upends any former literal reading of the symbolic content within *Gloria*, allowing the work's various narratives to not only unravel, but to also get weird.

> *Oh she looks so good, oh she looks so fine*
> *And I got this crazy feeling and then I'm gonna ah-ah make her mine*[10]

Rachel Harrison's penchant for bringing nearly any aspect of culture into her multidimensional work is well known. Harrison's sculptures, with their encrusted multicolored surfaces of acrylic paint atop cement-covered polystyrene, have a very particular and peculiar way of luring objects, events, and personalities into discussion, whether it is through their incorporation of everyday items like a Babyphat purse or a ski pole, their pointed titles (*Al Gore*, *Frumpy at 38*, *Voyage of the Beagle*), or the various ways in which they engage the gallery space around them, drawing in the viewer with seeming nonchalance.

For instance, *Slipknot* (2002; p. 35) is a monochromatic sculpture that lies low to the ground, its form seeming to stem from that of a coffee table. This domesticity and ripeness for display is underlined by a wooden African totem placed on the work's surface. Hanging onto one side of *Slipknot* is a photograph of the costumed guitarist from the late-1990s alt-metal band of the same name. The curious dichotomy between these two elements can be elucidated by a quote from Harrison, "A photograph of a celebrity is a thing, not a picture. It's a mundane cultural artifact."[11]

The differences between a Harrison and a Rauschenberg may have already become apparent. In fact, many over the past decade have strongly cautioned against pairing the two artists.[12] In the words of writer and curator Jack Bankowsky, "Despite the affinity suggested by the plastic and retinal qualities Rauschenberg brought to his scavenging, a Harrison never really feels like a Rauschenbergian 'Combine.'"[13] While this observation is correct, it isn't to say that Harrison and Rauschenberg don't have similar interests or goals, even if they explore them through the perspective of sculpture and painting, respectively. Yet the same sly self-awareness that characterizes *Gloria*, with its institution-revealing cutout, can be witnessed in Harrison's work. In *Legitimo* (2012; p. 87), for instance, a runway carpet engages the entire length of a gallery, while the trash can propping up the rest of the sculpture, including a can of air freshener, nods to the labor and material spent in maintaining such an environment. Referring to the psychological charge often possessed by Harrison's work, one writer astutely pointed out that if Rauschenberg's works should be called Combines, then it would be apt to refer to Harrison's as Complexes.[14]

When a Harrison dons celebrity skin, its multiple personalities act in a surprisingly orderly fashion. The 1990s boy band Hanson makes an appearance in *Stella 1* (2006; p. 25), reflecting the viewer behind their pubescent faces (a Lacanian joke about recognition and objecthood if there ever was one). While the painting of the totemic sculpture is precisely executed, its style recalls the push/pull of Hans Hoffmann's palette much more so than the work of the titular inspiration, artist Frank Stella. Here, the combination of title and object recalls a photo of a young Stella—wearing a slightly baggy suit, looking quite ready for a bank teller's first day on the job—which appeared in the catalogue for the landmark exhibition *Sixteen Americans* (1959).[15]

The most pleasurable *and* most infuriating part about having a conversation with Harrison's work is that the topic switches on you without you even realizing it. *Hans Haacke with Sculpture* (2005; p. 23) misleads while leading us on. At first we see a portrait of Ronald Reagan,

New York Daily Mirror, August 28, 1956, p. 1.

4¢ FINAL EDITION ★★★★★

Daily Mirror

FINAL EDITION 4¢ ★★★★★

Vol. 33. No. 58. C NEW YORK 17, N. Y., TUESDAY, AUGUST 28, 1956 Weather: Partly Cloudy

TWO IN RIESEL PROBE TALKING

. . . Story on Page 2

Gloria Weds Third Time

Radiantly happy Gloria Vanderbilt and TV director Sidney Lumet cut cake after their marriage Monday by Supreme Court Justice Say-pol at [illegible] St. It's the third marriage for Gloria [illegible] of conductor Leopold Stokow[illegible] [illegible] and second for Lumet. [illegible]

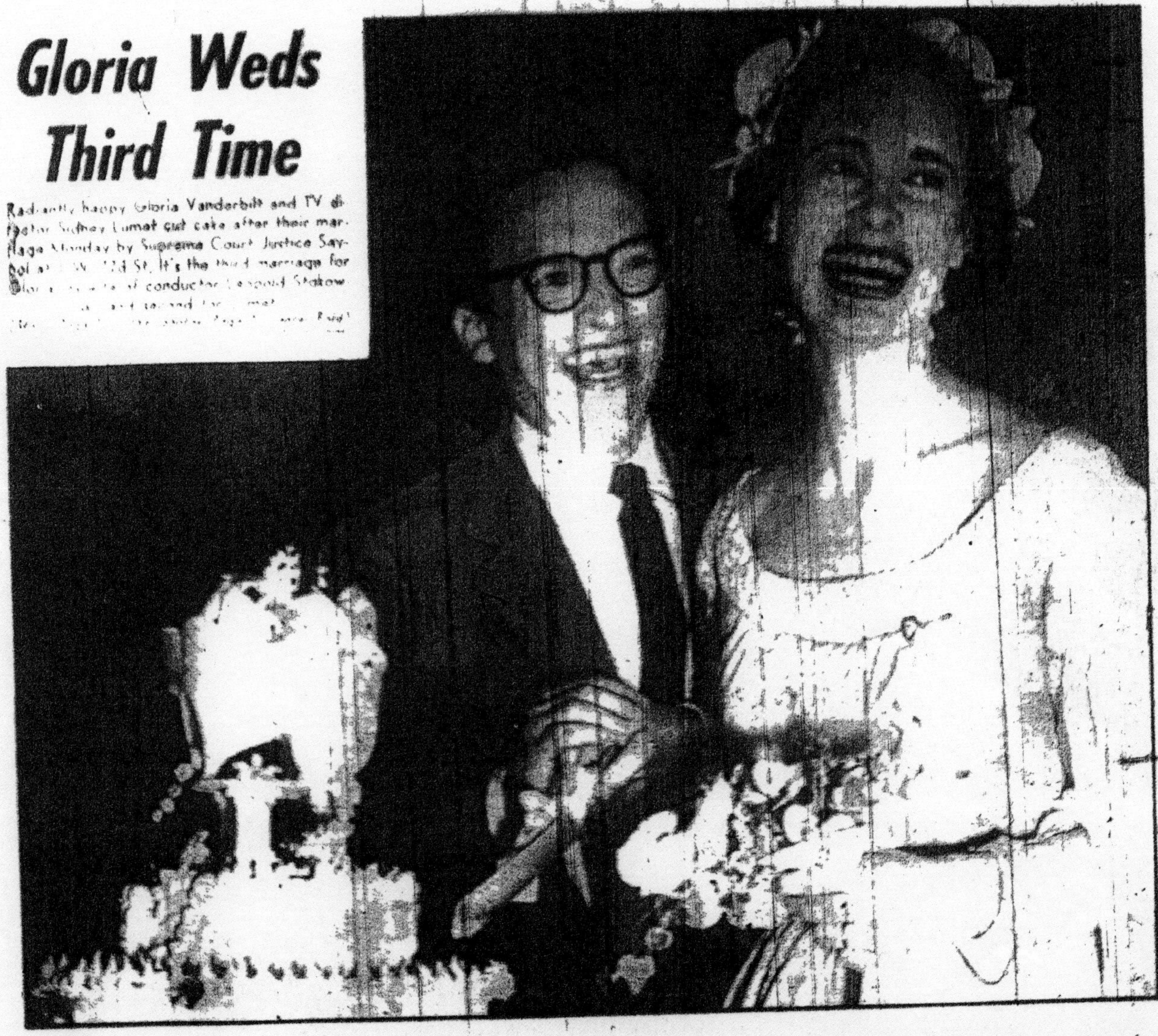

the former president and conservative icon, best known for his embrace of trickle-down economic theory. Yet the framed copy of Reagan's image is actually an enlarged scan of a catalogue featuring the famous work *Oelgemaelde, Hommage à Marcel Broodthaers* (1982), which conceptual artist Hans Haacke created for Documenta 7. The scan hangs on a leaning, door-sized piece of plywood that is sitting upon a dolly. The pull of gravity is stopped by an abstract cement-covered form (one recognizable aspect of Harrison's repertoire) that quite literally props Reagan up. With its bipolar paint job, the dual-minded sculpture is half bubblegum pink, like a snack to be chewed on at the movies, and half iridescent gold—perhaps evoking wealth, whether Reagan's own or that accumulated by the elite during his presidency.

As early as 1961, John Cage saw past a literal reading of Rauschenberg's work in his brilliant essay "On Robert Rauschenberg, Artist, and His Work" with the following question: "Is Gloria V. a subject or an idea? Then, tell us: How many times was she married and what do you do when she divorces you?"[16] In Harrison's practice, the same could also be asked of Reagan, Fats Domino, Petra von Kant, and (the most akin to Gloria V.) Amy Winehouse. In the fastidious drawing *Untitled* (2012; p. 98), Winehouse, the infamous chanteuse and icon of the suffering artist genius, appears alongside Willem de Kooning's *Woman V*. Making quite the fashionable appearance, the attention-grabbing duo enters together, Amy exuding her standard rock-and-roll attitude in a lime-green bustier with matching lips, red nails, and signature beehive. *Woman* seems as frantic as ever. While Rauschenberg erased one of de Kooning's Women in 1953, Harrison brought the art-history starlet back to life, deliberately placing her alongside another readymade tragedy.

A comparison of Rauschenberg and Harrison seems almost too good to be true, which explains the knee-jerk reaction of many curators and scholars. Rauschenberg brought everything around him into his Combines: the dregs of popular culture, tire skids, taxidermy, radios, and so on. But in the half-century separating our current age from the 1950s, the conflation of popular culture with extremely advanced technology and manufacturing has swallowed up everyday life. By giving even our most banal, unexpected desires and interests physicality—a mirror printed with the image of your favorite musical talent, NASCAR-branded trash cans, a top hat–wearing ape made from a coconut—we have produced wayward and valueless objects that are ripe for the picking. This glut of half-baked goods attests to why Rachel Harrison's bad objects, produced during the Post-Fordist era, resound so strongly within her artwork—they are undeniably part of today's culture. For example, *Gloria* was created during the golden age of print media; the use of newspaper clippings seems rather retardataire today, when an image can be dragged, dropped, and printed to any specificity. To this effect, Walter Benjamin once said that he wasn't interested in appropriating anything valuable, but that "the trivia, the trash" also wasn't worth taking stock of. Regarding seemingly worthless detritus, he urged, "Let it come into its own in the only way possible: use it."[17] When Harrison puts errant objects to highly specific use within her art, she reveals her startling ability of making anything around us hers.

NOTES

Epigraph: "Gloria," by Patti Smith from the album *Horses* (Arista Records, 1975).

1. *TIME*, September 10, 1956.
2. The journalist was popular *Mirror* columnist Victor Riesel. The attack stemmed from his reportage of labor policy.
3. Alvin Doyle and James McGlincy, "Gloria Weds Again, to Man Her Own Age," *New York Daily Mirror*, August 28, 1956, early edition, 3.
4. *Newsweek*, September 10, 1956, 71.
5. "Babies Got on Her Nerves, So Nurse Shook 3 to Death," *New York Daily Mirror*, August 28, 1956, 3.
6. See Kenneth E. Silver, "Modes of Disclosure: The Construction of Gay Identity and the Rise of Pop Art," in *Hand-Painted Pop: American Art in Transition, 1955–62*, ed. Russell Ferguson, exh. cat. (Los Angeles: Museum of Contemporary Art; New York: Rizzoli, 1992). Jonathan Katz, Jill Johnston, and James Meyer have also written to this effect.
7. See Branden W. Joseph, "The Gap and the Frame," *October* 117 (Summer 2006): 66. Joseph has also smartly described the hole as "acting like the blind spot in the middle of the retina." Branden W. Joseph, "BL(U)BROB TRRRCRRAATCHURBUP: Bob Rauschenberg in Swedish Bird Call," *Konsthistorisk tidskrift/Journal of Art History* 76 (2007): 19.
8. Doyle and McGlincy, "Gloria Weds Again."
9. Many writers misidentified Jaspers as an unknown man, Lumet, or a "nurse-turned-kidnapper" who was foiled by "Detective Jasper." See Edward B. Henning, "Robert Rauschenberg, Gloria," *Bulletin of the Cleveland Museum of Art* 56 (February 1969): 76; Roni Feinstein, "Random Order: The First Fifteen Years of Rauschenberg's Art: 1949–1964" (PhD diss., New York University, 1990), 218–19.
10. Smith, "Gloria."
11. Rachel Harrison, "Empire State," *Artforum* (October 2004): 146.
12. A comparison between Rauschenberg and Harrison is not unprecedented—writers such as Jack Bankowsky, Laura Hoptman, Branden W. Joseph, and John Kelsey have made such claims. See also Branden W. Joseph, "Ambition: A Telegraphic Voyage through Thirty Years of Rauschenberg's Art," in *Robert Rauschenberg: Travelling '70/'76*, ed. Mirta D'Argenzio, exh. cat. (Milan: Electa, 2008), 164–65.
13. Jack Bankowsky, "Monkey House Blessing Potpourri," in *Rachel Harrison: Museum without Walls*, ed. Eric Banks and Sarah Valdez, exh. cat. (Annandale-on-Hudson, NY: Center for Curatorial Studies, Bard College; London: Whitechapel Gallery Ventures; Frankfurt am Main: Portikus, 2010), 140.
14. John Kelsey, "Sculpture in an Abandoned Field," in *Rachel Harrison: If I Did It*, ed. Heike Munder and Ellen Seifermann, exh. cat. (Zurich: JRP/Ringier, 2007), 120.
15. For this image, see Dorothy C. Miller, ed., *Sixteen Americans*, exh. cat. (New York: Museum of Modern Art, 1960), 76.
16. John Cage, *Silence: Lectures and Writings* (Middletown, CT: Wesleyan University Press, 1961), 99.
17. Walter Benjamin, "N [Theoretics of Knowledge: Theory of Progress]," *Philosophical Review* 15, nos. 1–2 (1983–84): 5.

New York Daily Mirror, August 28, 1956, p. 3.

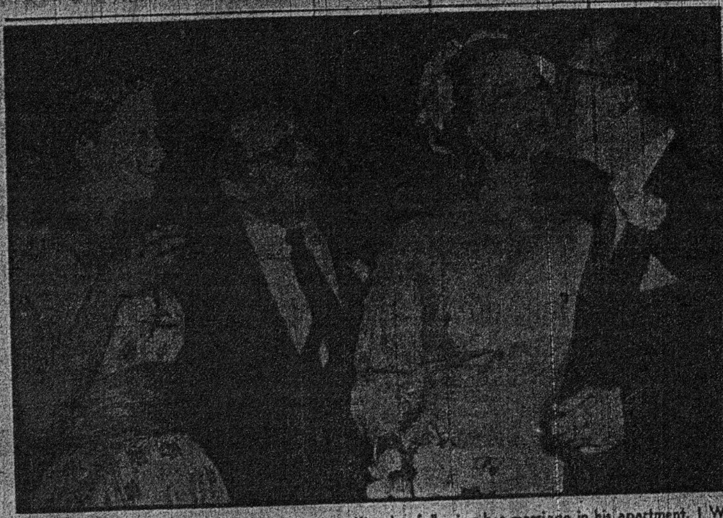

Gloria Vanderbilt is kissed by playwright Sidney Kingsley following her marriage in his apartment, 1 W. 72nd St. Looking on are Carol Grace, Gloria's attendant, and the bridegroom, director Sidney Lumet. (Mirror Photo by Barney Coons)

(Other Photos on Page 1 and Center Fold)

Gloria Weds Again, to Man Her Own Age

By ALVIN DOYLE and JAMES McGLINCY

Gloria Vanderbilt, who once upon a time was a poor, little rich girl, pondered for two years about whether to marry for a third time and then, mind made up, rushed out Monday and did it in a big hurry with Sidney Lumet, a Lower East Side boy who played a "Dead End" kid on Broadway and grew up to be a hot-shot television and theatre director.

They were married by Supreme Court Justice Saypol in the 1 W. 72d St. apartment of Sidney Kingsley, who wrote "Dead End," the play that started Lumet on his career.

* * *

"WAS THIS A SUDDEN decision?" reporters asked the couple, who were wed within two hours of taking out their license.

"Oh, no," they chorused.

"I've been thinking about it for two years," Gloria added. Two years ago both were still married, she to her second husband, conductor Leopold Stokowski, and he to his first wife, actress Rita Gam. Lumet recalled he met Gloria on March 4, 1955, at a friend's apartment.

"Will you give up your career?" Gloria was asked. This presumably referred to her acting. She also paints and writes poetry.

"Oh, no," said the newlyweds again.

Kingsley was Lumet's best man. Carol Grace, former wife of writer William Saroyan, was Gloria's attendant. Mrs. Emily Prescott, Gloria's childhood nurse, was among the handful of friends.

* * *

GLORIA WORE A crownlet of orchids in her hair and a 19th century French period dress in beige silk. Lumet wore a charcoal gray Summer suit.

The honeymoon, they said, will be delayed because Gloria is appearing in "The Spa," at the Paper Mill Playhouse in Millbank, N. J., and Lumet has conferences in Hollywood scheduled. He had been due to fly to the Coast Monday night, but the studio gave him leave to spend his wedding night with his bride when they heard the news.

The Lumets said they will live in Gloria's 18-room apartment at 10 Gracie Square. Stokowski, now 68, also used to live there. This time Gloria picked a spouse her own age, 32.

In Hollywood, Stowkowski said: "I wish her every happiness—as always."

* * *

BLACK-TRESSED Gloria and Lumet, a thin, intenese man slightly shorter than she, took out their marriage license at 2:30 p.m. and said they wanted to be wed right away. Deputy City Clerk George Whitfield explained they needed a waiver to avoid the standard waiting period.

With her lawyer, Arnold Krakower, leading interference they tore up Centre St. to the chambers of Justice Saypol who not only issued the waiver but agreed to officiate.

Lumet divorced Rita Gam in Mexico on July 14, 1955, and she since has rewed.

* * *

GLORIA'S FIRST marriage, at 17, was to actor's agent Pat De Cicco. She divorced him in Nevada in April, 1945. About a year later she married Stokowski. They had two children, Stanislaw, 6, and Christopher, 5.

* * *

GLORIA WAS divorced from Stokowski in Mexico City on Oct. 31, 1955.

Gloria inherited $5,000,000 from her father, the late Reginald C. Vanderbilt when she was 21. As a child she was the pawn in a headline-making court battle for her custody between her mother, Gloria Morgan Vanderbilt, and her aunt, Mrs. Harry Payne Whitney.

Lumet is the son of Baruch Lumet, a well-known Yiddish playwright.

SONNY'S BLOOPERS GET HIM FIRED

Recurring "blooper" trouble got Sonny Fox, master of ceremonies of the CBS-TV show "The $64,000 Challenge," fired Monday.

Fox has been in hot water several times this year for mistakes of the tongue, including the occasion when he let slip part of the answer to a contestant for the big money. CBS replaced him for the Sunday evening show with Ralph Storey, who runs an early morning program in Los Angeles.

Babies Got on Her Nerves, So Nurse Shook 3 to Death

(Special to the Mirror)

NEW HAVEN, Conn., Aug. 27. — A six-foot, 260-pound pediatric nurse who admitted her infant charges sometimes "get on my nerves," has confessed that she had beaten or shaken three babies to death, Coroner James J. Corrigan announced Monday night.

A fourth death is being investigated, Police Chief Francis McManus said.

* * *

THE NURSE was identified as Virginia B. Jaspers, 33, daughter of a county political leader and railroad official. She was being held on a technical charge pending an autopsy on the 11-day-old daughter of Mr. and Mrs. Allen Kapsinow, 65 Brookside St., New Haven

"It was all uncontrollable," the nurse was quoted. "I didn't know why I did it. Children sometimes get on my nerves."

The police chief said:

"She has tremendous hands and probably doesn't know her own strength."

The Kapsinow baby died in her home last Thursday under circumstances that caused Dr. Sterling P. Taylor, medical examiner, to order an investigation.

* * *

When a reporter broke the news to Mrs. Kapsinow, she cried:

"Oh, my God! They told us our baby died of natural causes."

* * *

AFTER FIVE hours of questioning, the nurse, who was described as "distraught but cooperative," confessed she became enraged when the baby refused to take her formula, seized the child by both arms, pressed her thumbs against the tiny chest, and shook the baby violently.

The baby's head bobbed rapidly, Corrigan said, and when the nurse noted that breathing had become faint she put the child down. Death occurred shortly thereafter.

Corrigan said the nurse related she had similarly caused the deaths of another infant four or five years ago and a three-months-old girl in 1948.

Additionally, the coroner said, Miss Jaspers said she had broken the leg of a three-month-old girl last year.

Police said the child of Mrs. Alice Hubbard, now of Gilford, died suddenly seven years ago, and the baby of Mrs. Willard Malkins, now of New Canaan, died similarly four years ago, both while under Miss Jaspers' care.

The nurse, tear-reddened eyes blinking behind horn-rimmed glasses, was held overnight in the county jail for further questioning Tuesday. Chief McManus said the records of all babies she cared for will be checked.

* * *

THE NURSE'S FATHER, William Jaspers, of East Haven, former State Senator and an assistant personnel manager for the New Haven R. R., accompanied his daughter to the police station, but said the family is "as flabbergasted as anyone else" about the case.

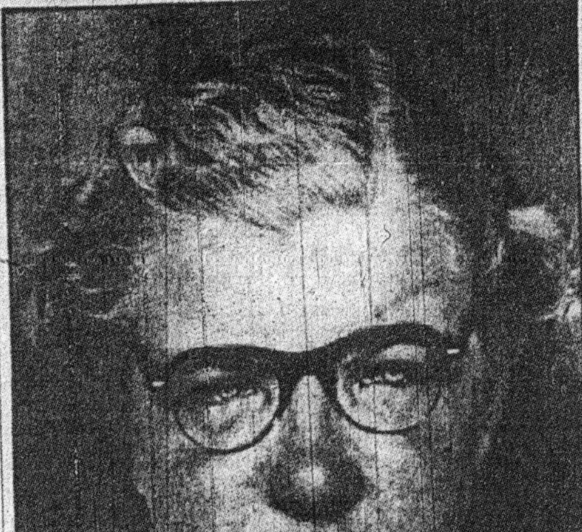

Virginia B. Jaspers . . . "Children sometimes get on my nerves." (AP WIREphoto)

GOP WOMEN URGED BY IKE TO WORK

WASHINGTON, Aug. 27 (UP).—President Eisenhower called on Republican women Tuesday to go out and "Win enthusiastic support" in the coming campaign for the GOP program of "peace and prosperity."

The President's appeal was in a letter to Mrs. Carroll D. Kearns, president of the National Federation of Republican Women, which holds its ninth biennial convention in Chicago Sept. 5-7.

3 Sanmen Save Her $500

A Bronx candy-store owner mistakenly threw out $530 Monday and it took three Sanitation Department men a half-hour of sifting through two tons of rubbish to find it.

Mrs. Rosalie Mirabal, 32, whose store is at 401 E. 145th St., had put $500 in bills and $30 in checks in an envelope to take to the bank. Somehow the envelope got into the garbage which she put out a short time later.

* * *

SHE MISSED the envelope even as the Sanitation Department truck was picking up her rubbish. She ran after the truck and told the crew her plight. Nicholas Minutolo, Albert Cook and Andrew Paterno obligingly dumped their load of garbage on the street and began to go through it. Meantime, Mrs. Mirabal prayed.

After a half-hour one of the men triumphantly held aloft the envelope. Mrs. Mirabal gave them $5—to split three ways.

Heir Fresheners

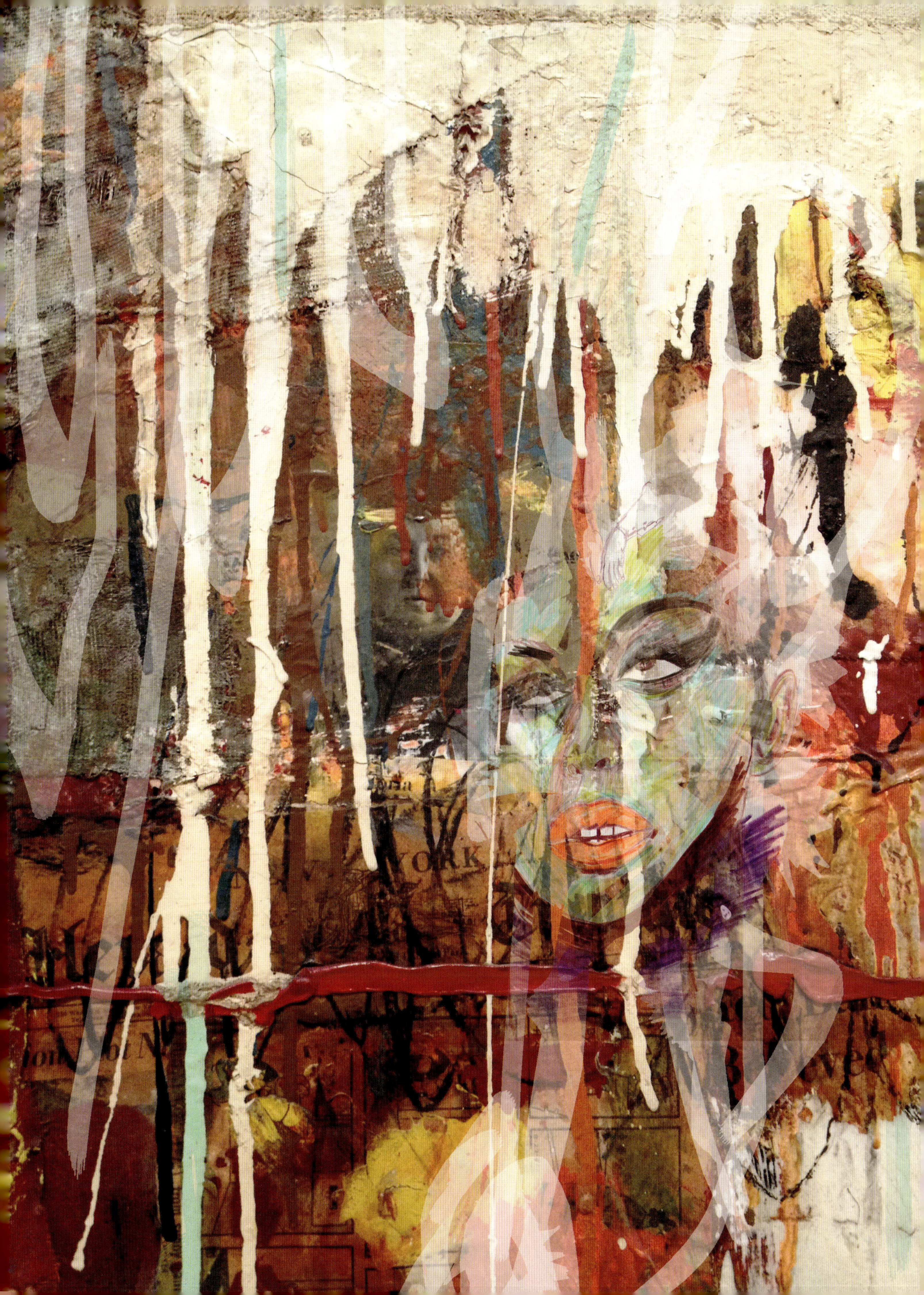
YORK

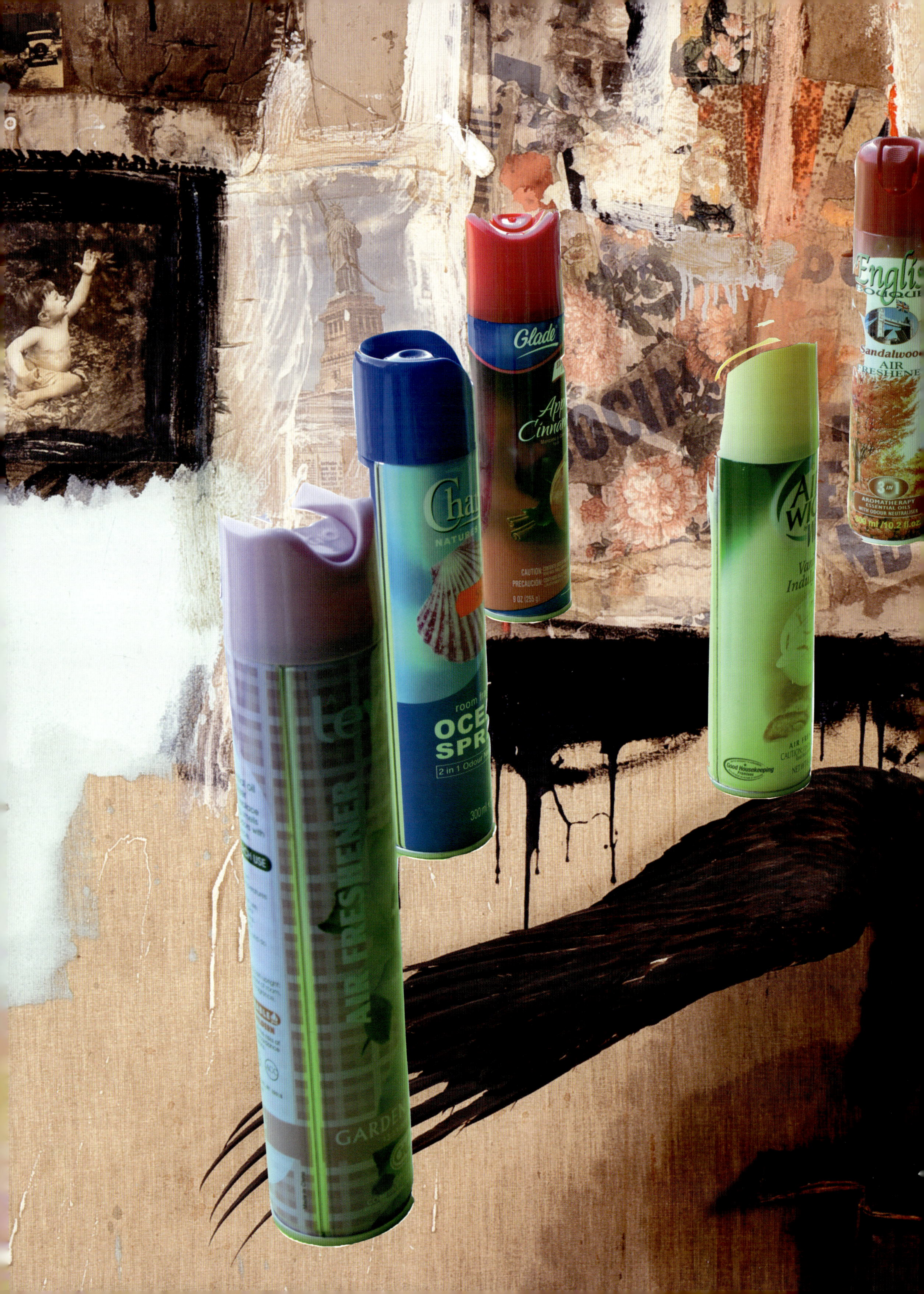
Glade
AIR FRESHENER
AROMATHERAPY
Good Housekeeping

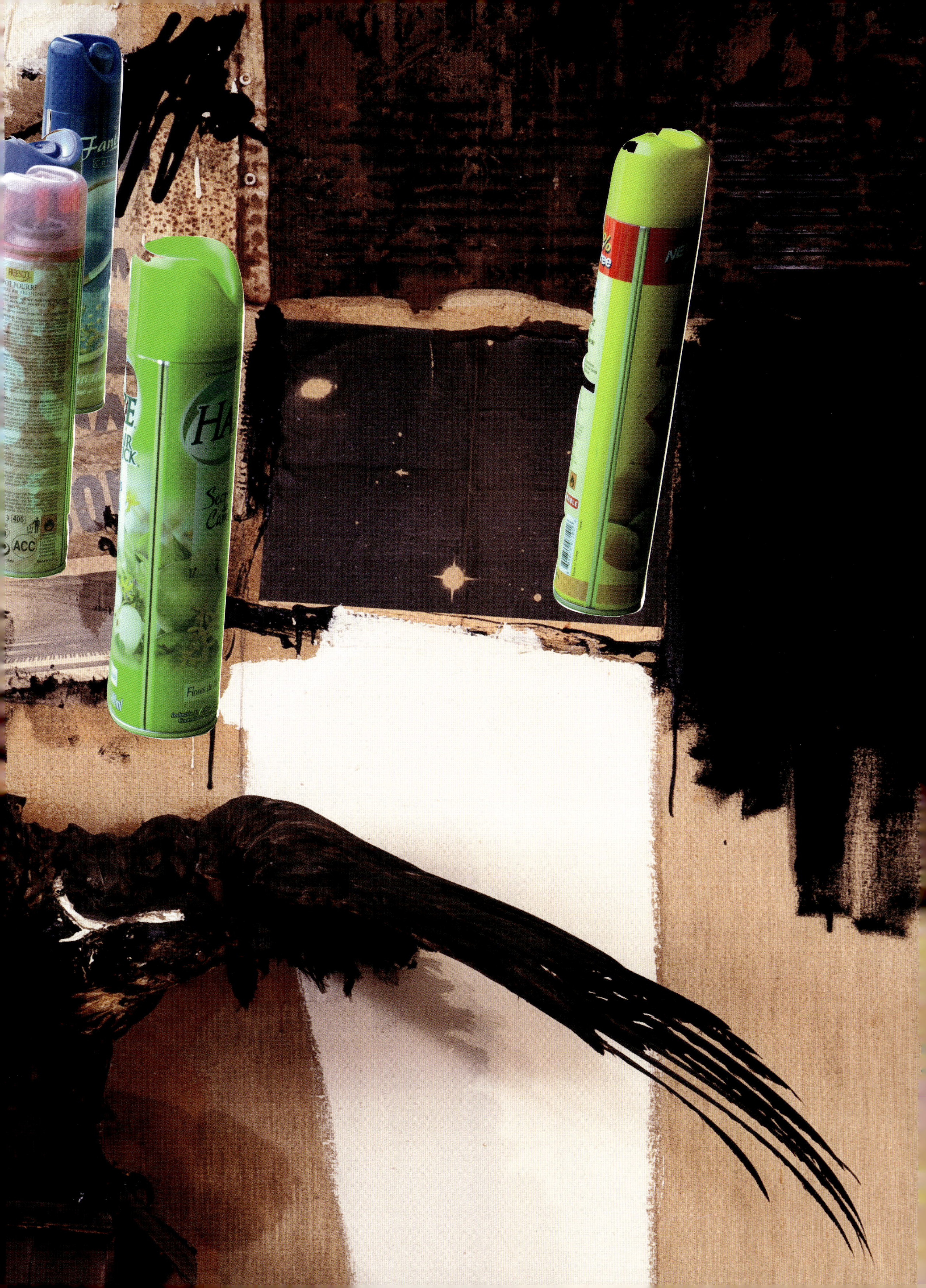
FREESCO
POT POURRI
ACC
Flores de

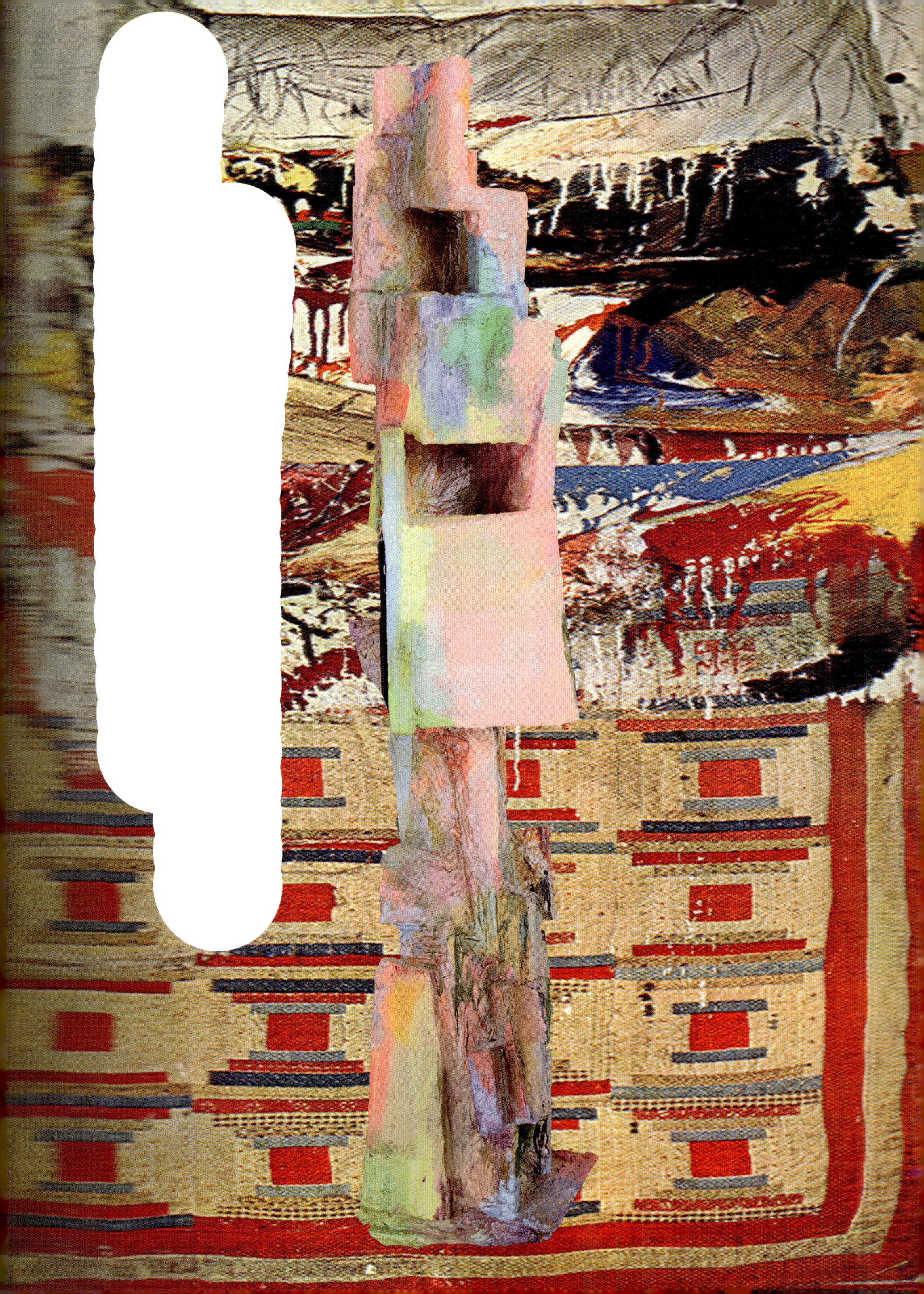

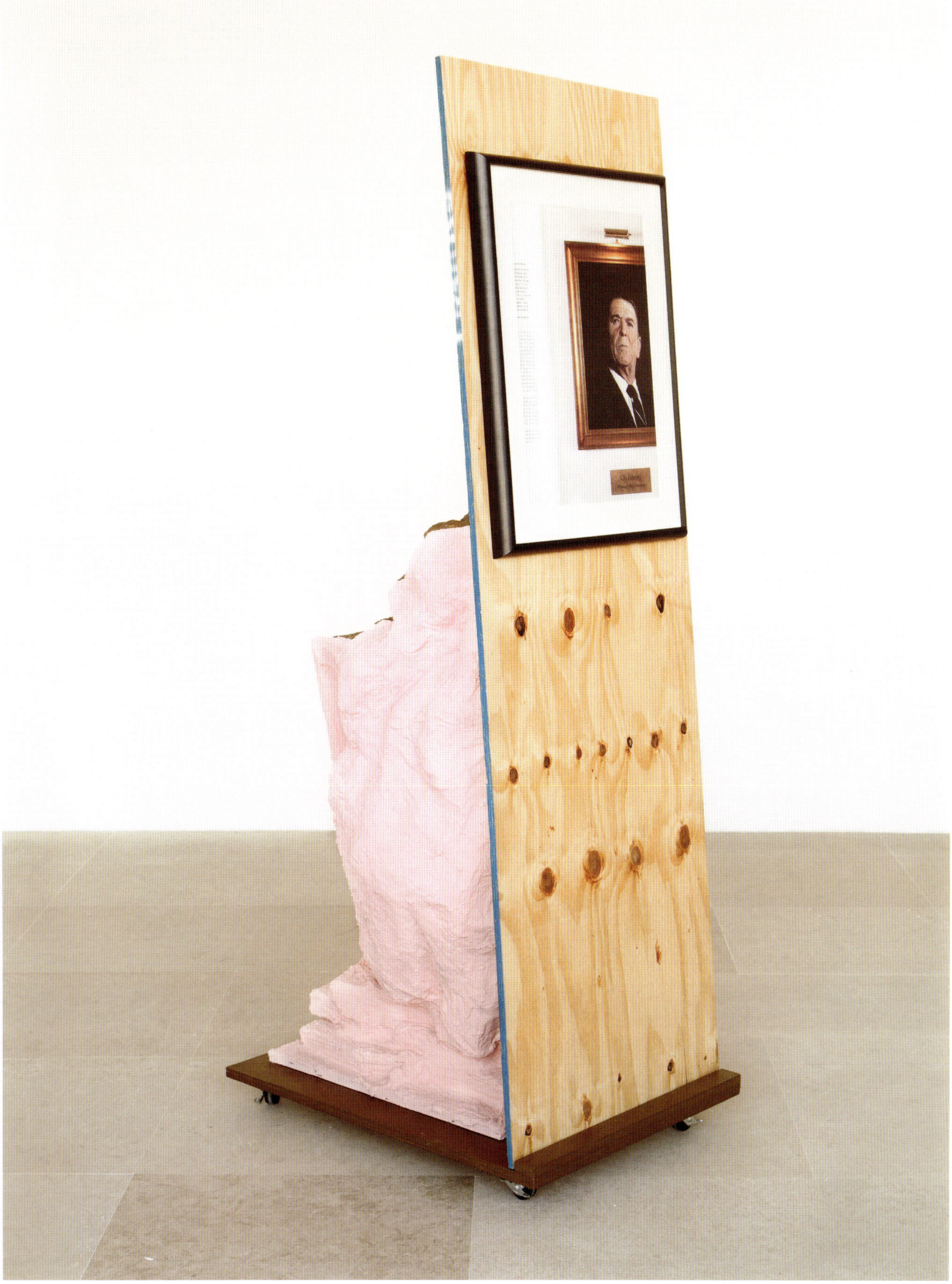

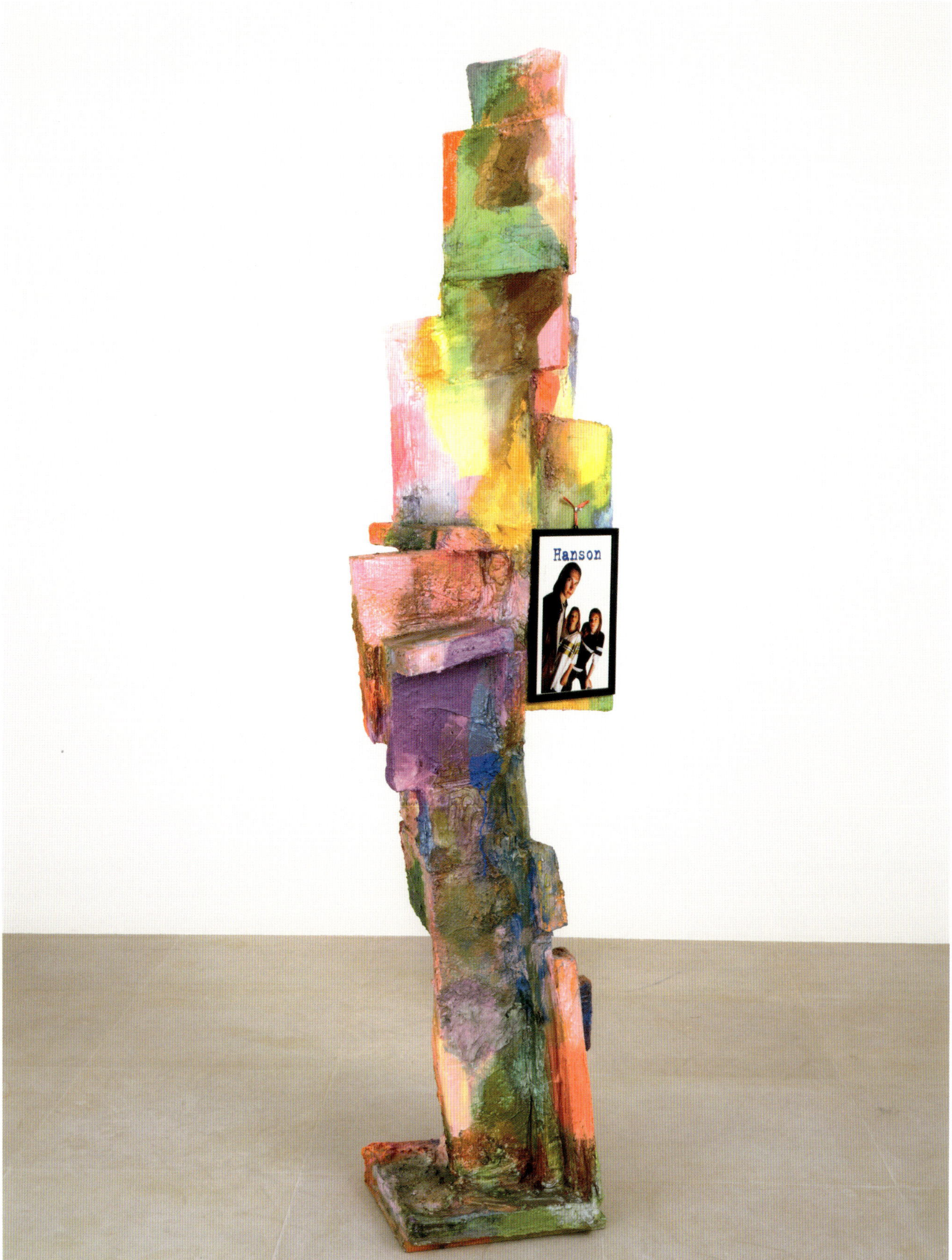
Hanson

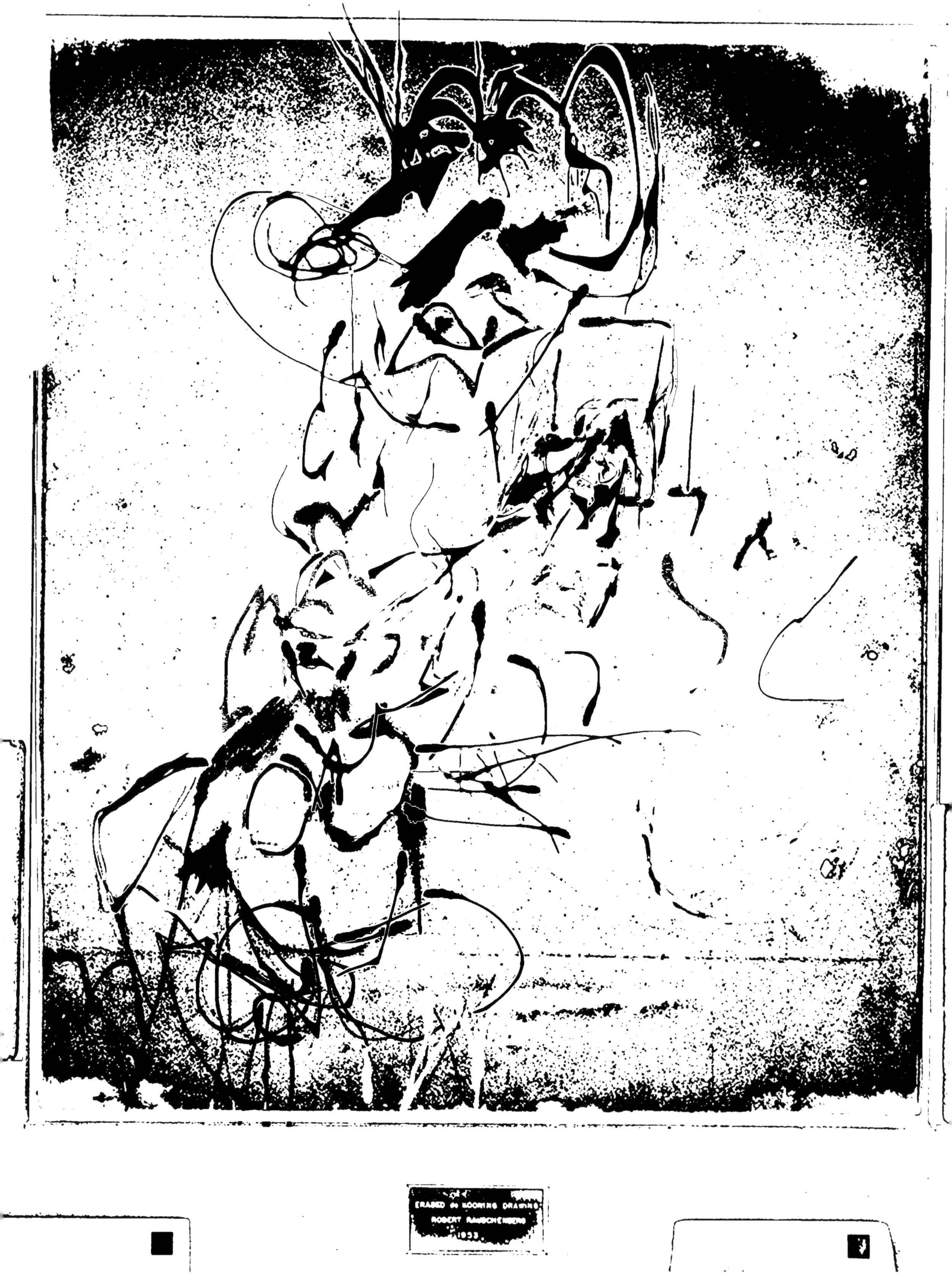
ERASED de KOONING DRAWING
ROBERT RAUSCHENBERG
1953

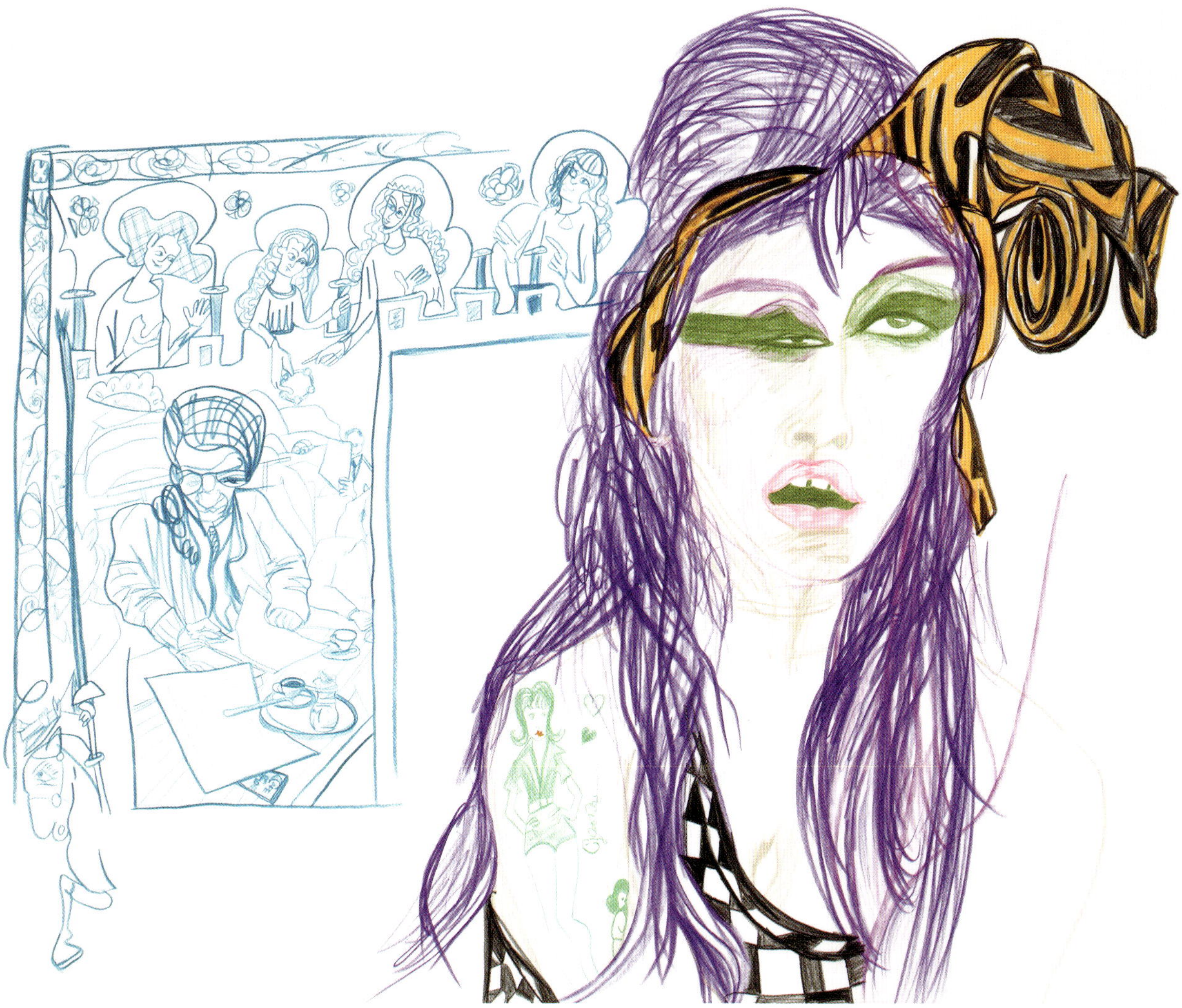

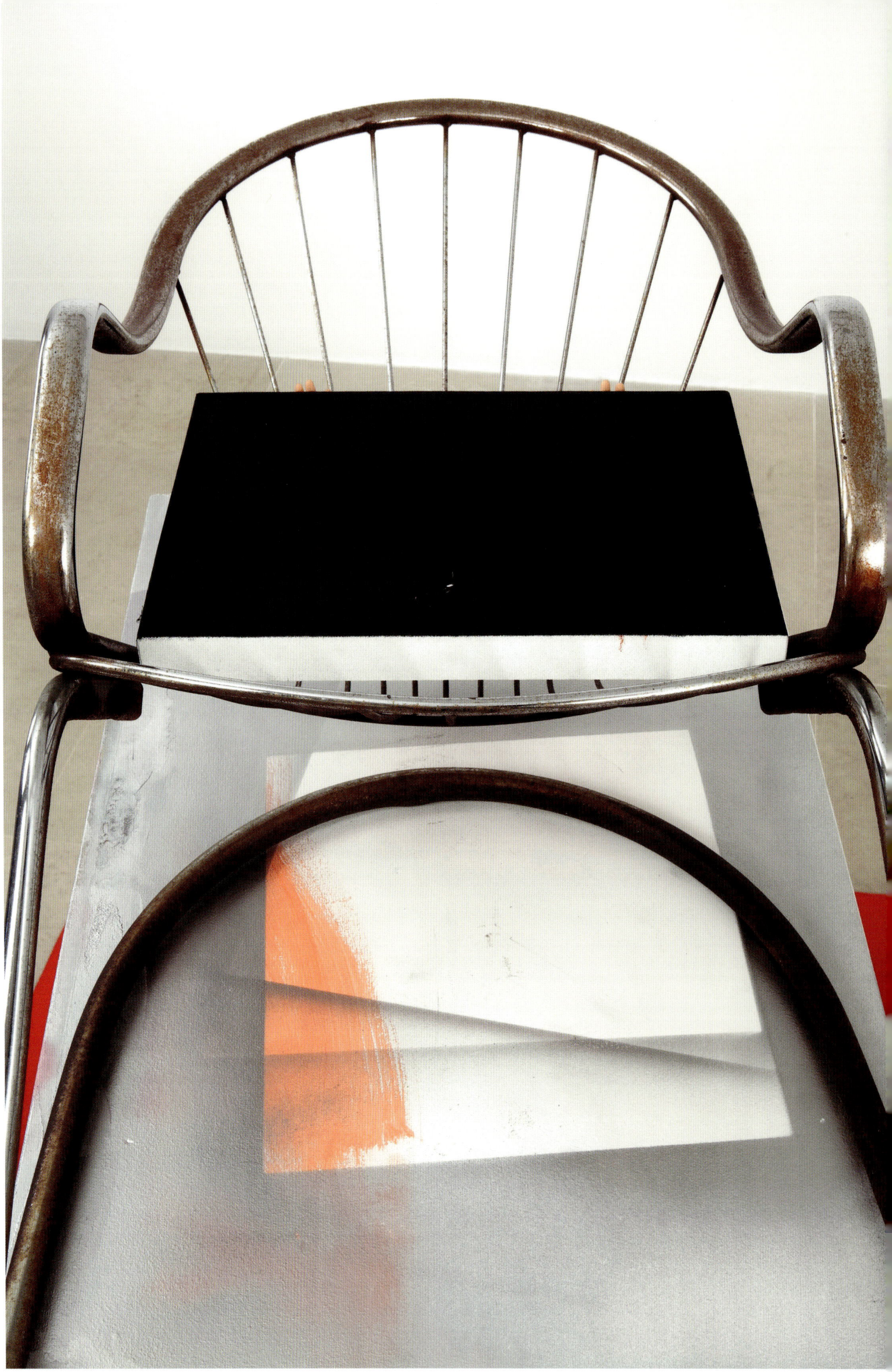

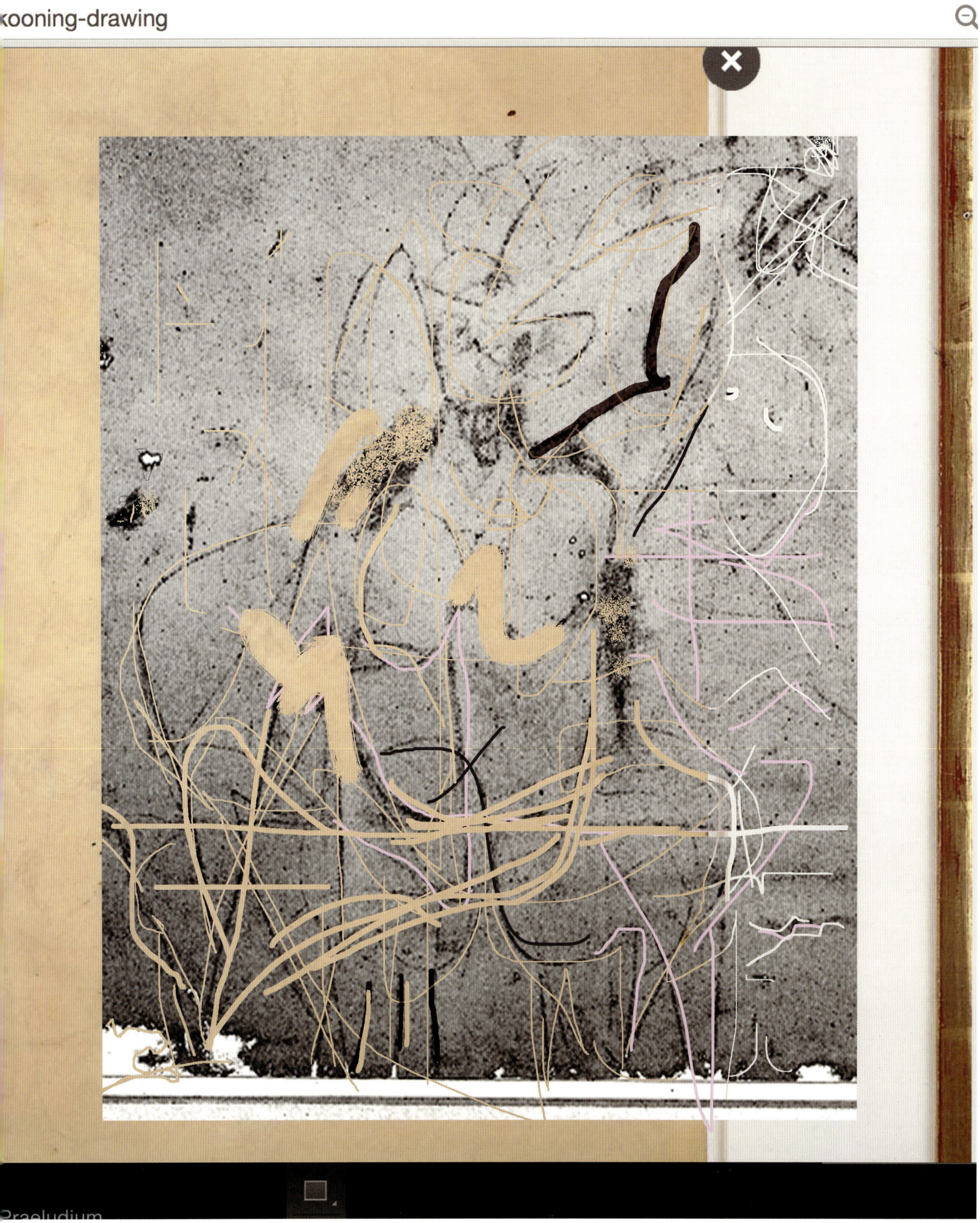
kooning-drawing
Praeludium

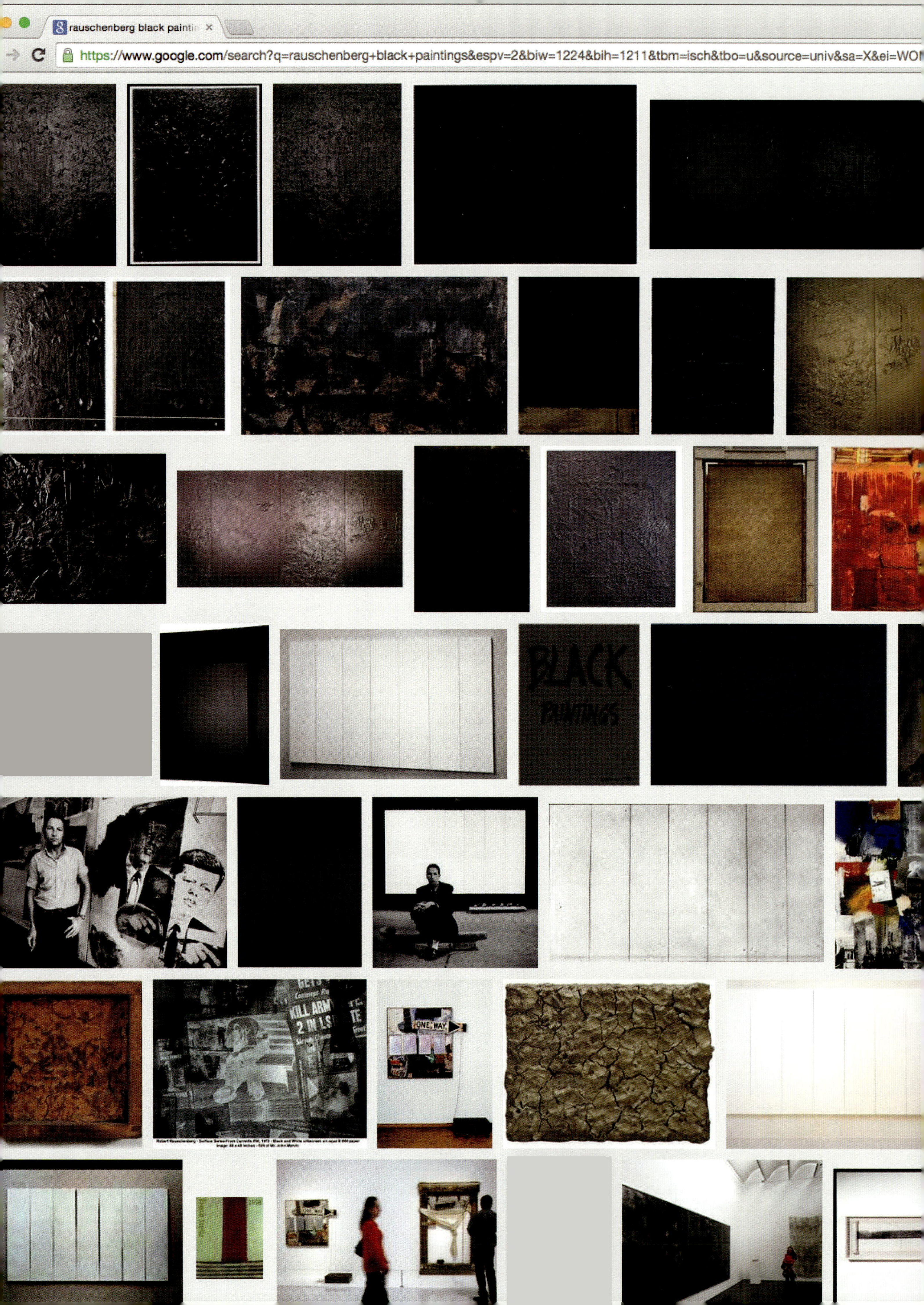
rauschenberg black paintin
https://www.google.com/search?q=rauschenberg+black+paintings&espv=2&biw=1224&bih=1211&tbm=isch&tbo=u&source=univ&sa=X&ei=WO
BLACK
PAINTINGS
ONE WAY

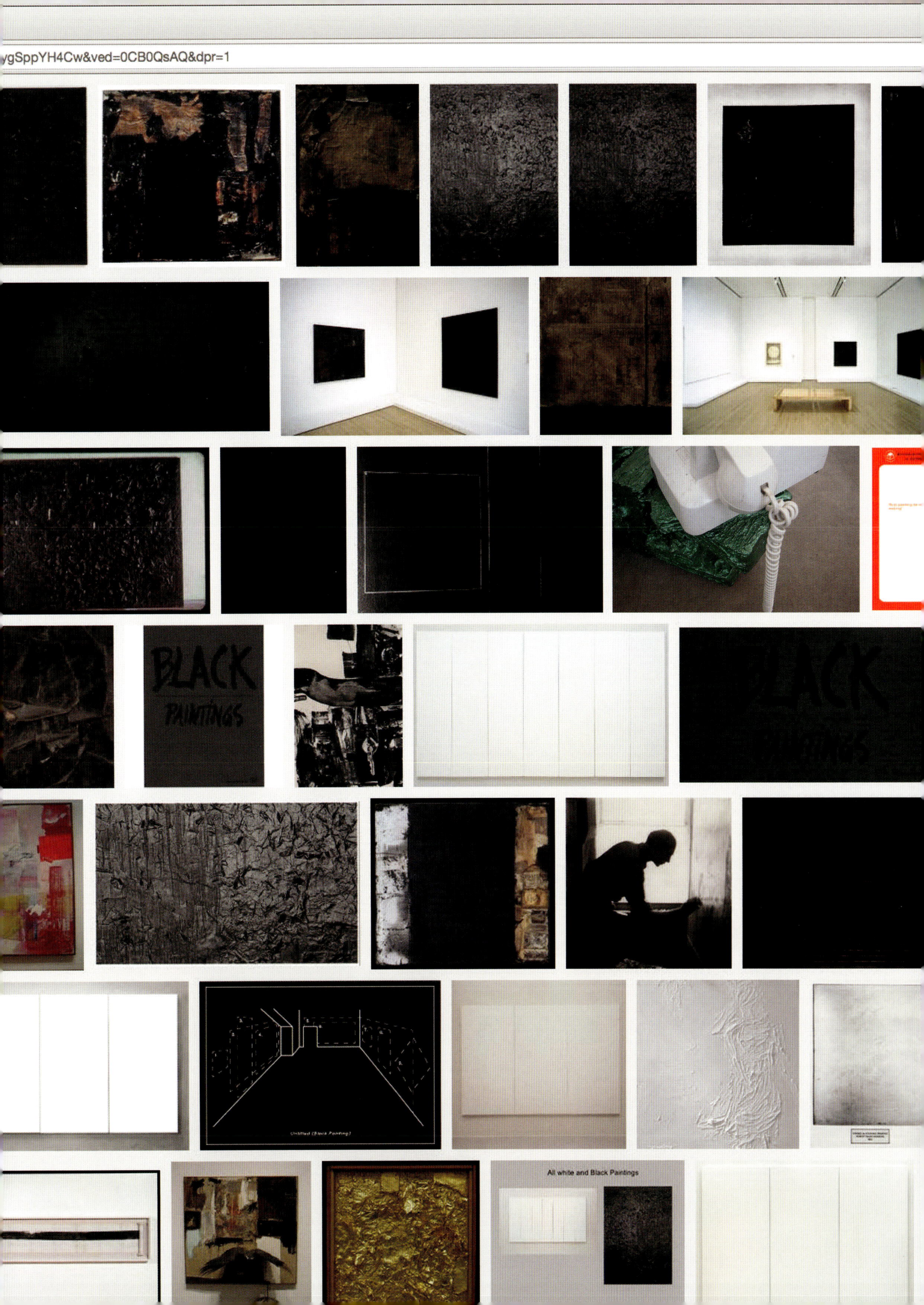

ygSppYH4Cw&ved=0CB0QsAQ&dpr=1
BLACK
PAINTINGS
All white and Black Paintings

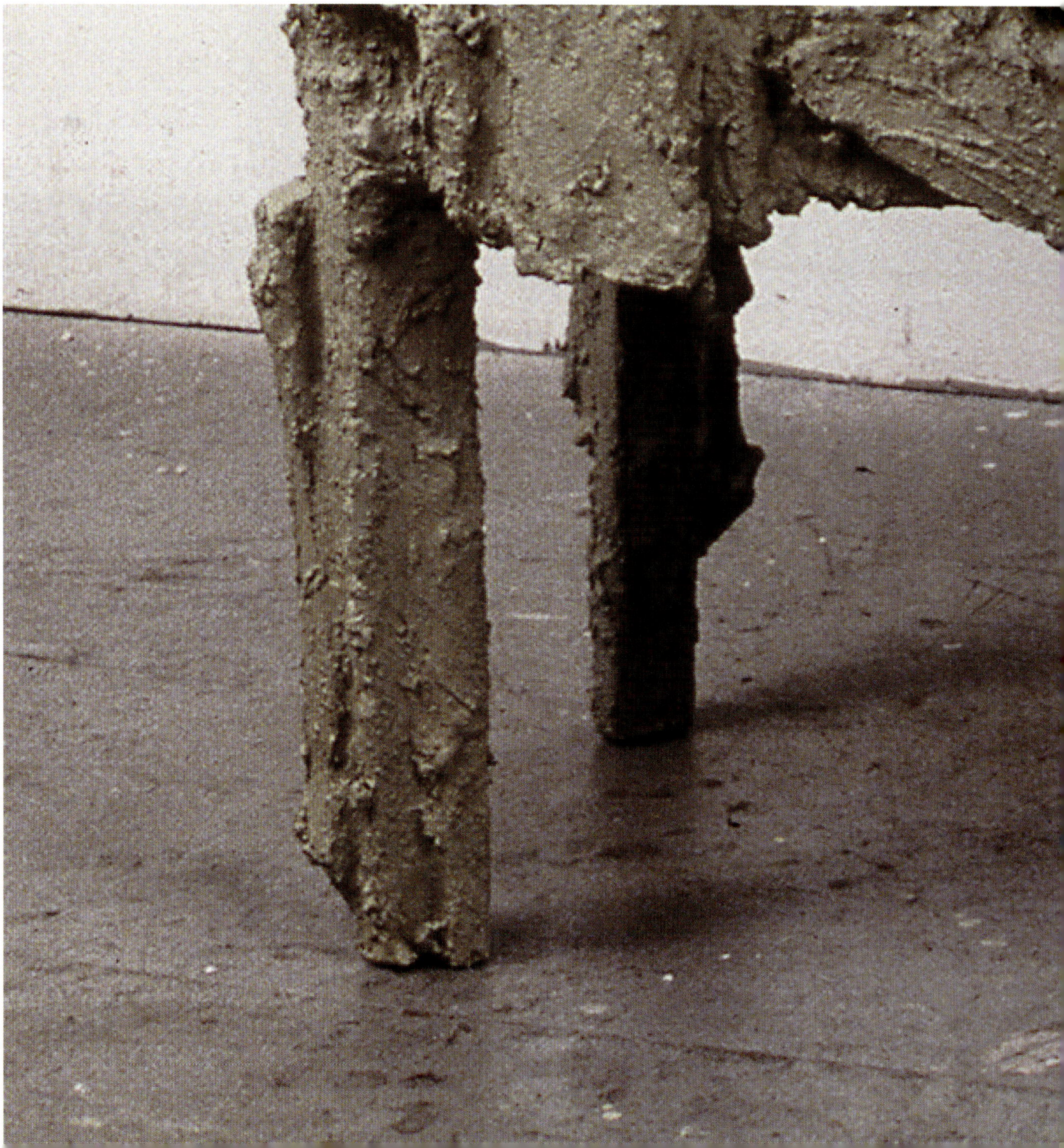

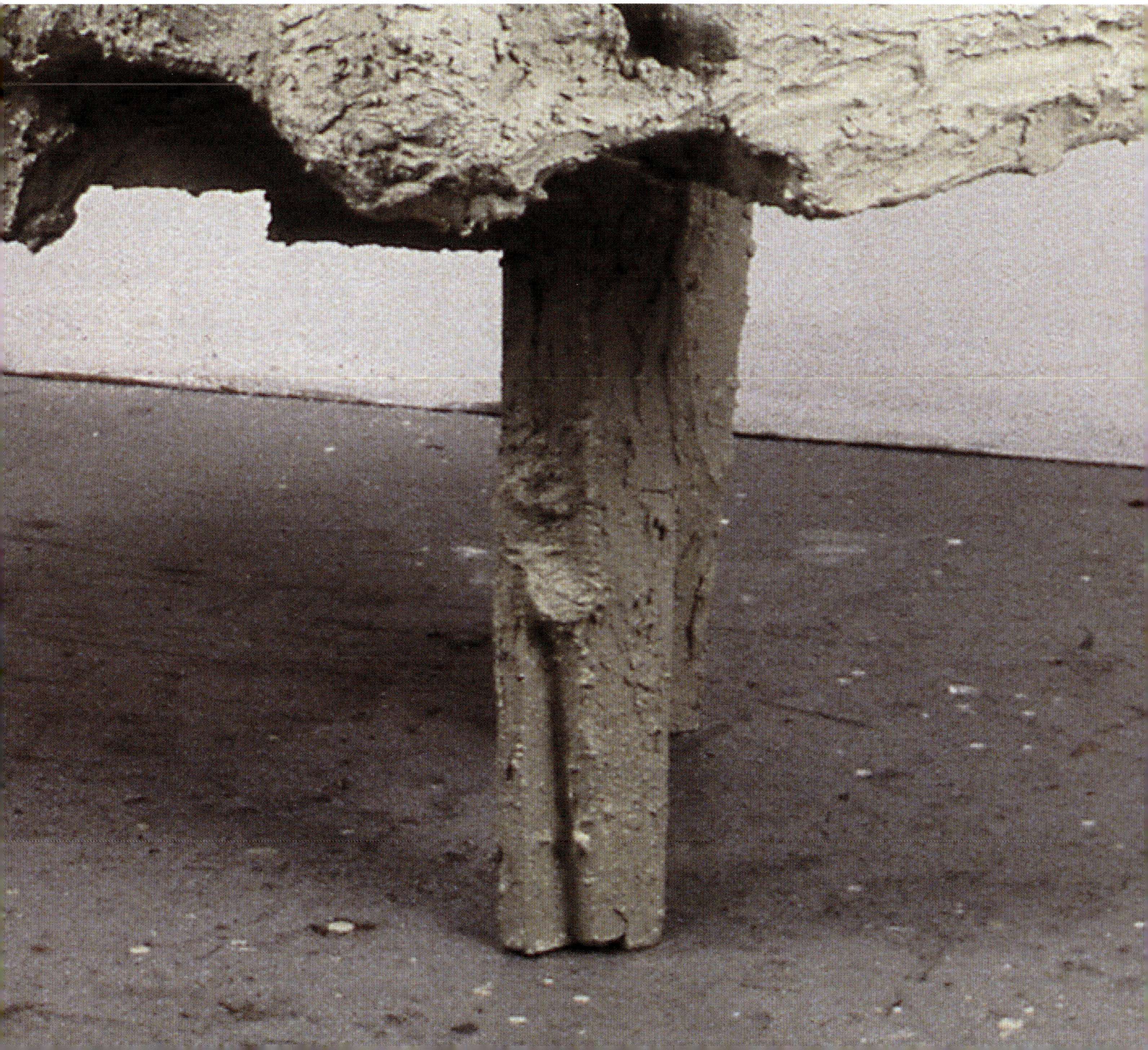

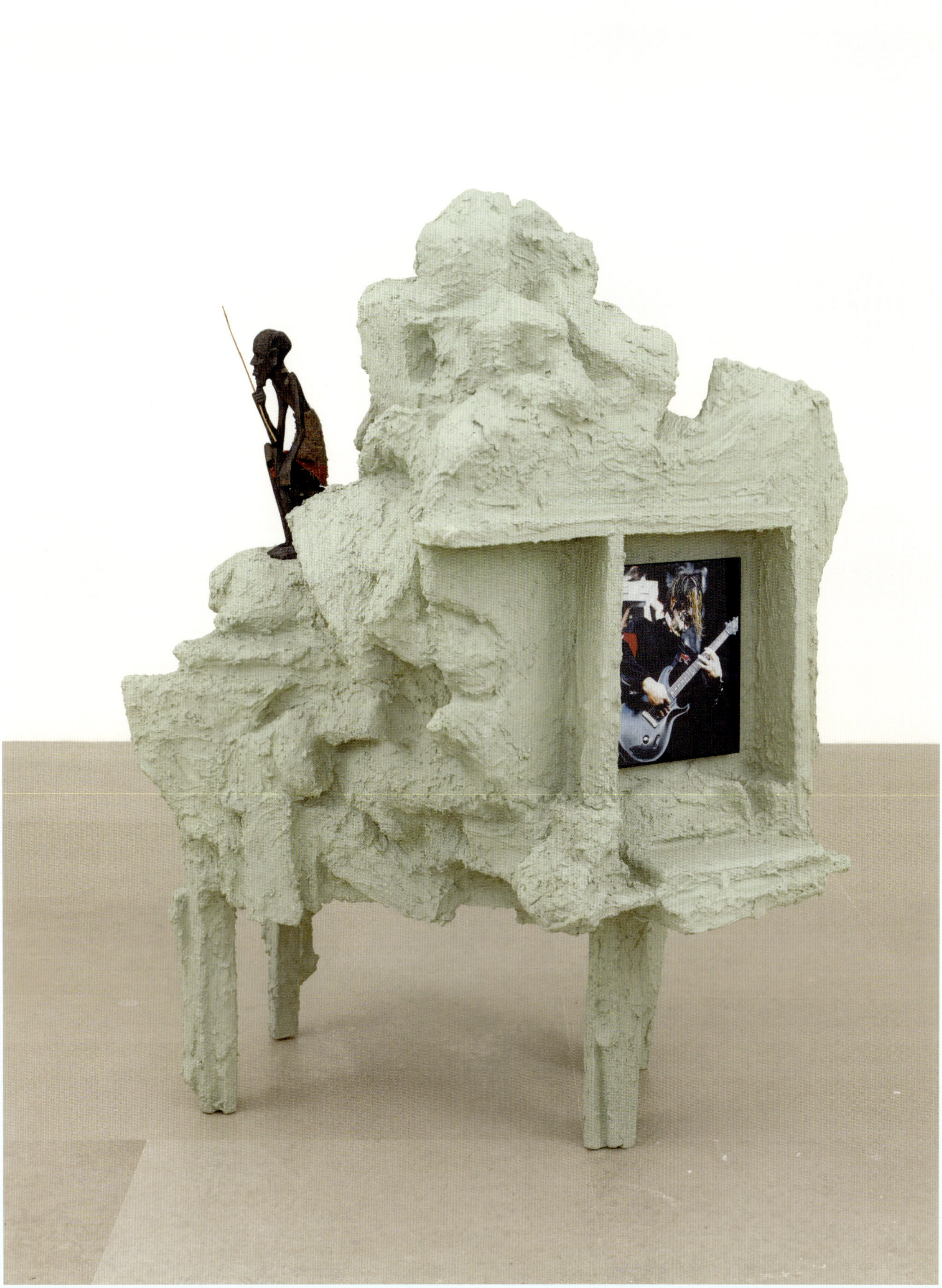

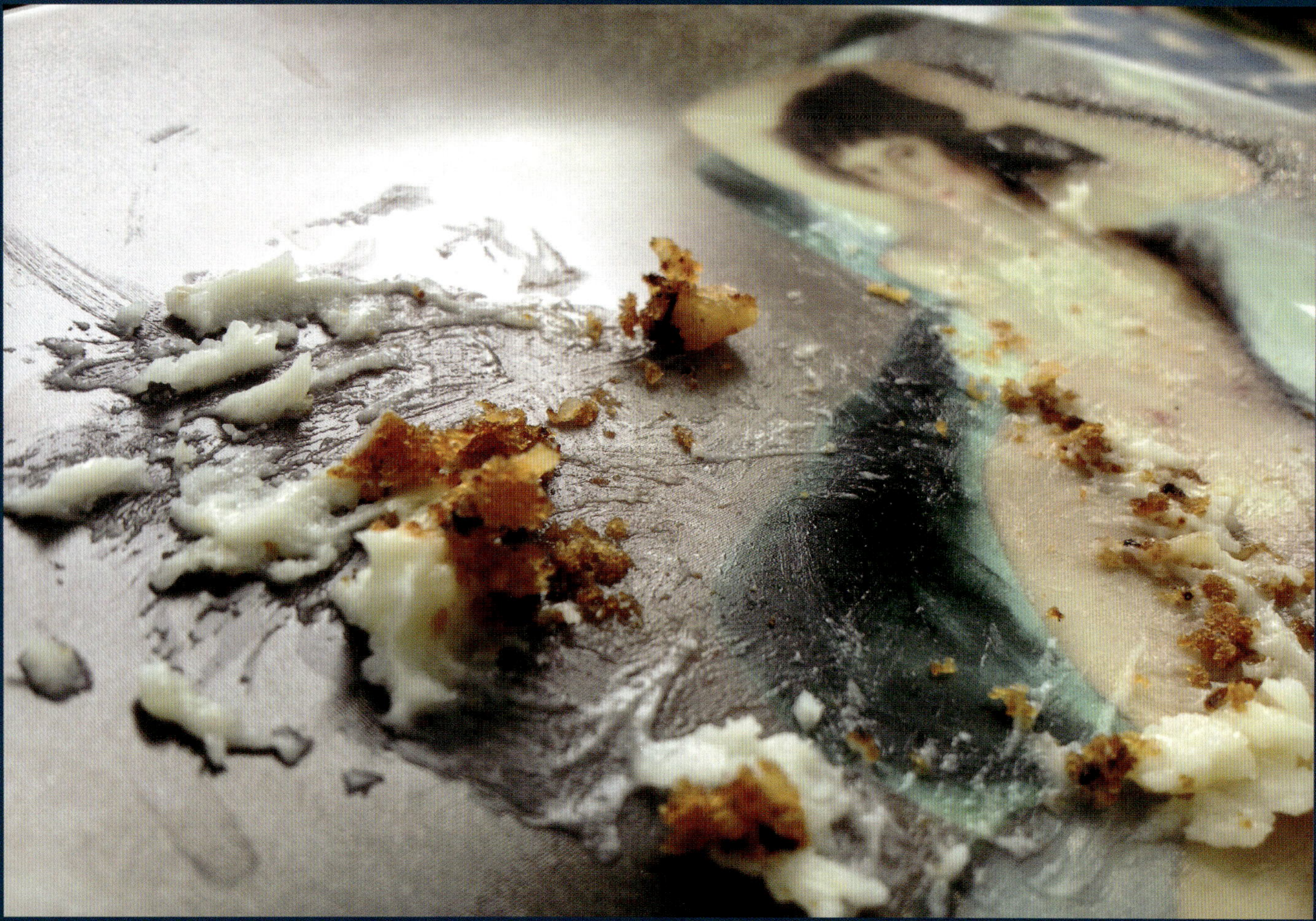

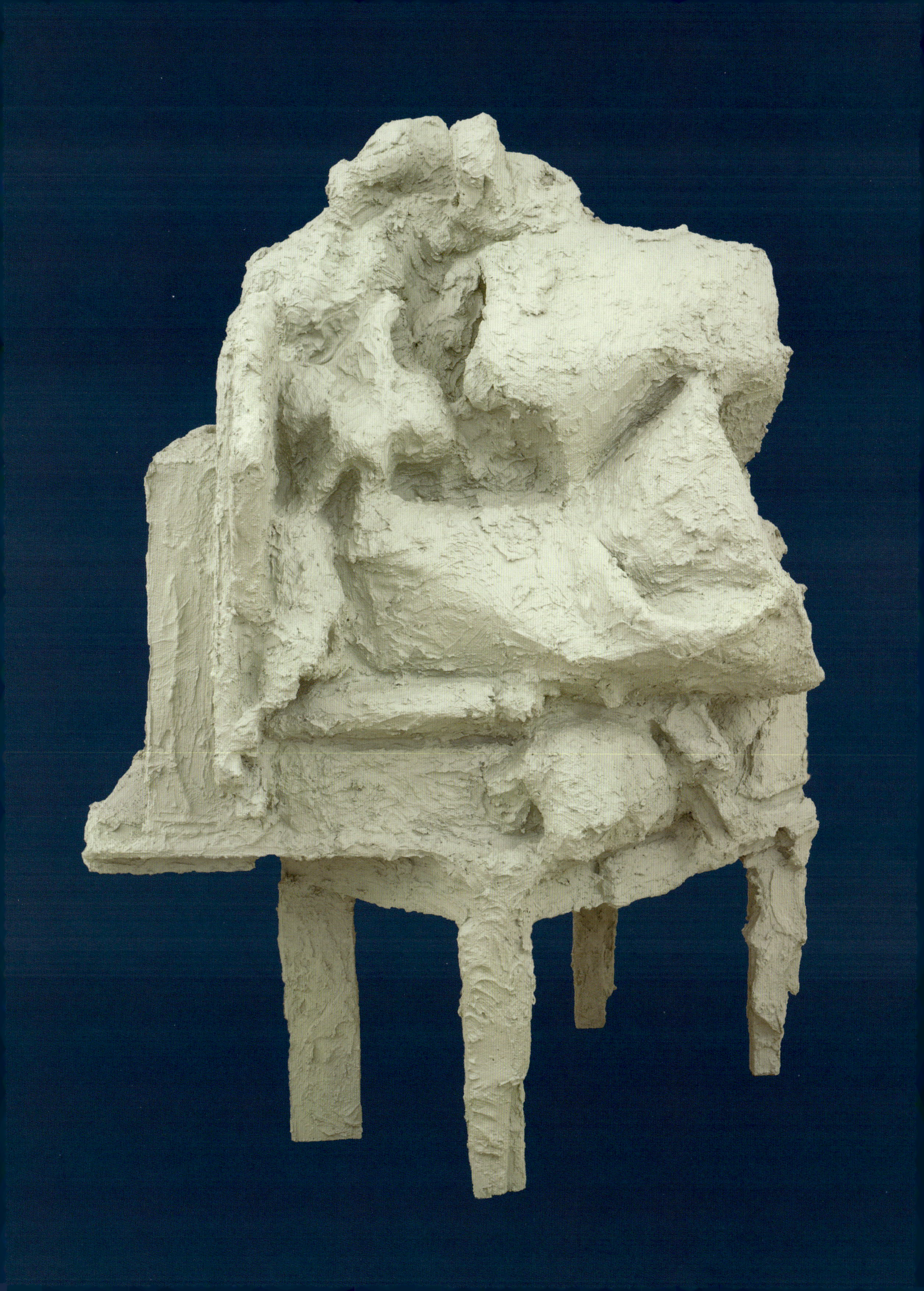

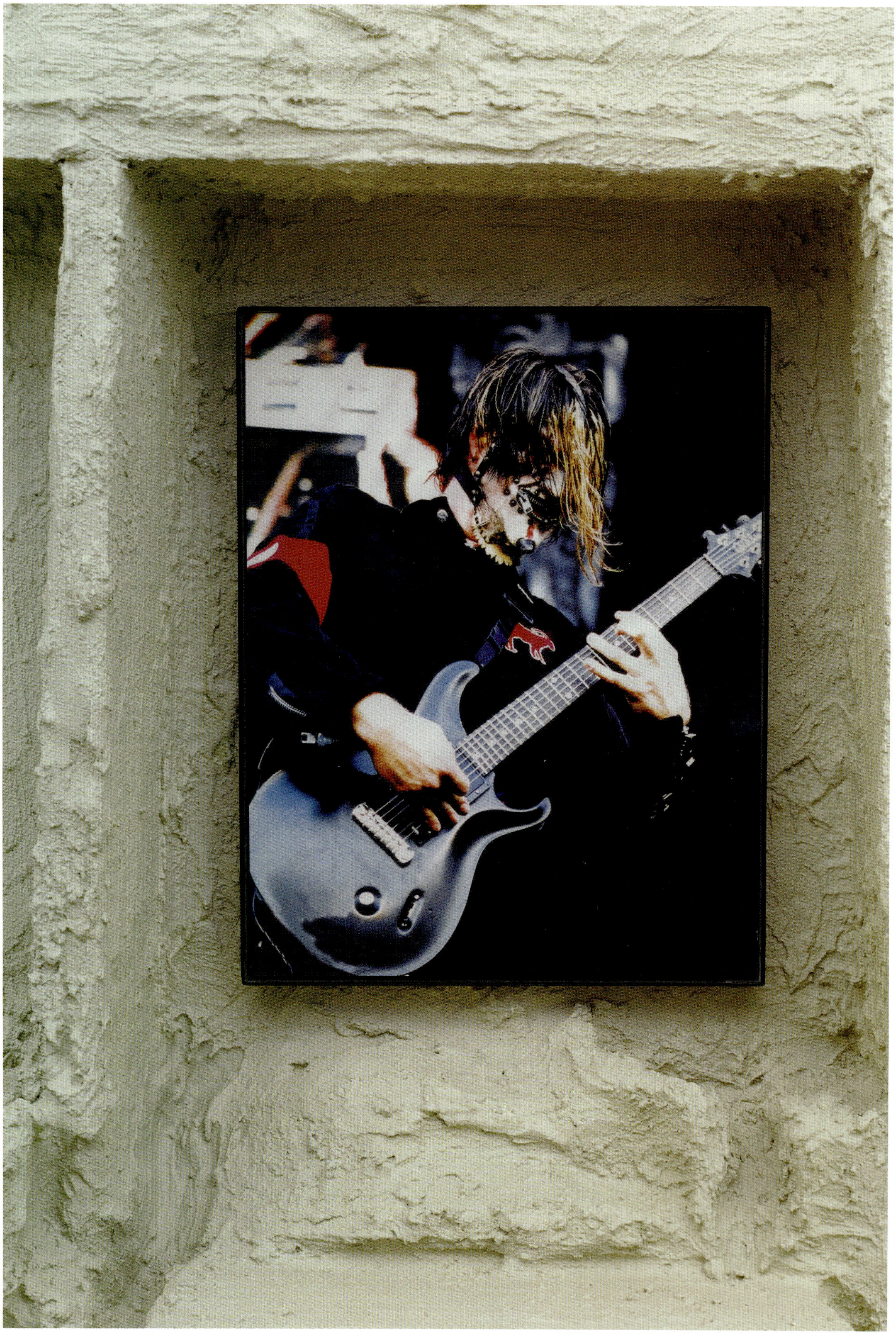

Broodthaers

sions determined
nting in gold
plaque, brass
rope, red carpet.
35 1/2 x 29 in.
rame; carpet.
variable;
(11.4 x 30.4 cm);
iriable.
a 7, Kassel,
ber 28, 1982.
n Kassel by

Foundation.

ening of Docu-
t exhibition in
ered a speech to
of the Federal
to rally support
Pershing II mis-
ccompanied by a
iclear arms, the
Germany since
for the installa-
ocumenta 7 was
oration and res-
of painting.
of this work, the
umenta installa-
presenting local
taken by other

after the demon-
ing anti-nuclear
500,000 people,
f New York to
this rally, taken
venue overpass,
used for the first
n Weber Gallery,

nail Gorbachov
limination of all
siles their coun-
soil.

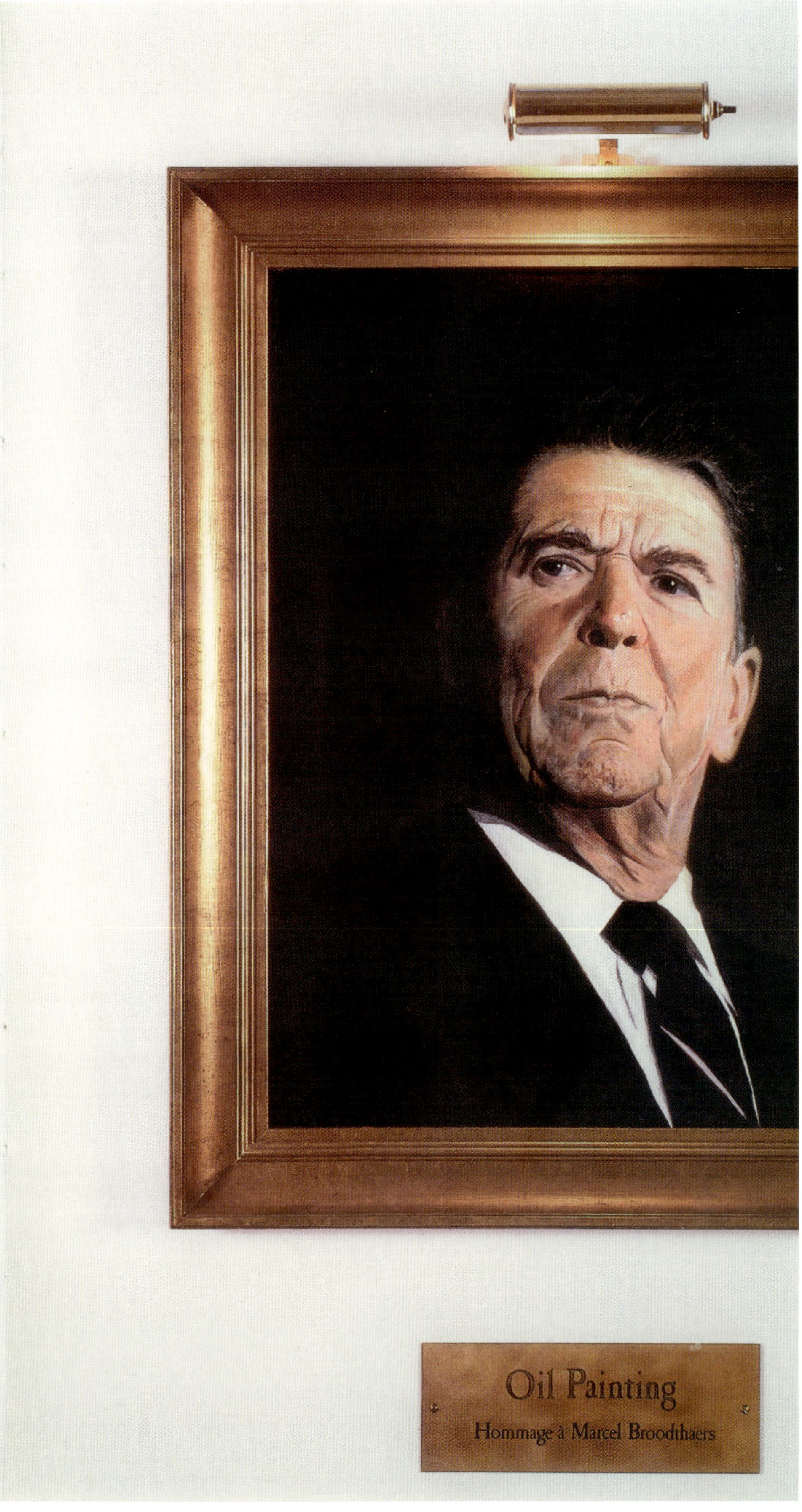

serious person, which I'm not at all. At first it was going to be a serious record. It was going to be more like Happy Days — real overtone serious. ...it just didn't ask for it once I ...ted recording. Once I put the ...al steel in there, I was like: oh no, something else."

...all its surface prettiness and ...-day naïveté, *Bad Timing* ... plenty of connections with ...e's more experimental work. ...erpicking rarely locks into a ...d when it does, the tune ...dissolves into a longform ...is halted by organ swells ... interventions. Midway ...he final track "Happy ...example, a sombre solo ...ry blues is interrupted by ...hestral anthem. Two minutes later the horns, strings and drums slow and ...ving the acoustic guitar to take over briefly before joining the orchestra ...elancholy coda.

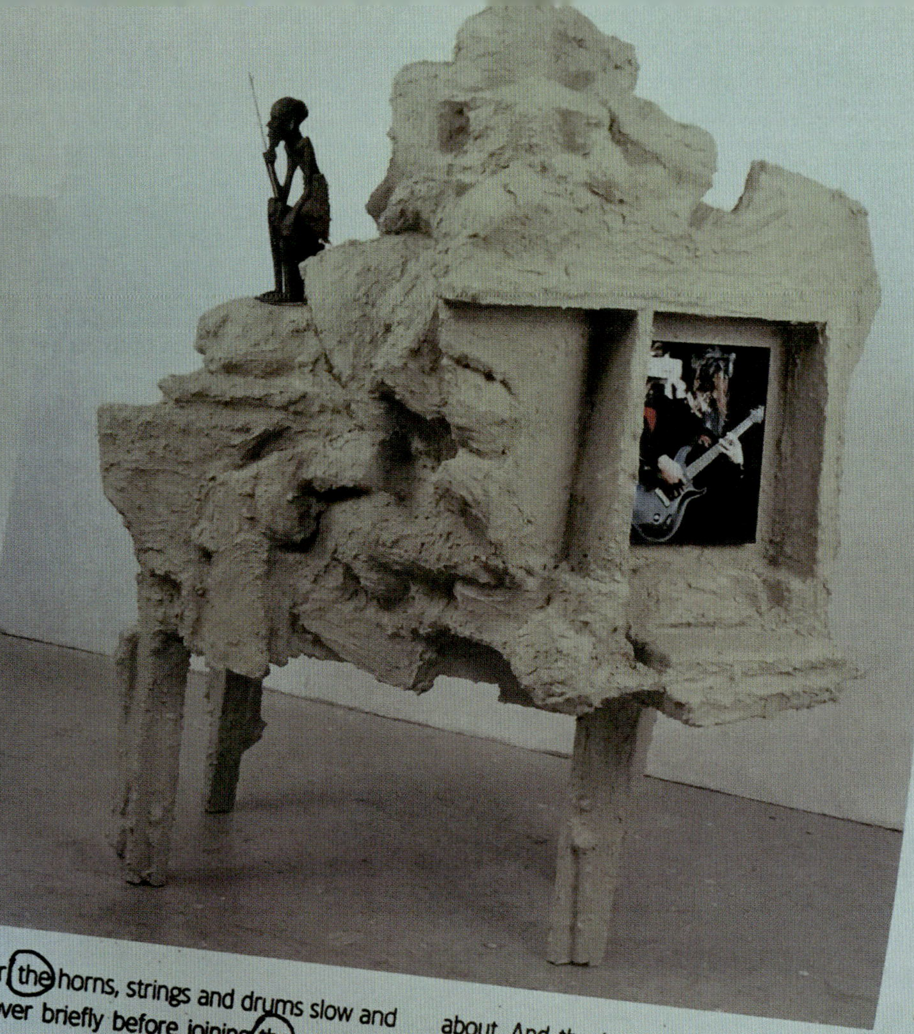

...acility with lush arrangements is also evident in O'Rourke's latest work ...oDeliSol, the avant rock group for which she is best known in the US. O'Rourke and David Grubbs with various guests, GastroDeliSol has ...utation for turning out ...chworks of repetitive guitar ...otifs, lyric fragments and ...ualls that toy with the very ...he pop song, and effect a ...

"I'm always glad when someone makes me uncomfortable. There are very few people who really hassle themselves on a regular basis"

...t year's *Upgrade And Afterlife* attracted plenty of mainstream press ...nd had the duo touring and performing for much of the year. ...cation to a single project and aesthetic seems to conflict with O'Rourke's ...sibilities; and sure enough, upon completion of the group's forthcoming ...*ofleur* she left GastroDeliSol. "Gastro had become almost some damn ... says. "I couldn't do anything else. It was just too much. It was really giving

...t year, O'Rourke had also begun to feel that the group's experimental ...dened into a calculated and formulaic avant gardism. "*Upgrade And* ...pposed to be our pop record, but it ended up not being. When we were ... said, 'Can we please write a song that uses normal chords? We don't ...o that. Why are we continuing to do this?' I mean, I'm not interested in ... *Crackt, Or Fly* [the first Gastr Del Sol record] over four times."

GastroDeliSol's previous four records, *Camofleur* deliberately goes ...s multitracked vocals, sweet tunes and rich palette of trumpet, violin ...n and pedal steel recall Buffalo Springfield–era Neil Young (whose ...ses were notably produced and arranged by Jack Nitzsche) and ... with the angular austerity of those earlier records. "I'm sure a lot of ...g to think: oh, now I'm interested in all of this stuff," O'Rourke says. ...stening to Jack Nitzsche and Van Dyke Parks since I was a little kid. ...n these people. It just wasn't my place to do it yet."

...ne that *Camofleur* is some manifest bid for the top of the charts, it ...g that the record is also a collaboration with Oval's German audio ... for their ability to melt down any musical material into a digital soup ..., buzzes and clicks. Oval's contribution throws *Camofleur*'s pop ...er. Its low volume fits and starts provide an unsettling undercurrent

that is even more disturbi... fact that it isn't foregrounde... in the mix alongside jazzy and lilting pedal stee... conjunction that's as enigm... unnerving as anything Gast... has recorded.

Asked about his plans ... coming year, O'Rourke ... as if genuinely trying to rem... whether or not she'll be ... anything. After a mom... deliberation, she mentions that ... recently been asked to join D... Behrman and Takehisa Kosugi in Merce Cunningham Dan... Company's music ensemble. "Tha... kinda nifty," she muses, "to be part o... this tradition I grew up reading about. And they're really nice to think I'm OK enough to work with them." Having already completed production work on John Fahey's new Womblife records and Faust's Rien album, an assignment that turned into a year-long nightmare of tape edits (see *The Wire* 145) she now reels off a list of imminent production jobs, among them Edith Frost, Loren Mazzacane Connors, and Flying Saucer Attack. A 10" plunderphonics record, "Please Note Our Failure", will be out soon on Fire, a small Icelandic label. "I figured it was a way to put out something that otherwise I'd get sued for," she says. "Everything's lifted. There's nothing original on it." And following brilliant and wildly varying remixes for The Sea And Cake, Merzbow, Tortoise and Microstoria, O'Rourke is looking forward to more ...

"Everything I like doing is in one thing: I get material that's already culturally loaded, so I can deal with it in that regard; I get to do concrète stuff, which I love to do; it's always something different, so I have to really reconceptualise it every single time; I get to sit in my studio for two weeks working on a remix. I love it." Various other projects include a collaboration with sound and video artist John Duncan, and playing lap steel with digital noisemakers Peter Rehberg and Christian Fennesz from Vienna's Mego label. After this torrent, he pauses again, quickly runs through his mental agenda, and concludes: "That's about it." ☐ *Jim O'Rourke's Web site, "Hoobalaboobala", is at http://pages.ripco.com:8080/~muni/*

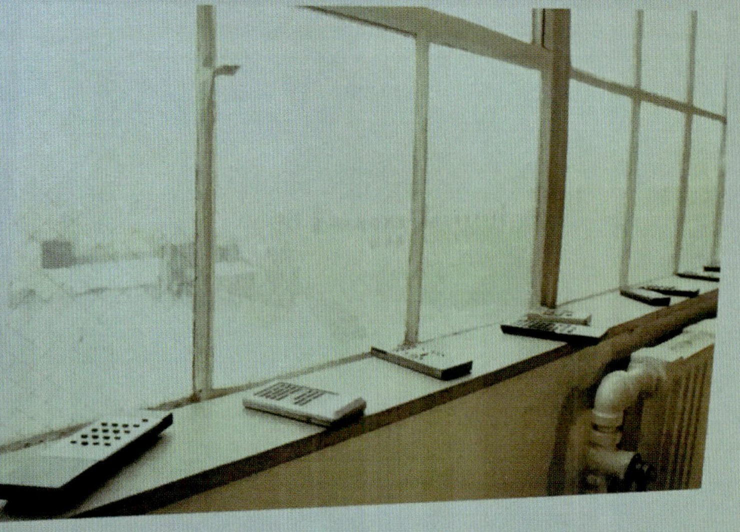

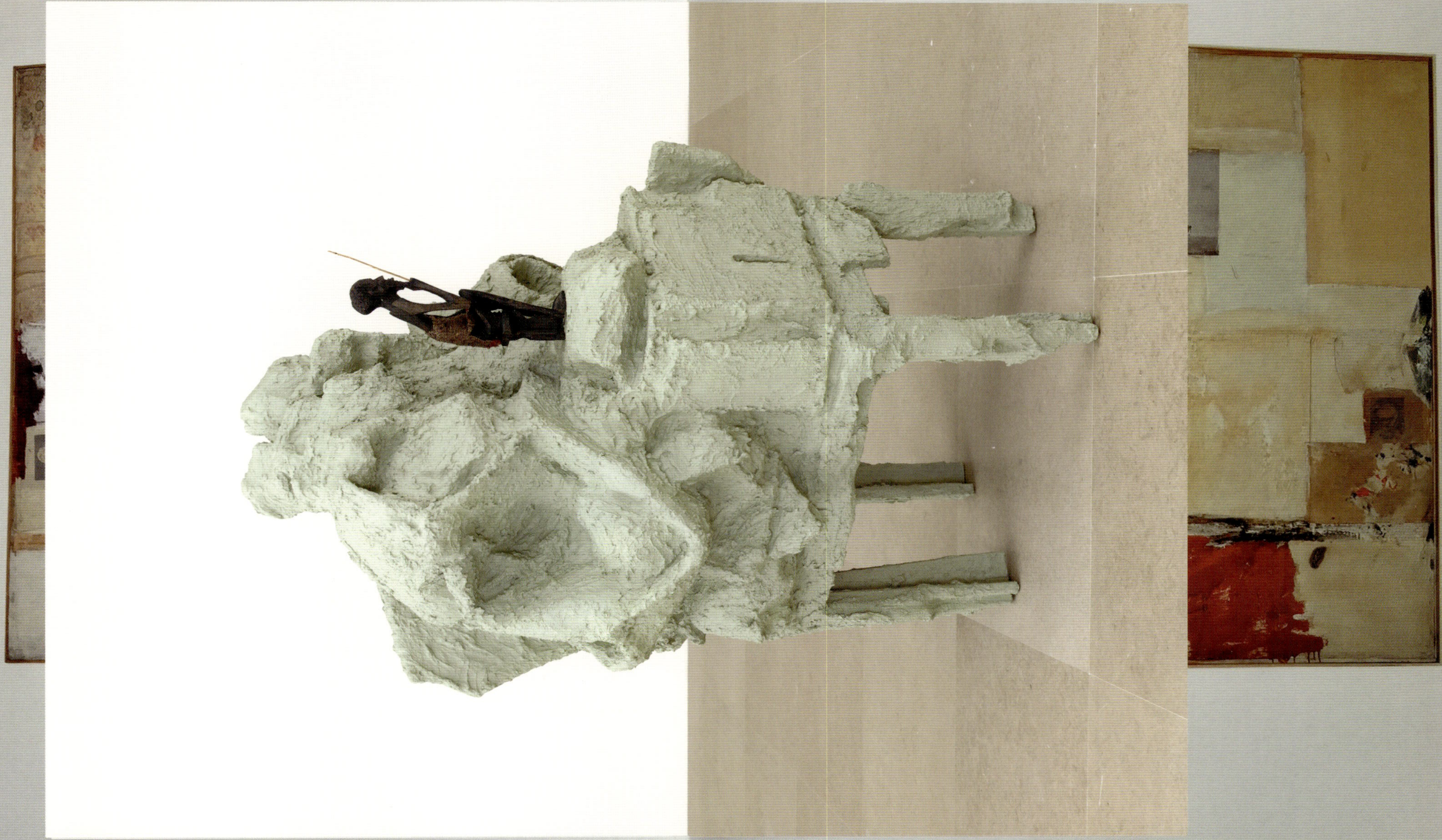

*

PLATE 35 **Honeysuckle**, 1956
Oil, paper, newspaper, printed reproductions, fabric, and ankle brace on canvas
48 x 48 inches
Collection Jasper Johns

PLATE 36 **Gloria**, 1956
Oil, paper, fabric, newspaper, printed paper, and printed reproductions on canvas
66½ x 63¾ inches
Cleveland Museum of Art
Gift of The Cleveland Society for Contemporary Art

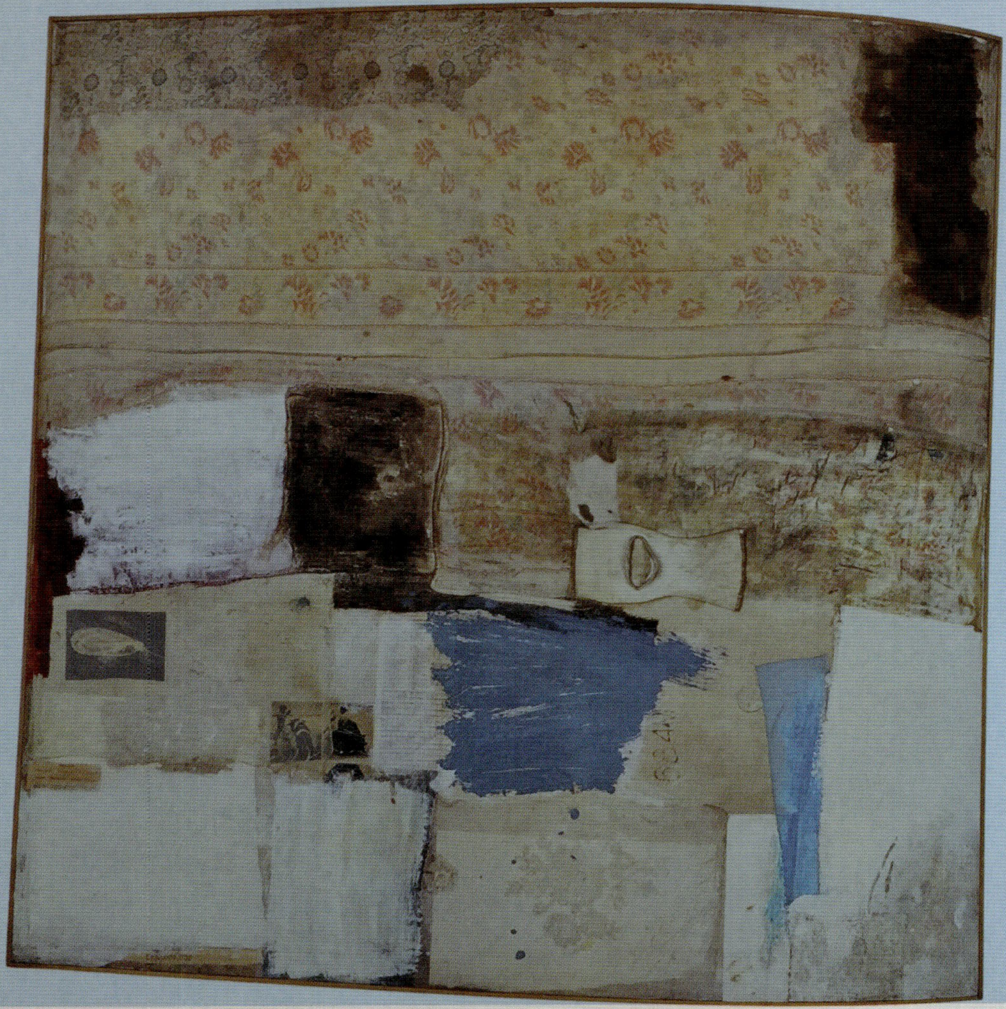

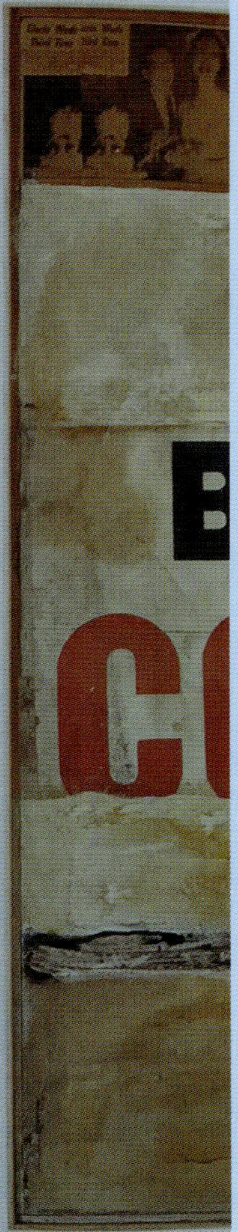

*
PLATE 35 **Honeysuckle**, 1956
Oil, paper, newspaper, printed reproductions,

sopranos
THEATRICAL TEAMSTERS
LOCAL 817
NEW YORK CITY

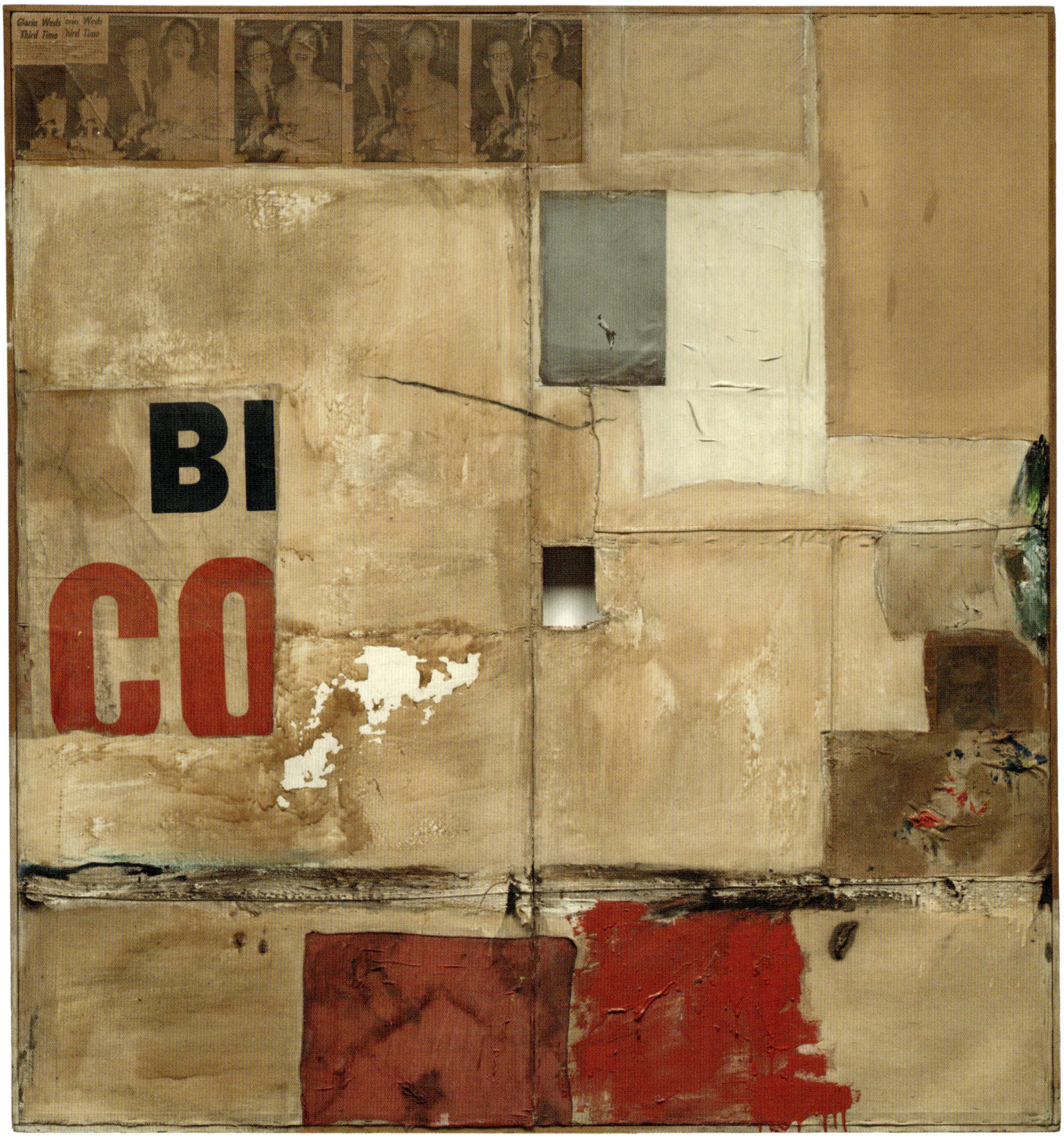
Gloria Weds
Third Time
BI
CO

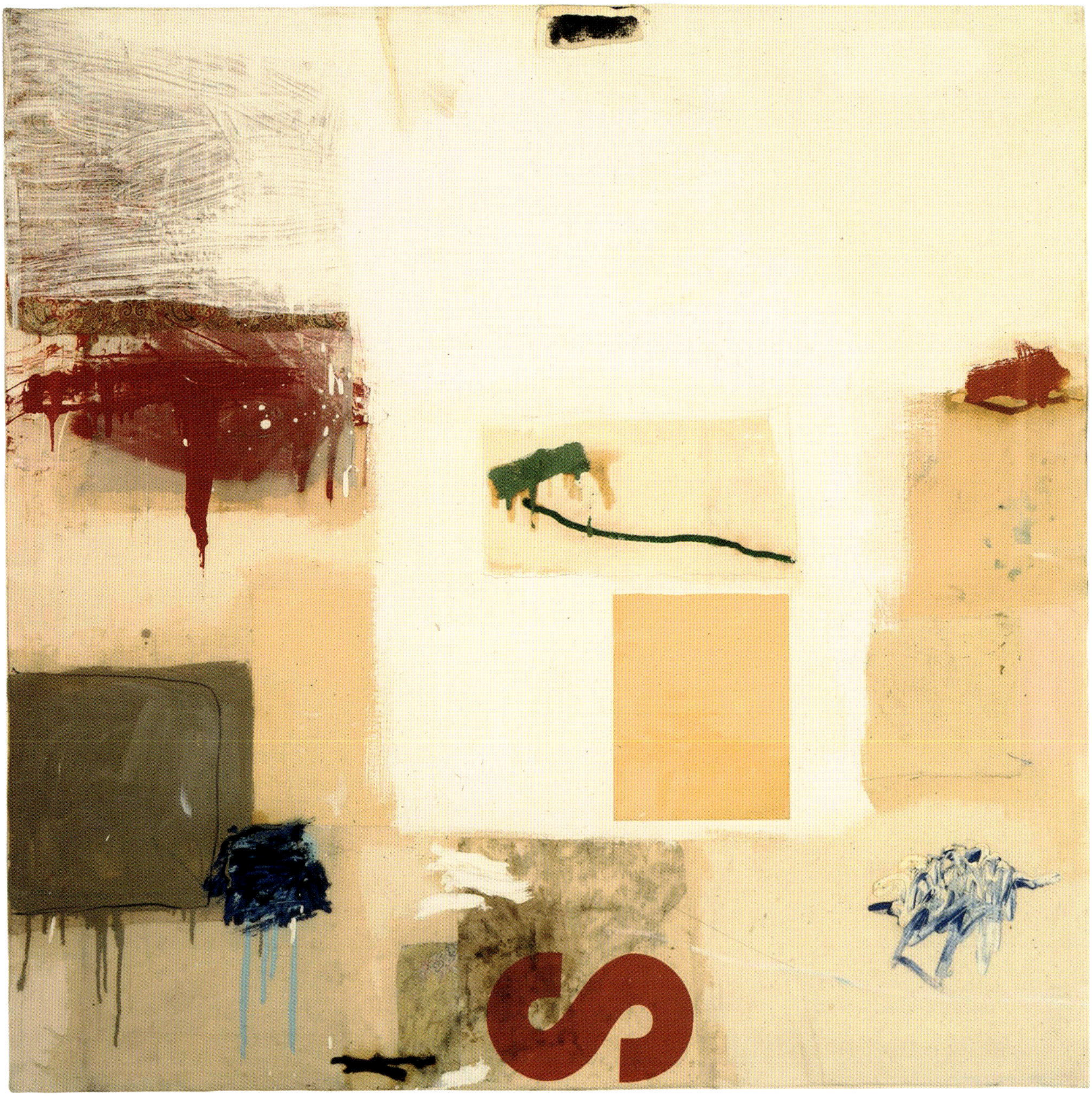
S

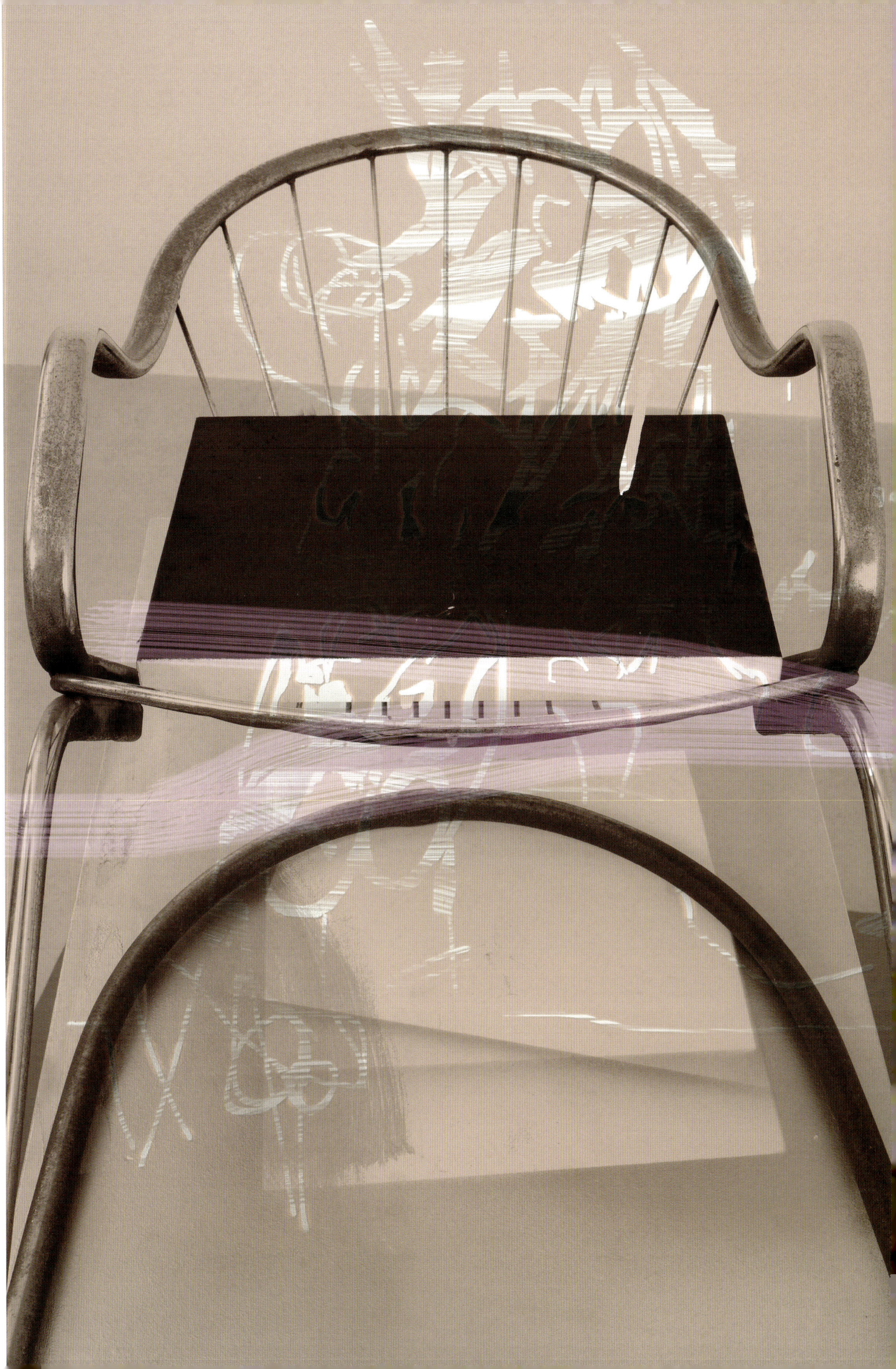

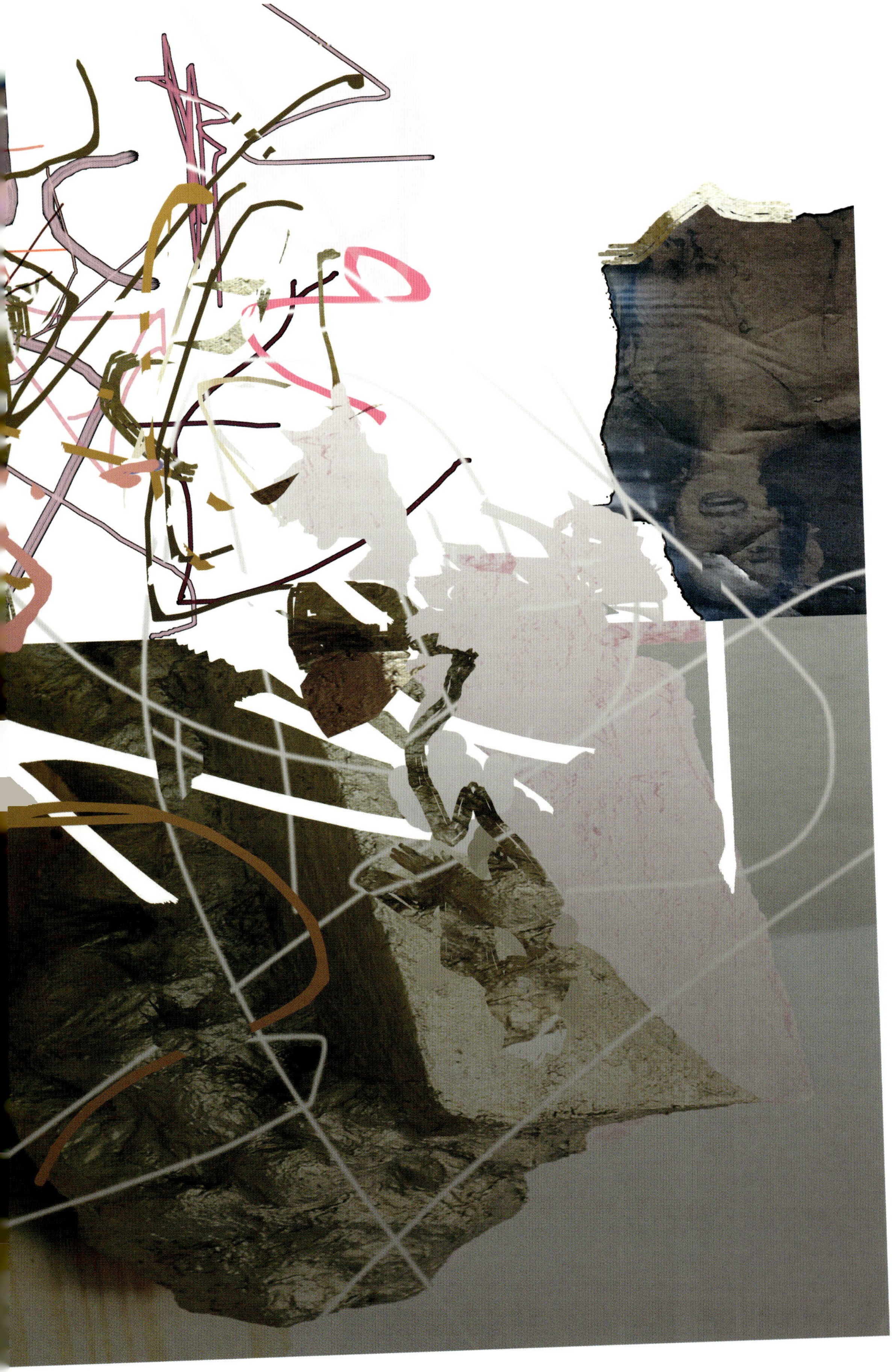

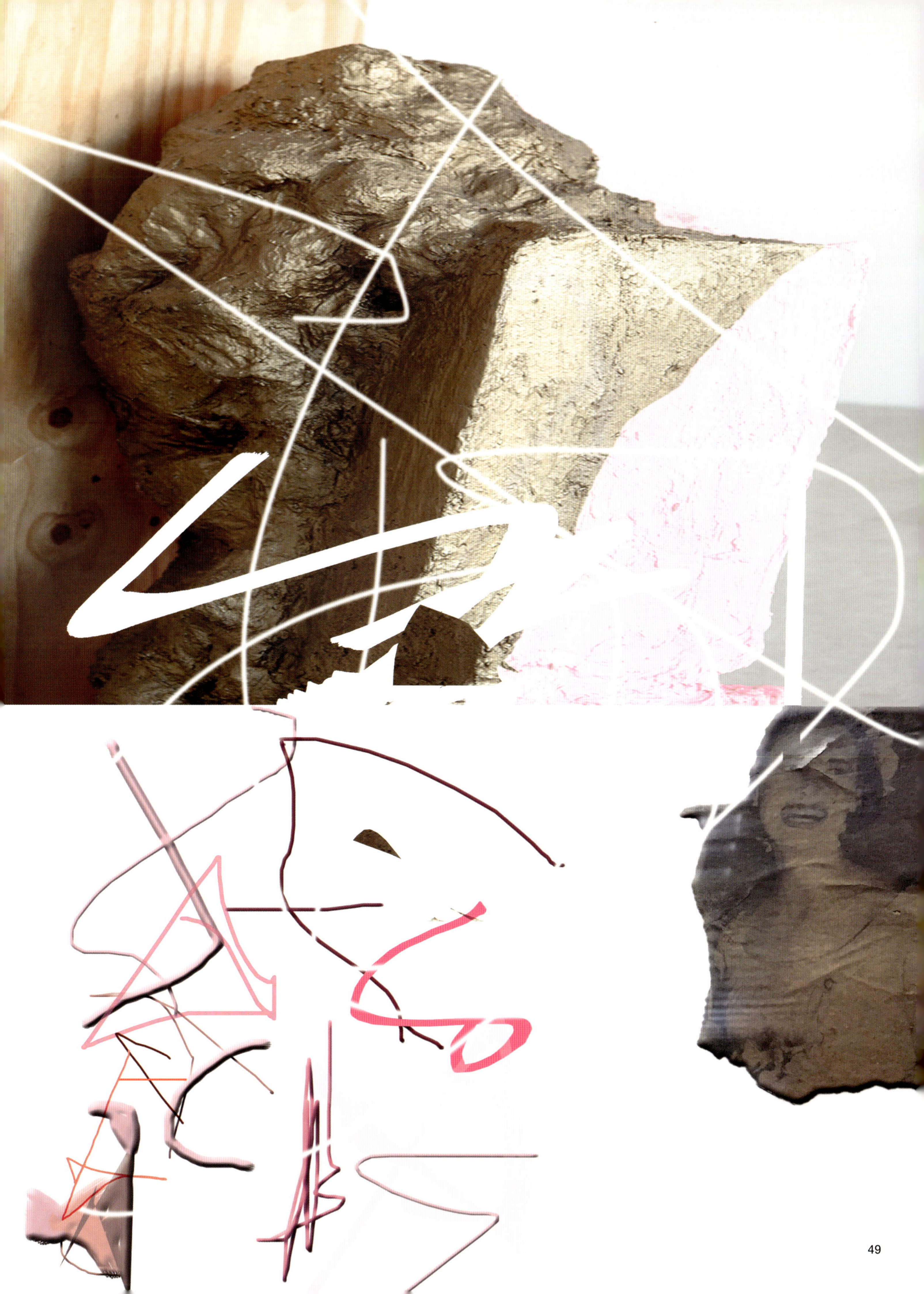

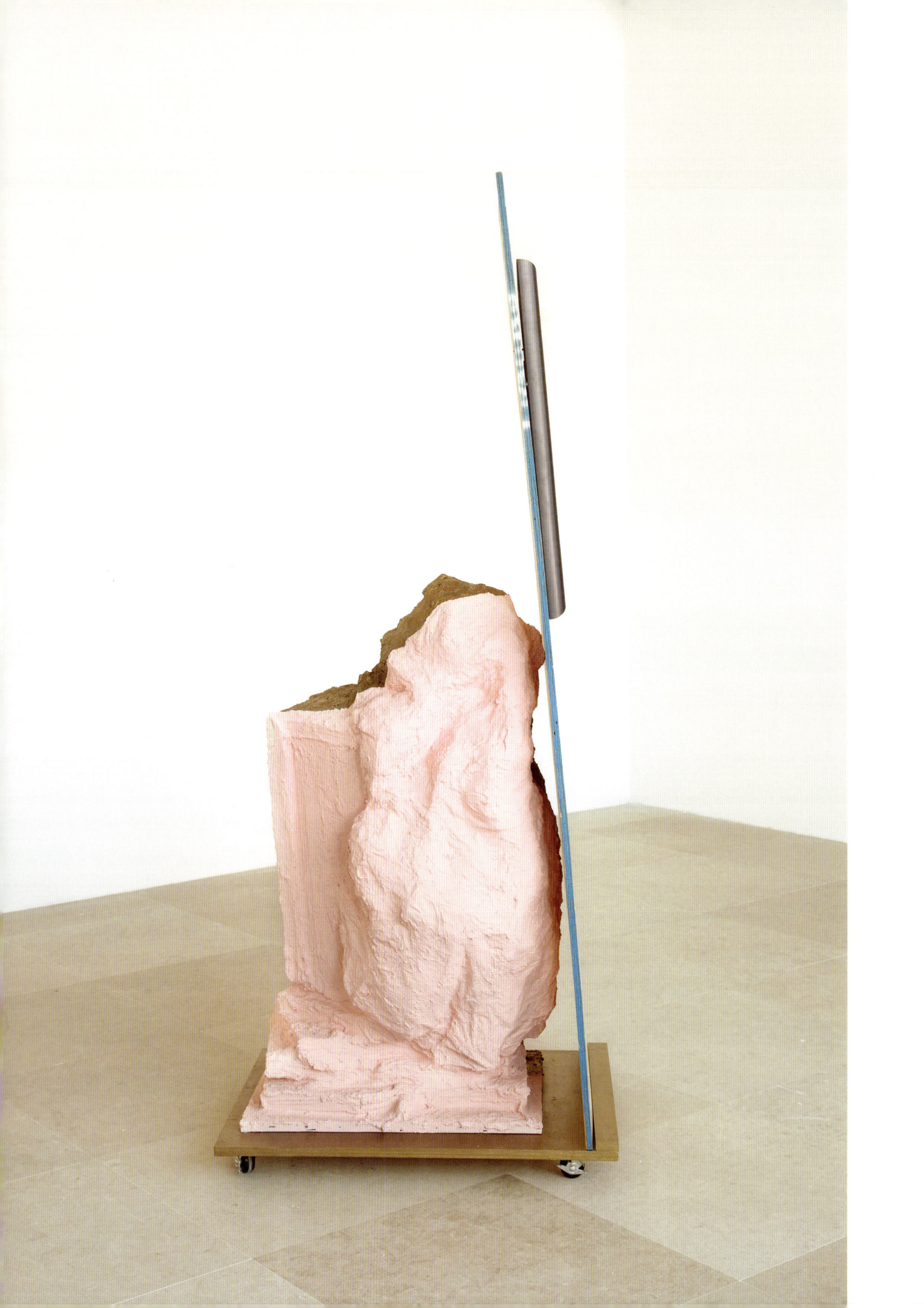

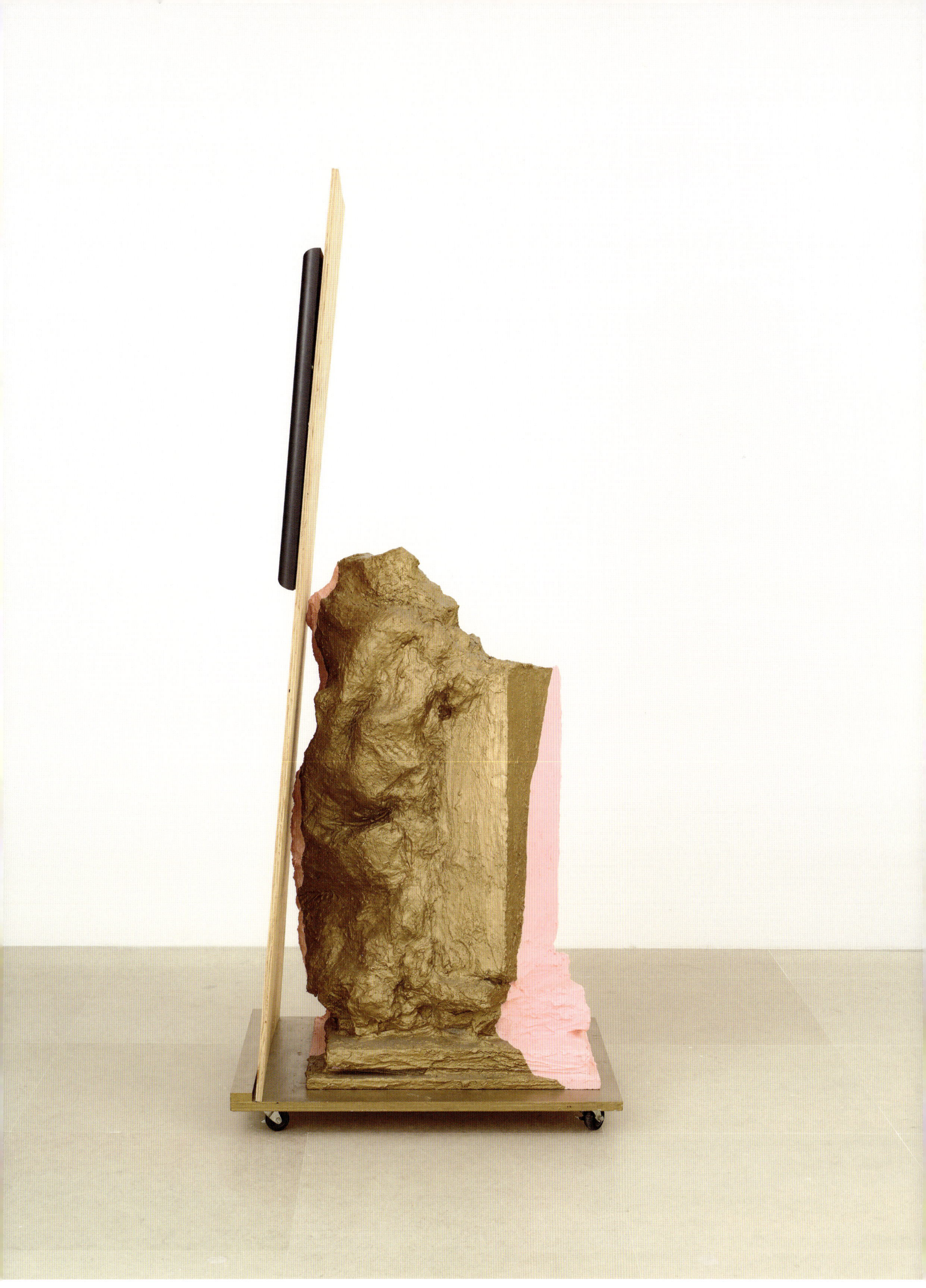

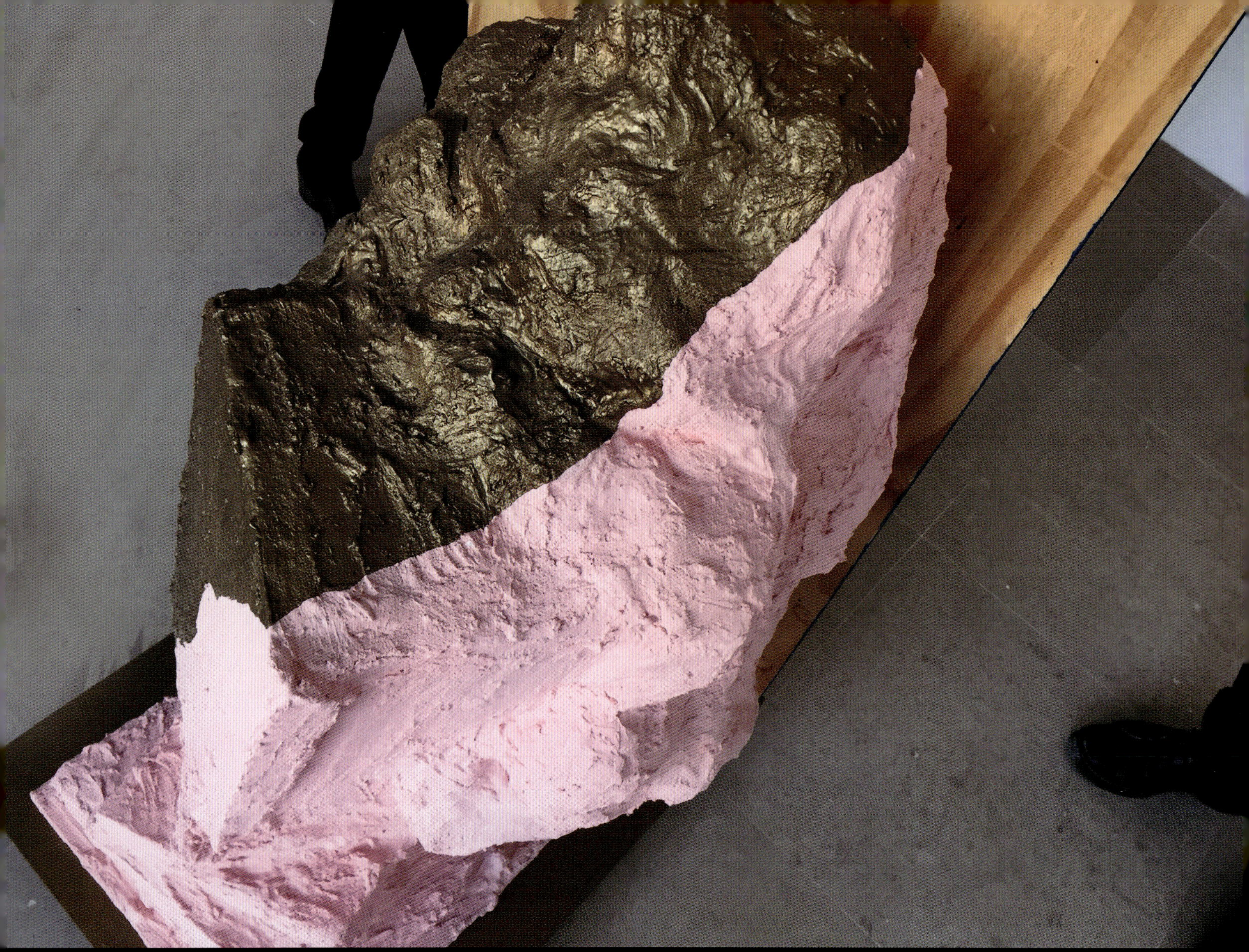

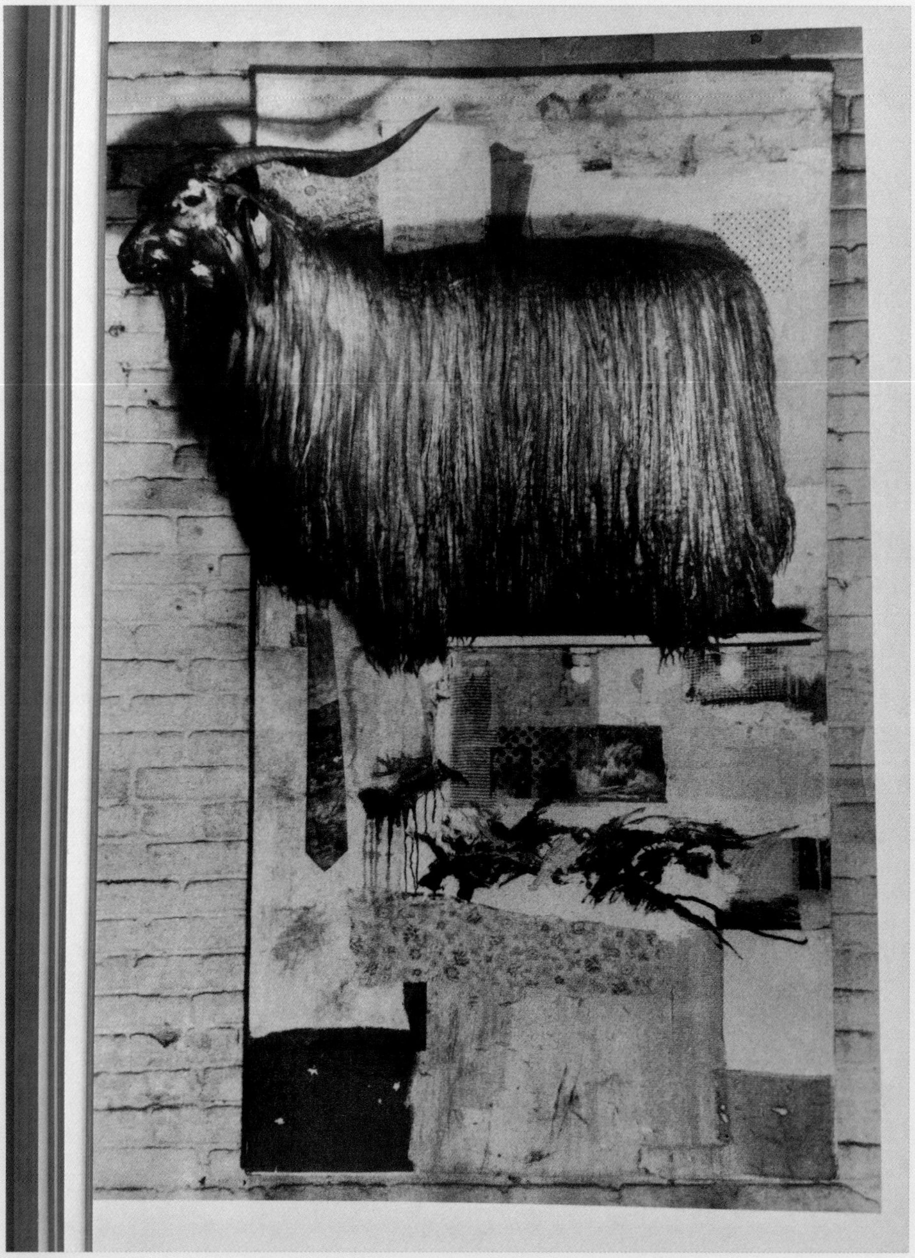

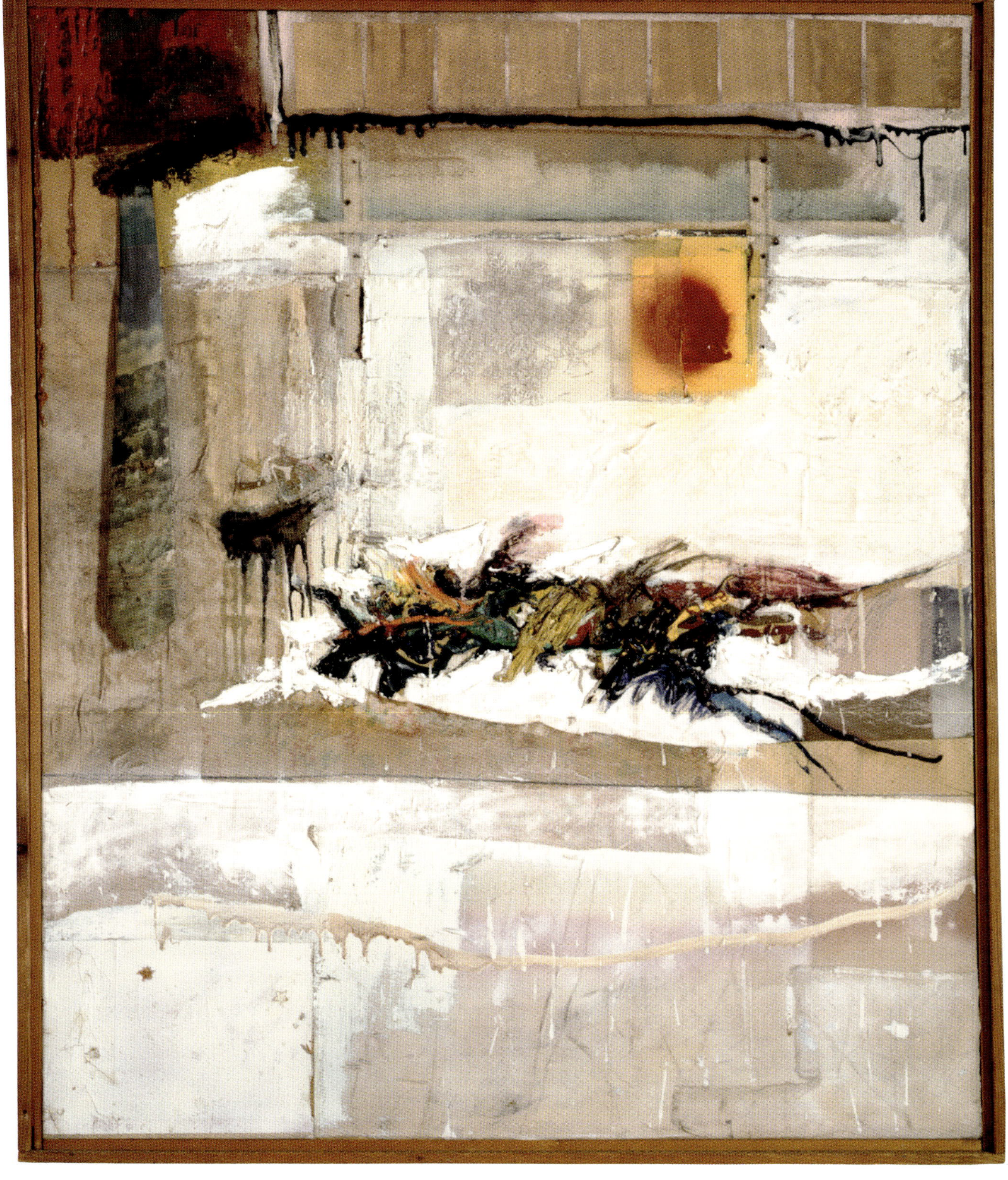

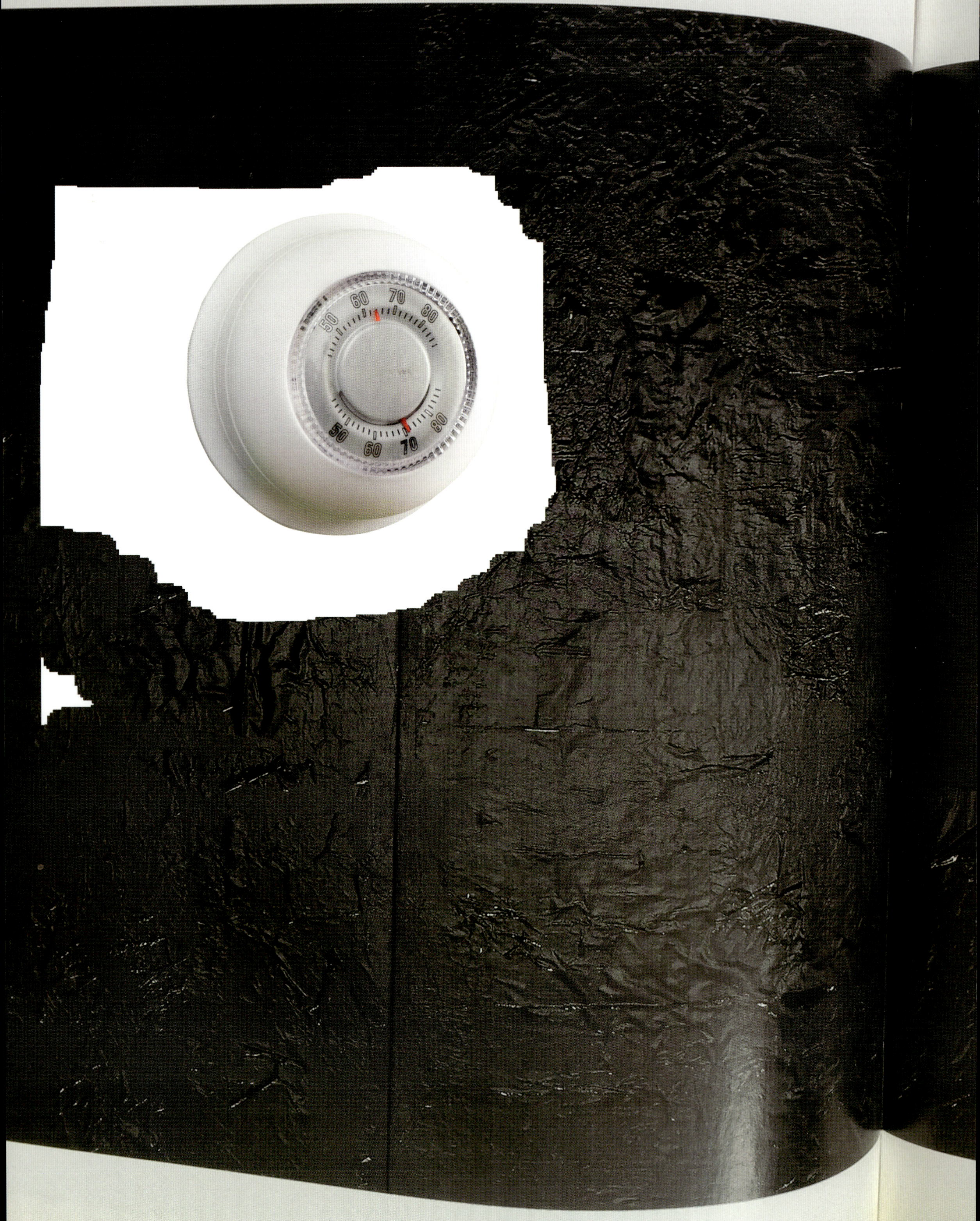
50 60 70 80
50 60 70 80

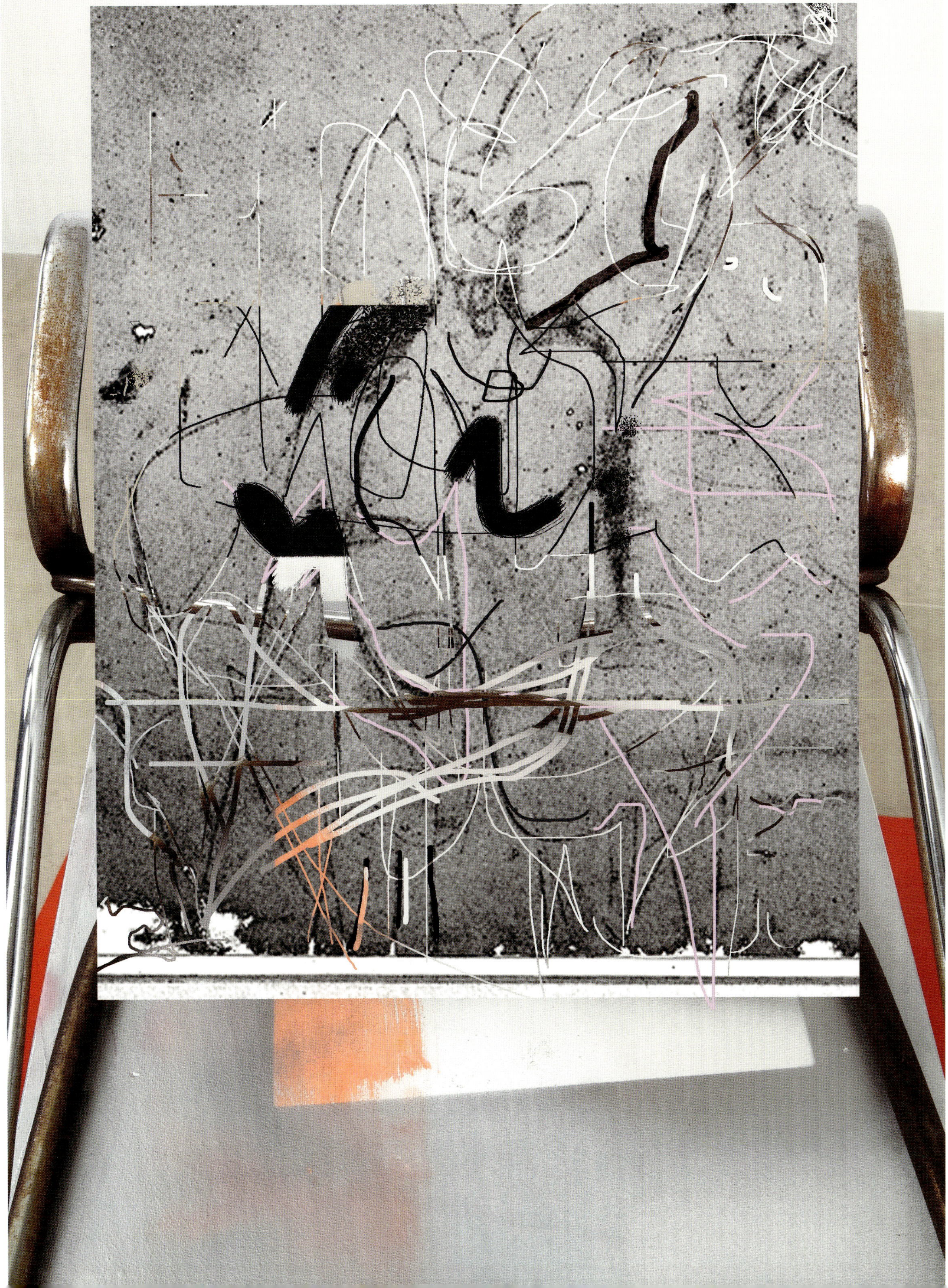

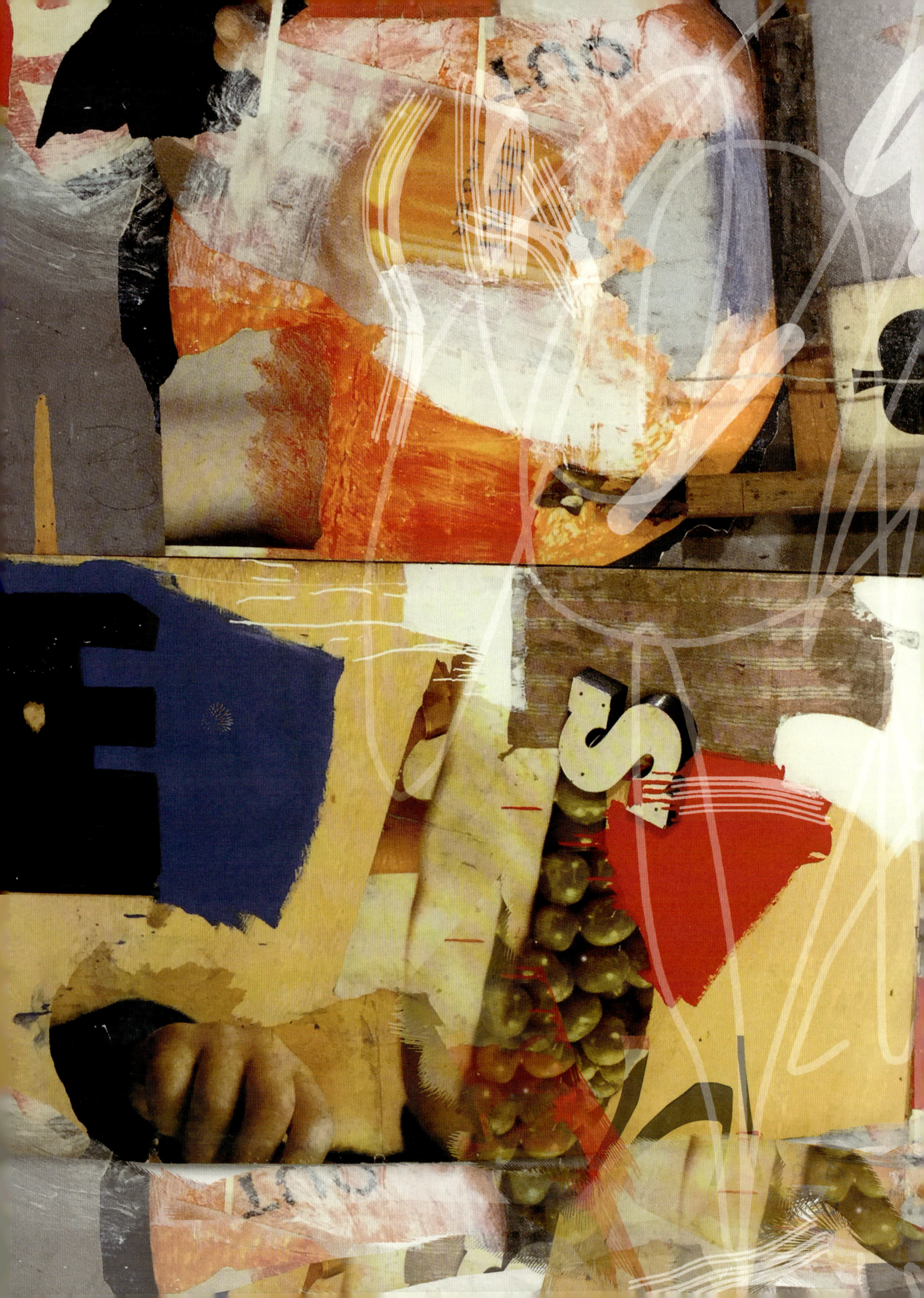

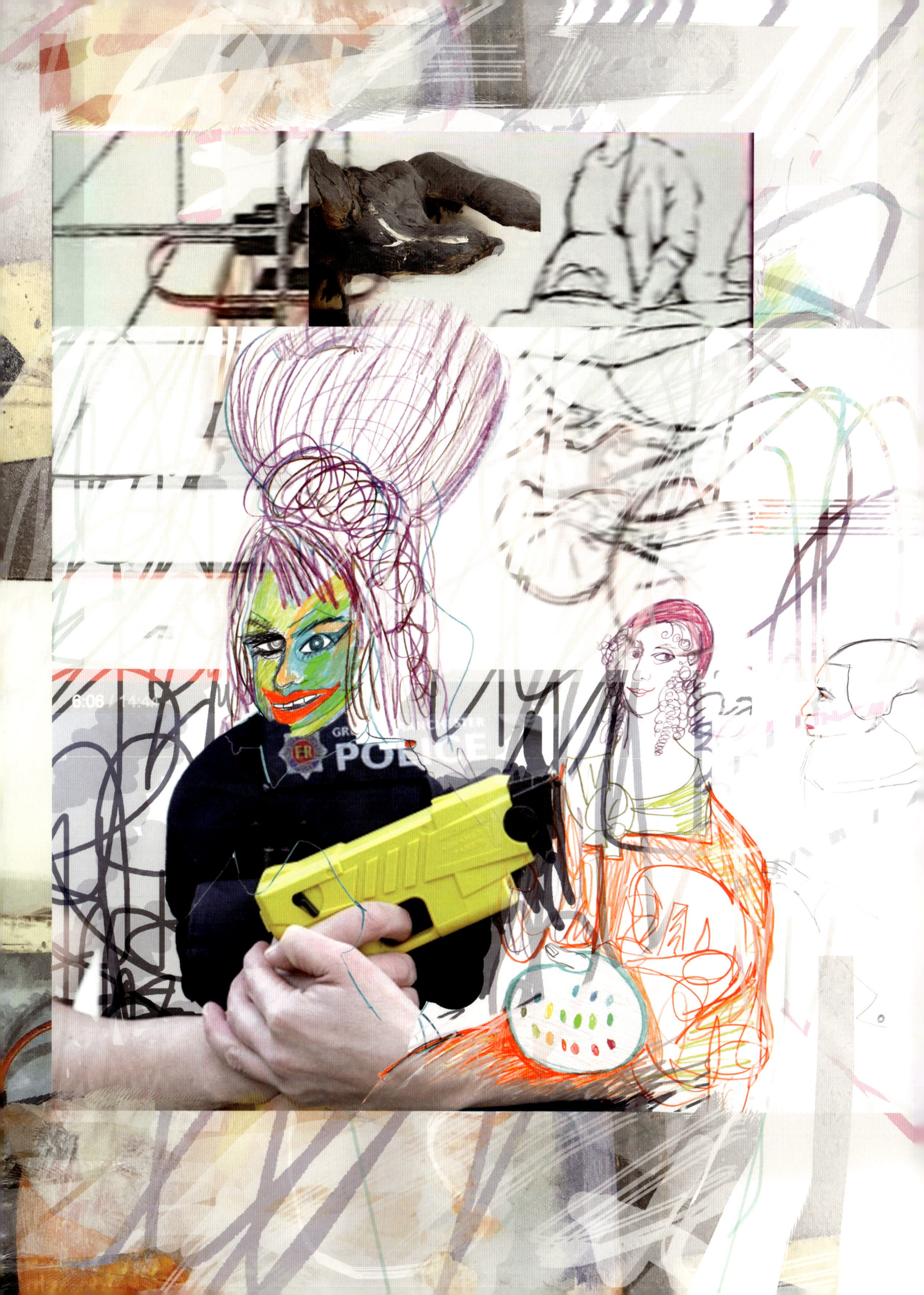
6:06

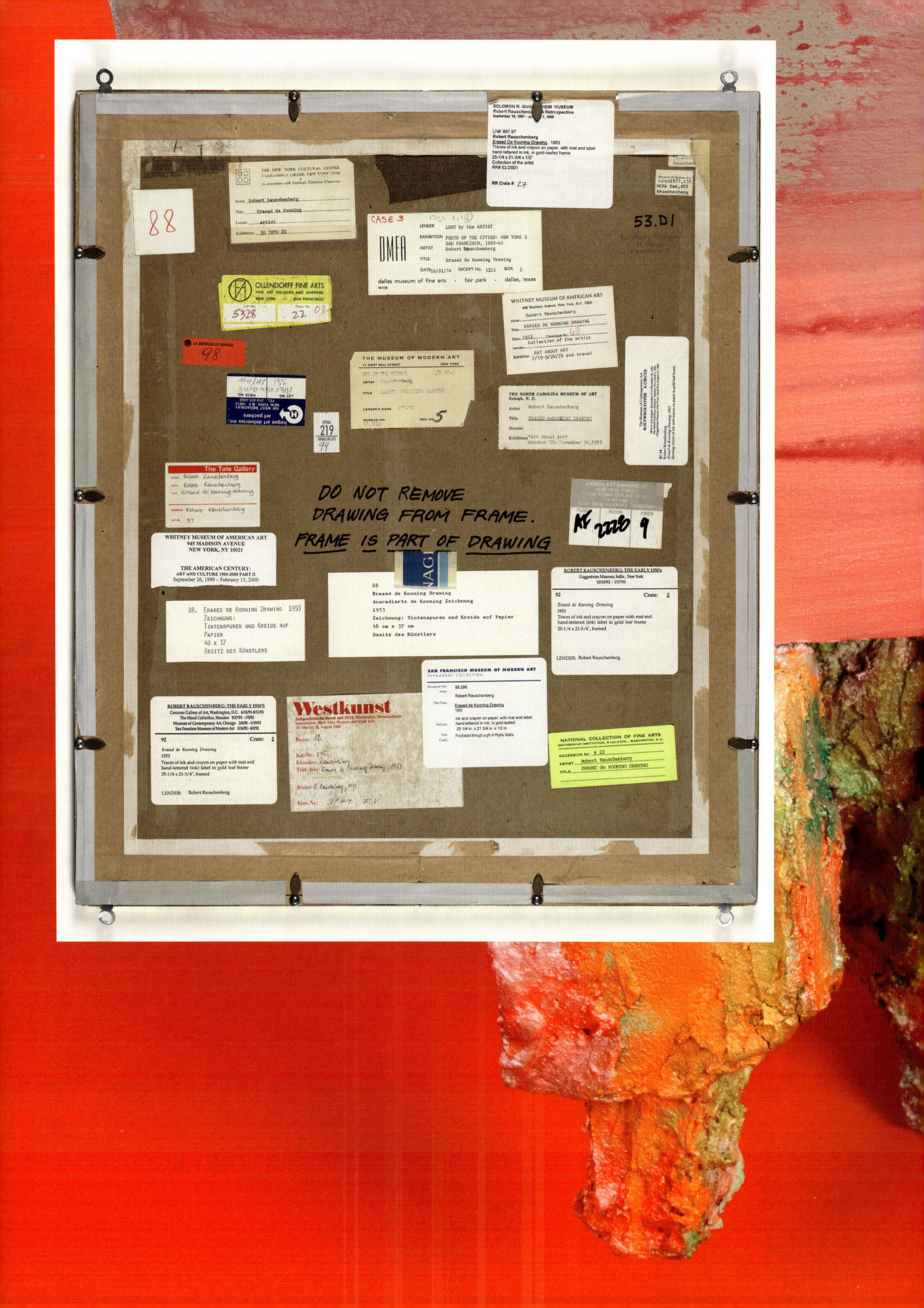

SOLOMON R. GUGGENHEIM MUSEUM
Robert Rauschenberg
Erased De Kooning Drawing, 1953
Traces of ink and crayon on paper, with mat and label hand-lettered in ink, in gold-leafed frame
25-1/4 x 21-3/4 x 1/2"
Collection of the artist
RR# 53.D001
RR Crate #: 27
88
THE NEW YORK CULTURAL CENTER
Artist Robert Rauschenberg
Title Erased de Kooning
Lender artist
53.D1
CASE 3
DMFA
LENDER LENT by the ARTIST
EXHIBITION POETS OF THE CITIES: NEW YORK & SAN FRANCISCO, 1950-65
ARTIST Robert Rauschenberg
TITLE Erased de Kooning Drawing
DATE 10/31/74 RECEIPT No. 1221 BOX 5
dallas museum of fine arts · fair park · dallas, texas
OLLENDORFF FINE ARTS
FINE ART PACKERS AND SHIPPERS
NEW YORK SAN FRANCISCO
5328
22
WHITNEY MUSEUM OF AMERICAN ART
945 Madison Avenue, New York, N.Y. 10021
Robert Rauschenberg
ERASED DE KOONING DRAWING
1953
Collection of the artist
ART ABOUT ART
7/19-9/24/78 and travel
98
THE MUSEUM OF MODERN ART
11 WEST 53RD STREET NEW YORK
5
hague art deliveries inc.
art packers
219
99
THE NORTH CAROLINA MUSEUM OF ART
Raleigh, N. C.
Artist Robert Rauschenberg
Title ERASED deKOONING DRAWING
Exhibition "Art About Art" October 22- November 26,1978
The Tate Gallery
Robert Rauschenberg
Erased de Kooning drawing
97
DO NOT REMOVE
DRAWING FROM FRAME.
FRAME IS PART OF DRAWING
9
WHITNEY MUSEUM OF AMERICAN ART
945 MADISON AVENUE
NEW YORK, NY 10021
THE AMERICAN CENTURY:
ART AND CULTURE 1900-2000 PART II
September 26, 1999 – February 13, 2000
88
Erased de Kooning Drawing
Ausradierte de Kooning Zeichnung
1953
Zeichnung: Tintenspuren und Kreide auf Papier
48 cm x 37 cm
Besitz des Künstlers
ROBERT RAUSCHENBERG: THE EARLY 1950's
Guggenheim Museum, SoHo, New York
92
Crate: 2
Erased de Kooning Drawing
1953
Traces of ink and crayon on paper with mat and hand-lettered (ink) label in gold leaf frame
25-1/4 x 21-3/4", framed
LENDER: Robert Rauschenberg
88. ERASED DE KOONING DRAWING 1953
ZEICHNUNG:
TINTENSPUREN UND KREIDE AUF PAPIER
48 x 37
BESITZ DES KÜNSTLERS
SAN FRANCISCO MUSEUM OF MODERN ART
PERMANENT COLLECTION
98.298
Robert Rauschenberg
Erased de Kooning Drawing
1953
ink and crayon on paper, with mat and label hand-lettered in ink, in gold-leafed frame
25 1/4 in. x 21 3/4 in. x 1/2 in.
Purchased through a gift of Phyllis Wattis
ROBERT RAUSCHENBERG: THE EARLY 1950's
92
Crate: 2
Erased de Kooning Drawing
1953
Traces of ink and crayon on paper with mat and hand-lettered (ink) label in gold leaf frame
25-1/4 x 21-3/4", framed
LENDER: Robert Rauschenberg
Westkunst
NATIONAL COLLECTION OF FINE ARTS
ACCESSION No. # 22
ARTIST Robert Rauschenberg
TITLE ERASED de KOONING DRAWING

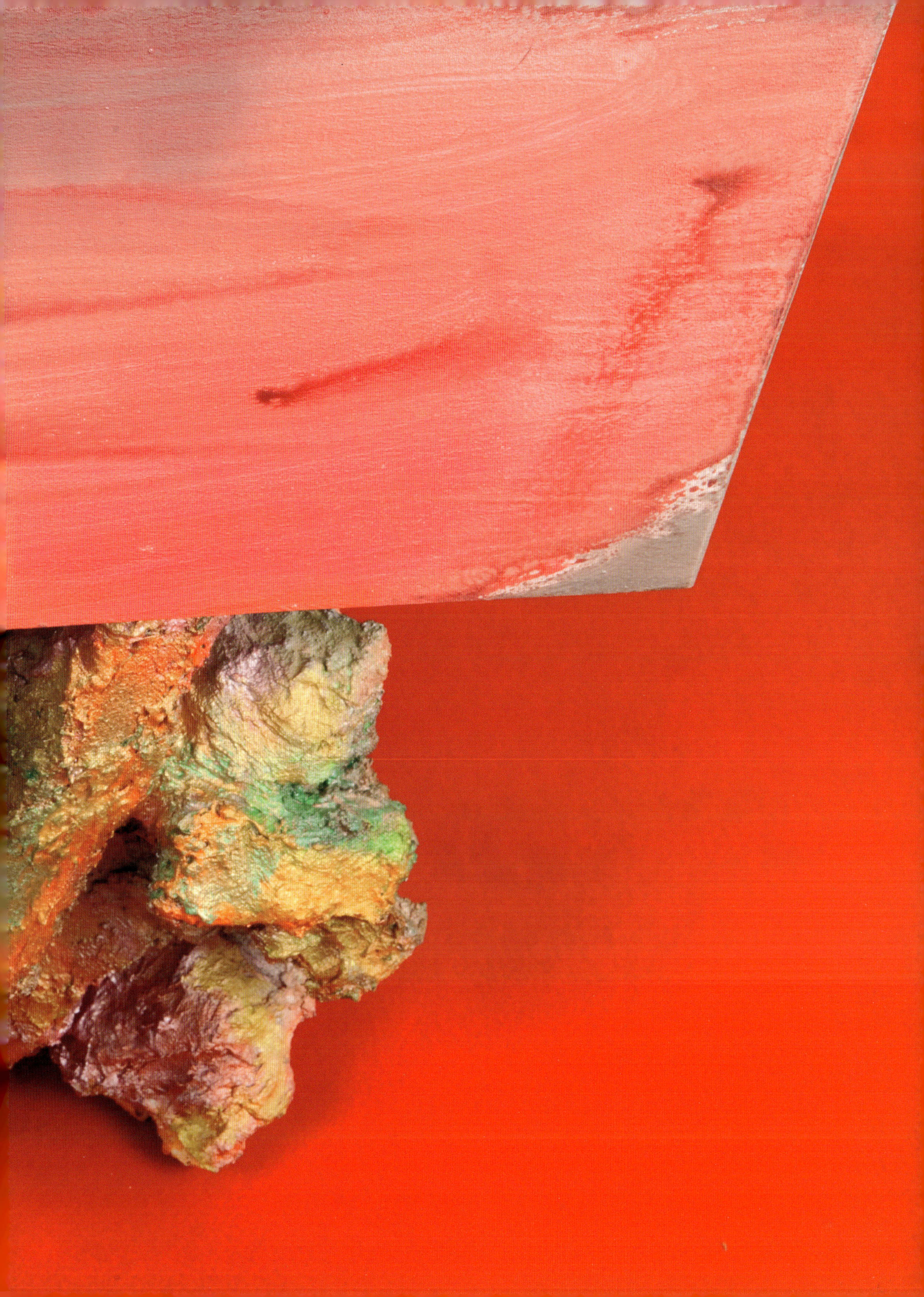

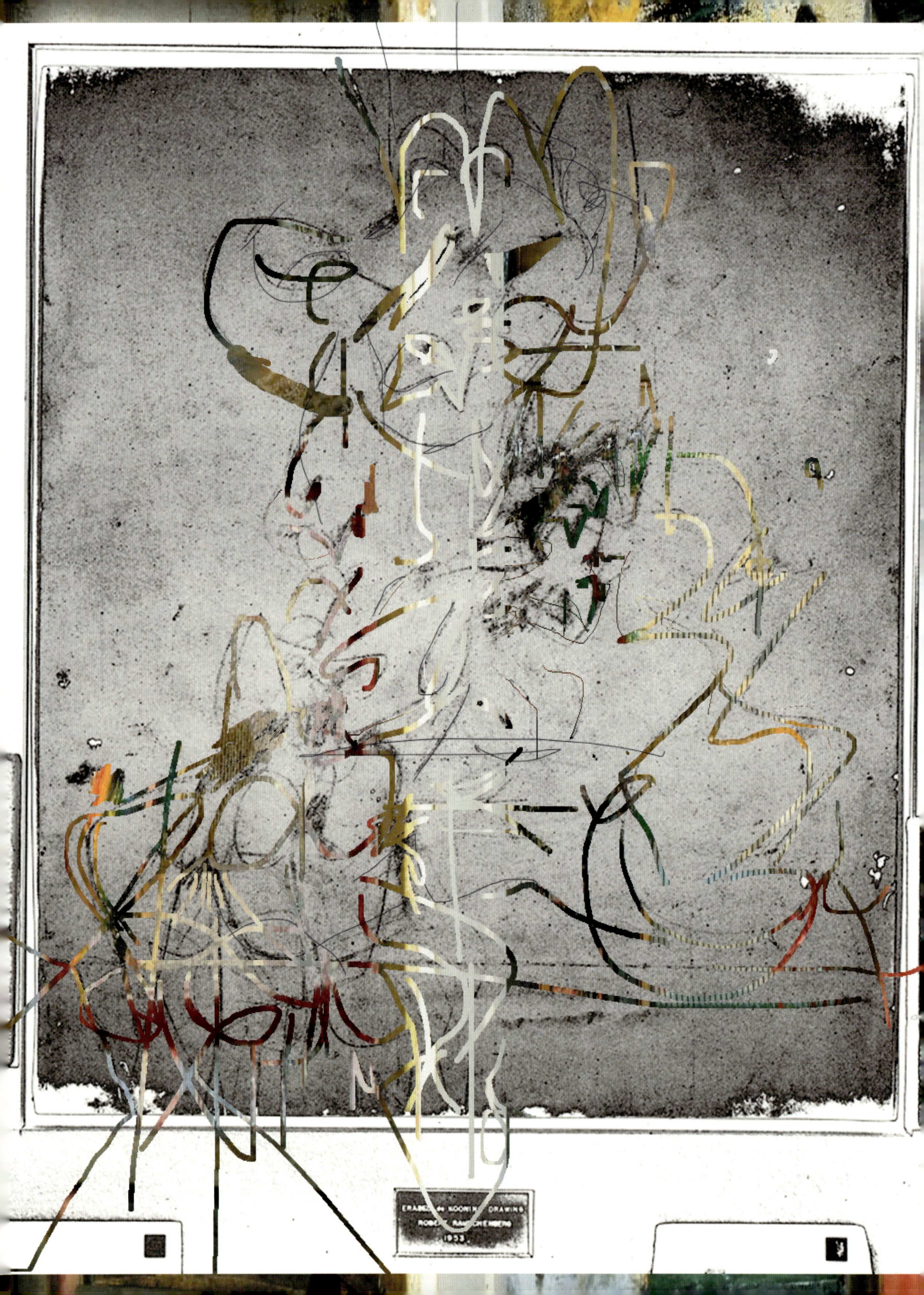
DRAWING
1953

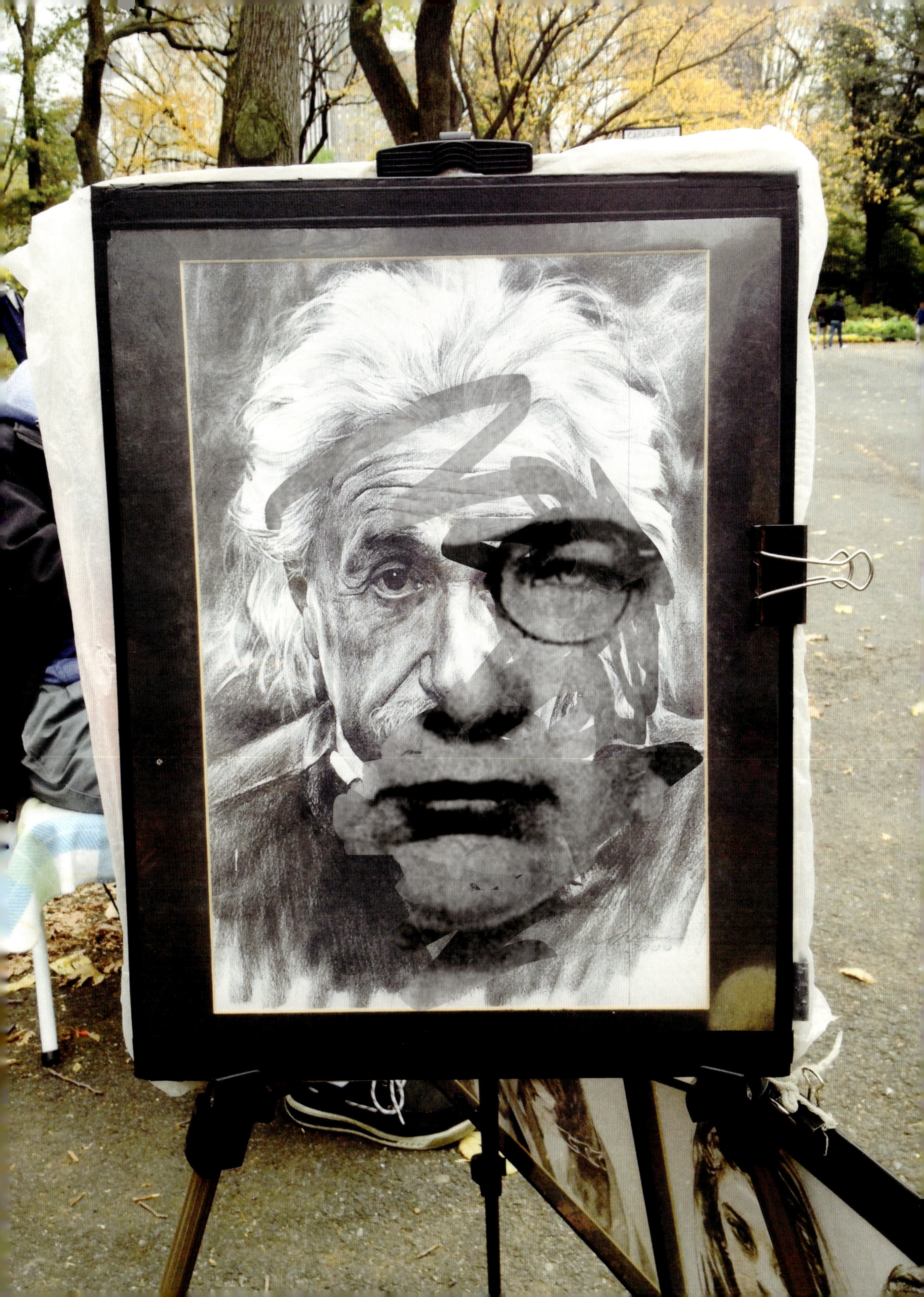
CARICATURE

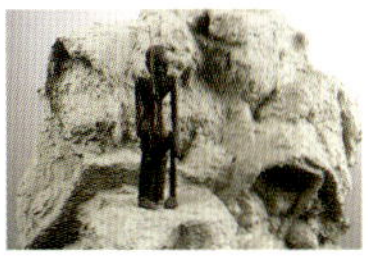

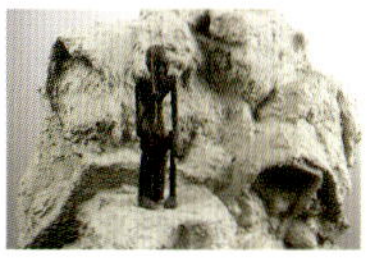

/artwork/untitled-gold-painting-3

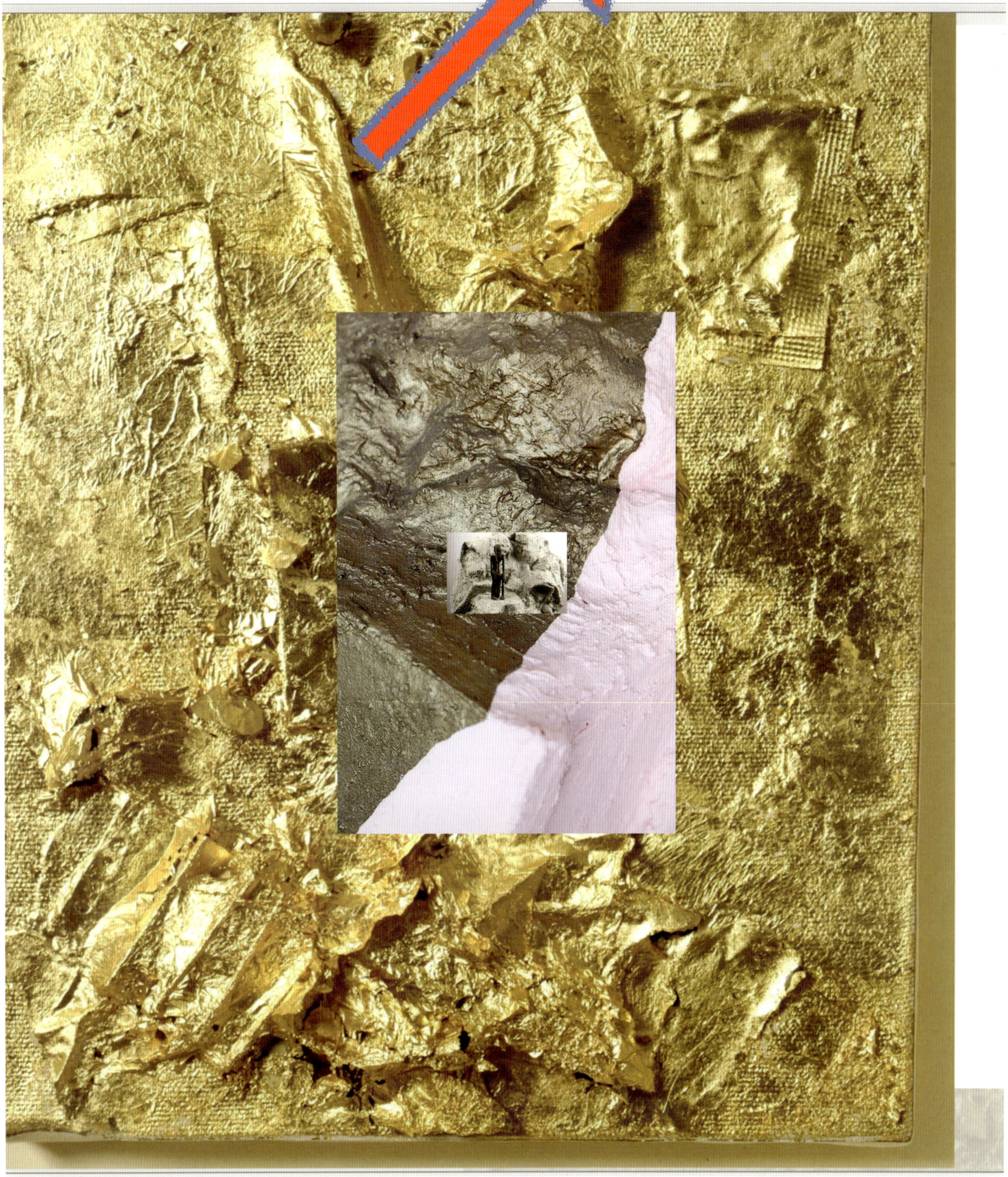

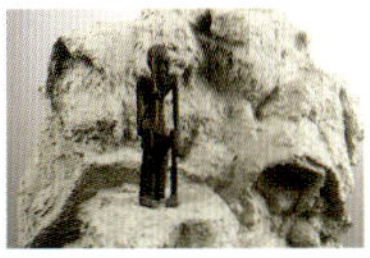

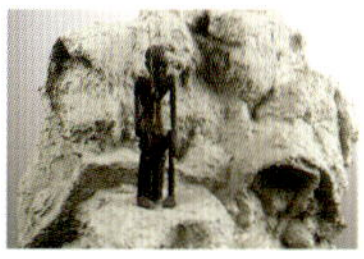

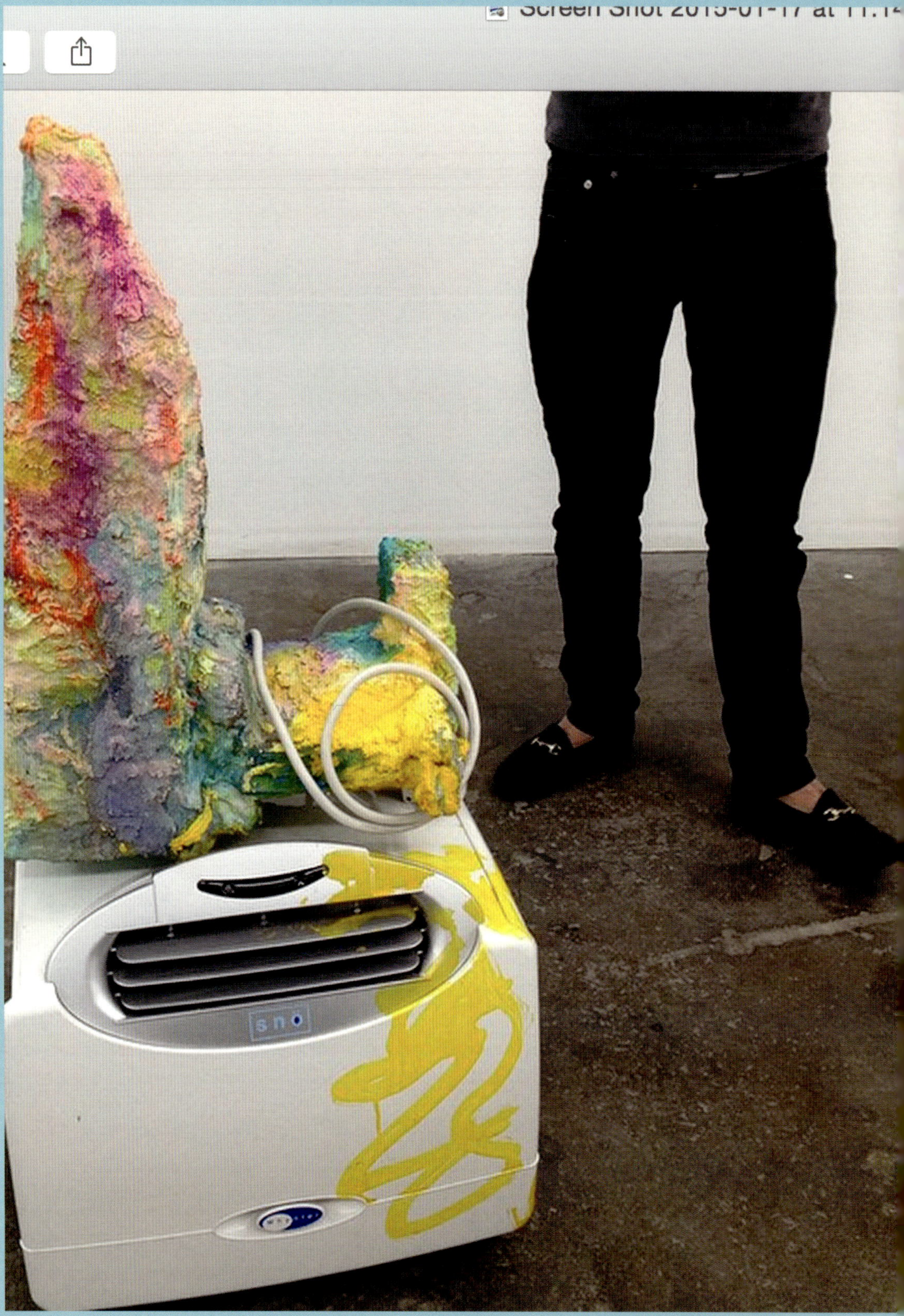
sno

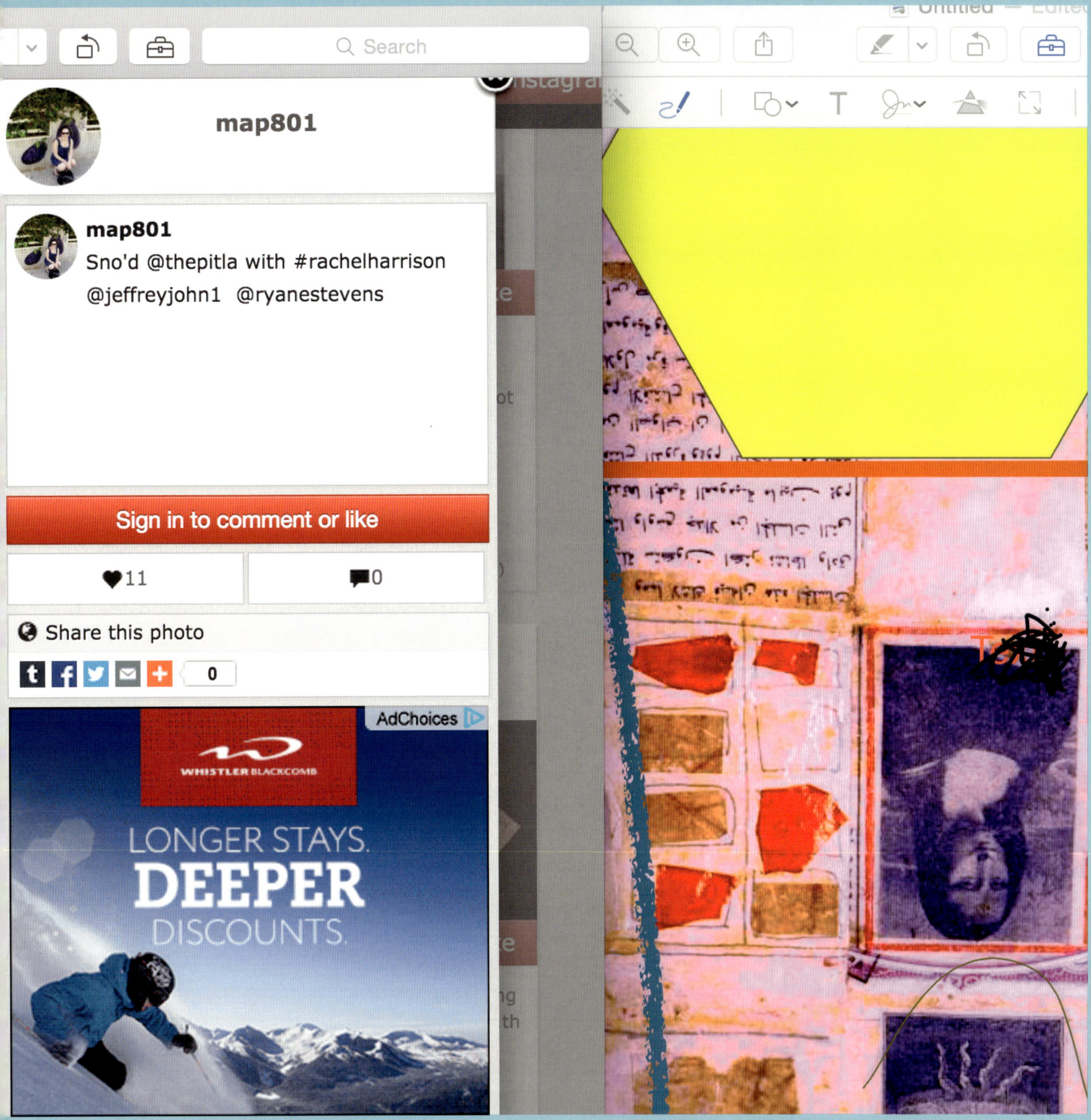

Search
map801
map801
Sno'd @thepitla with #rachelharrison
@jeffreyjohn1 @ryanestevens
Sign in to comment or like
11
0
Share this photo
0
AdChoices
WHISTLER BLACKCOMB
LONGER STAYS.
DEEPER
DISCOUNTS.

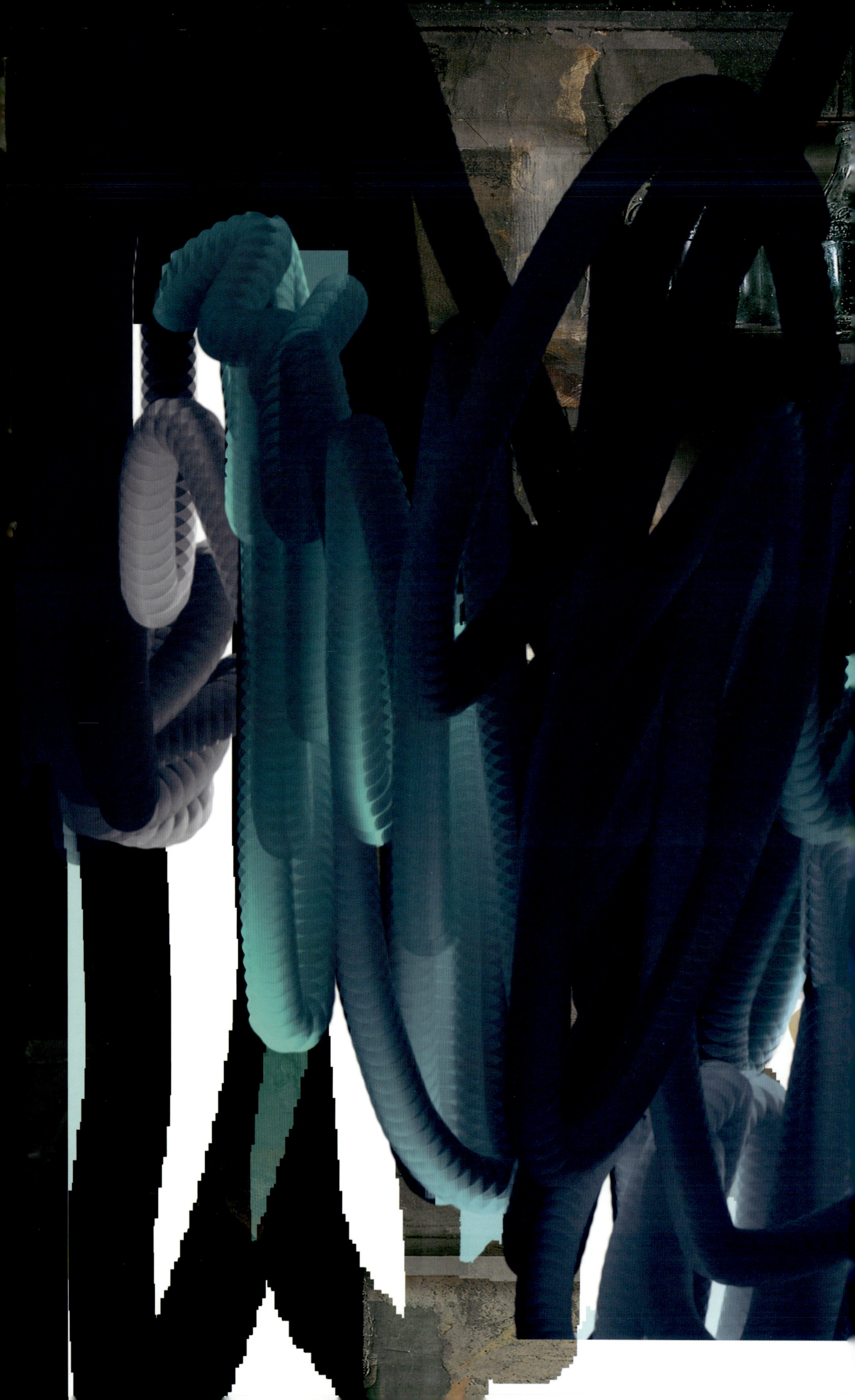

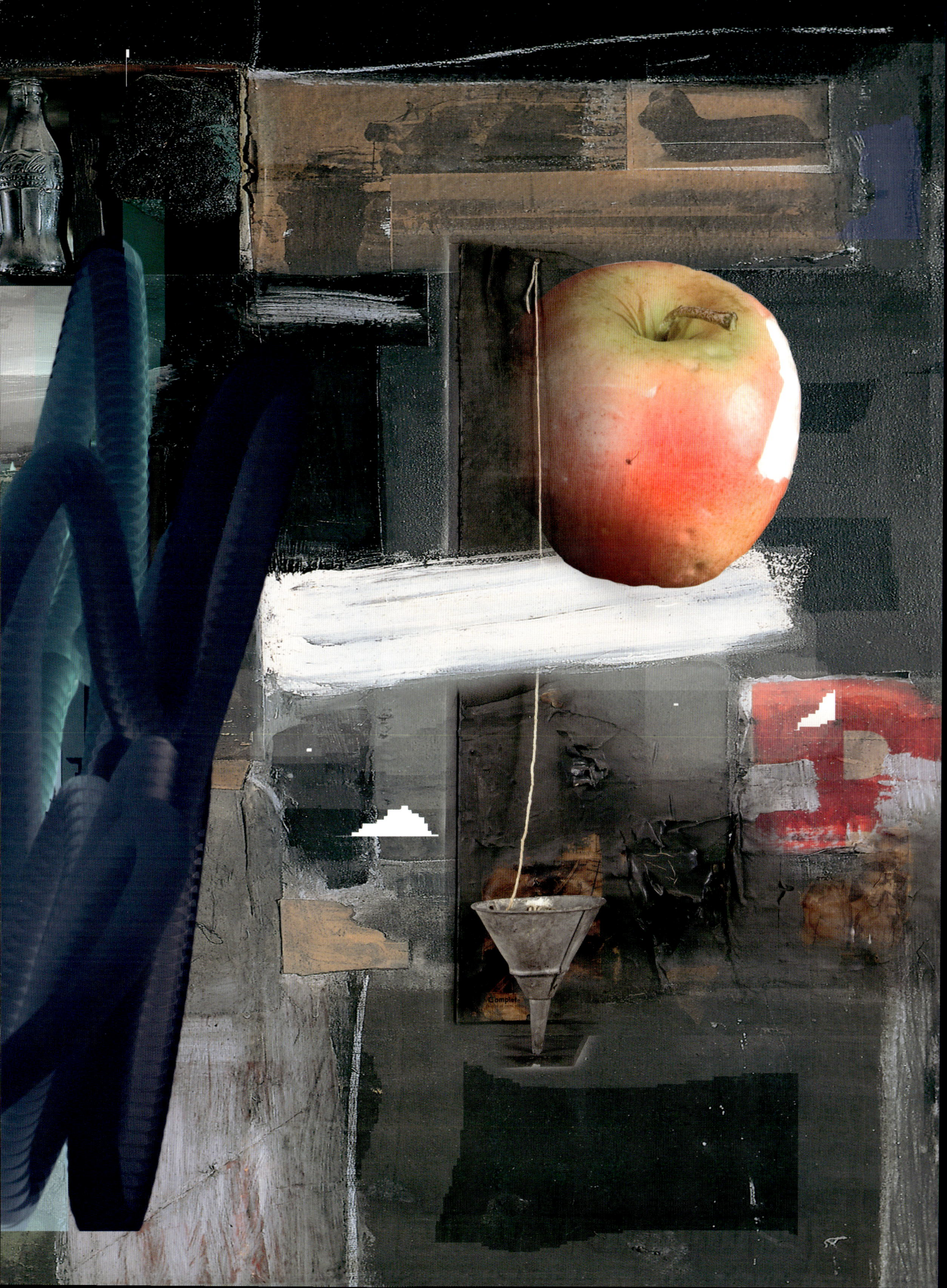

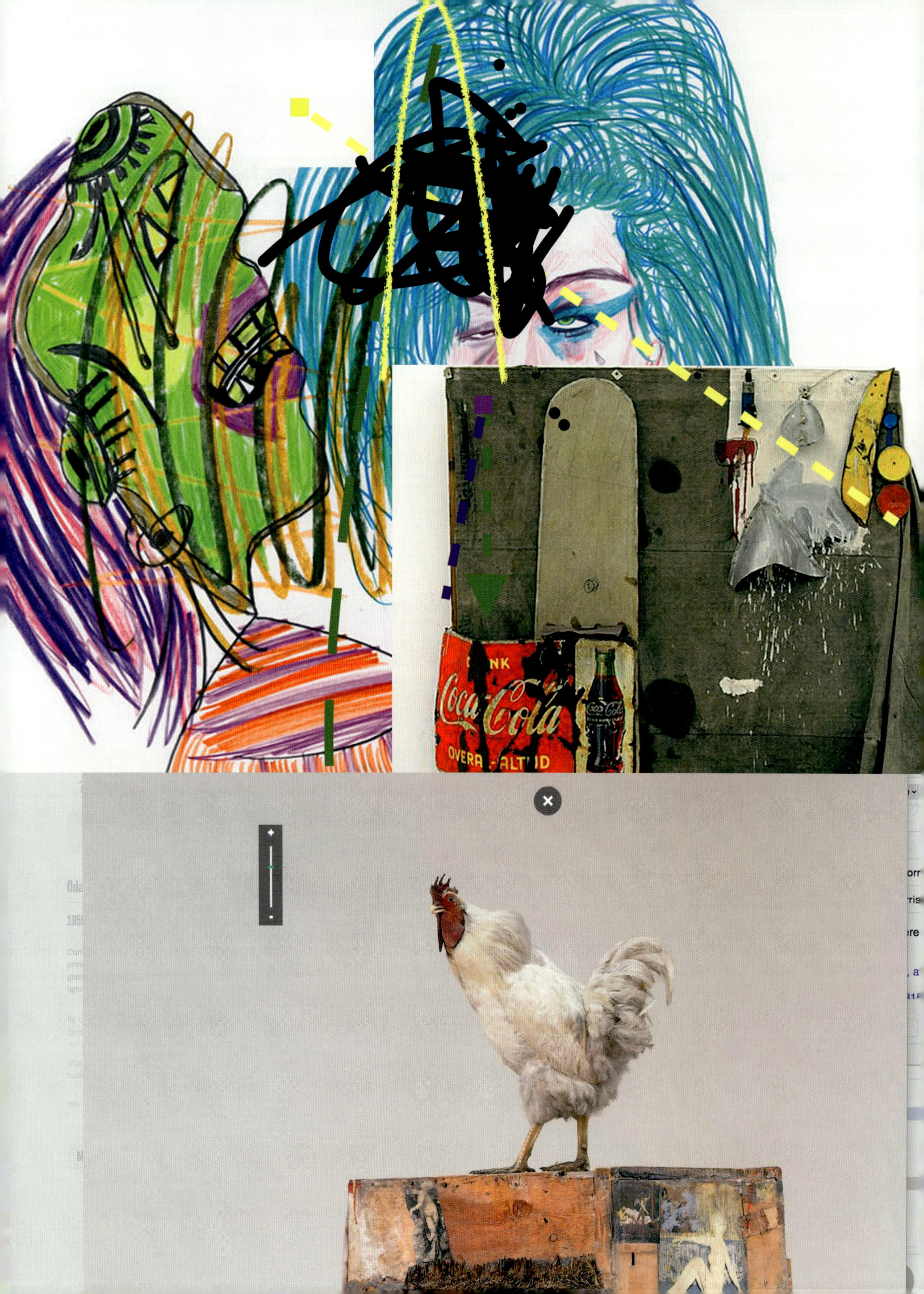
Coca-Cola

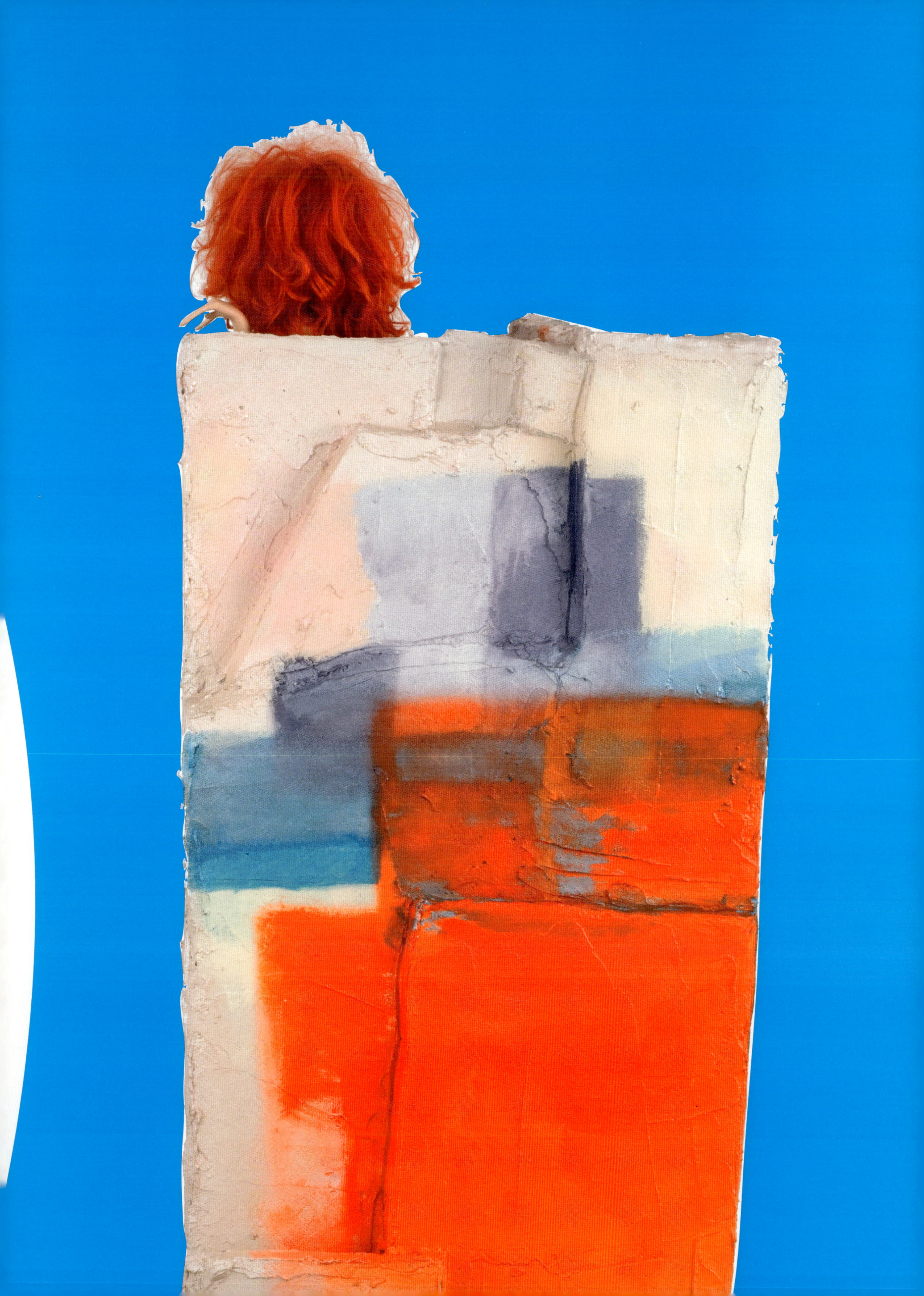

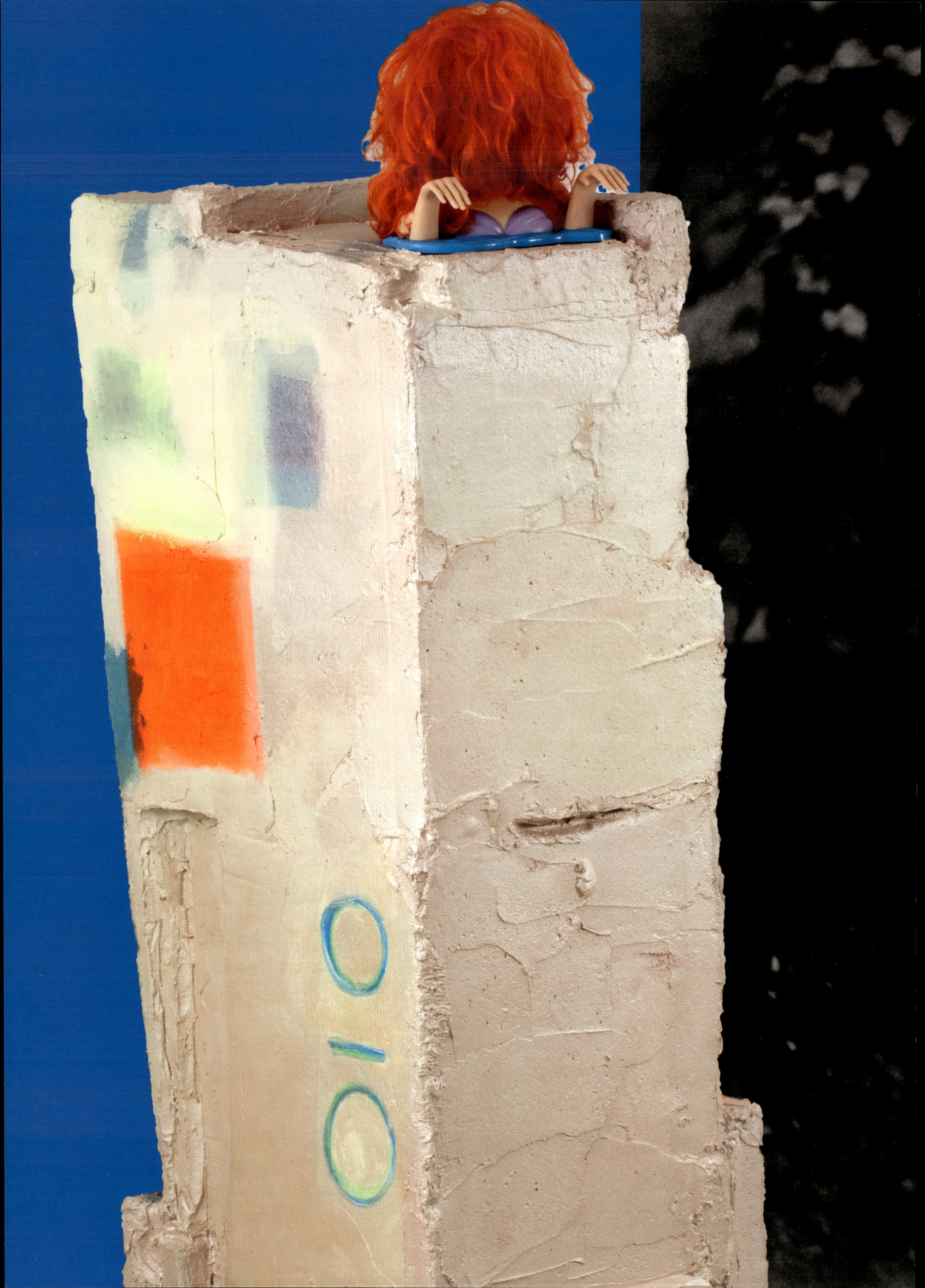

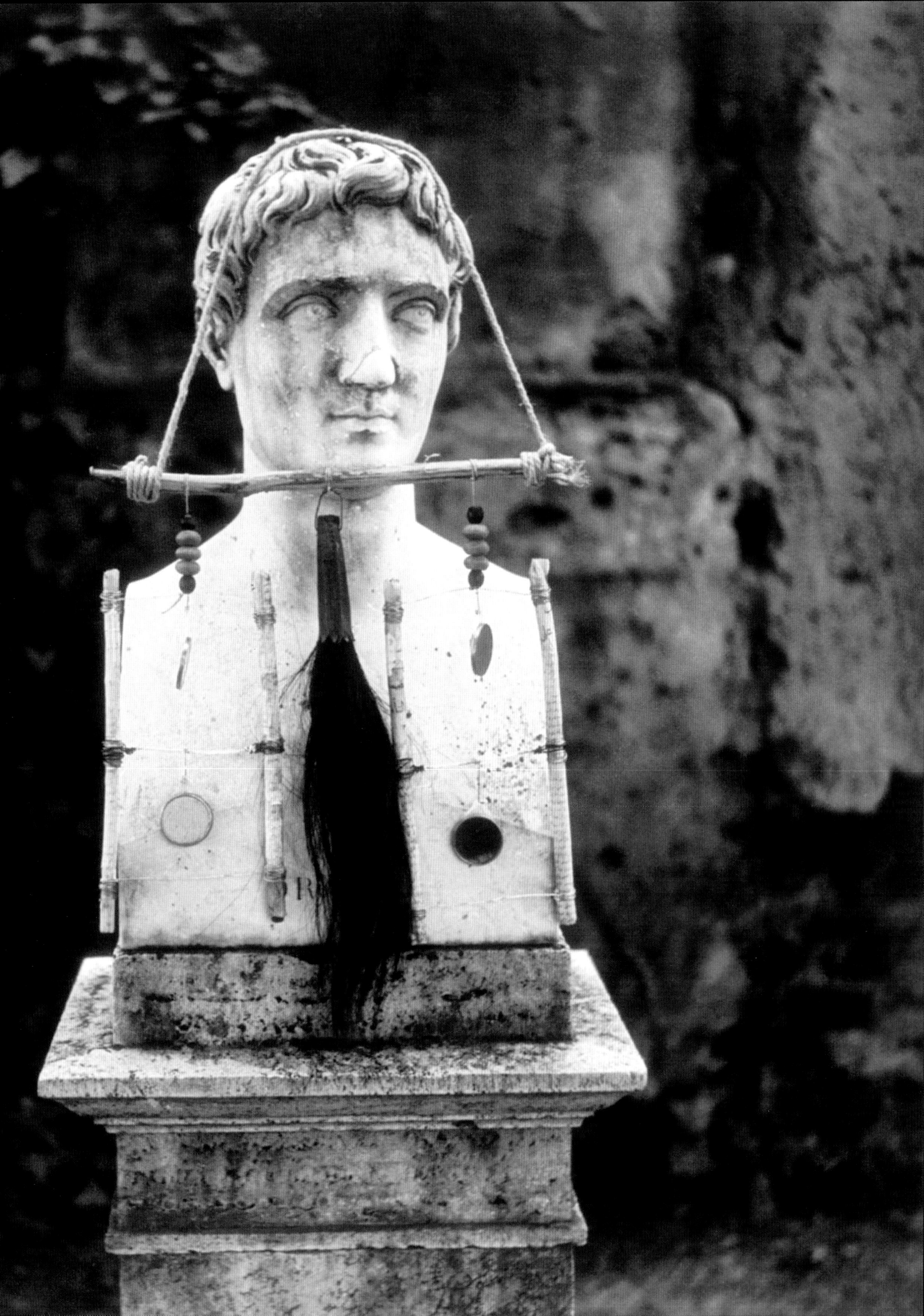

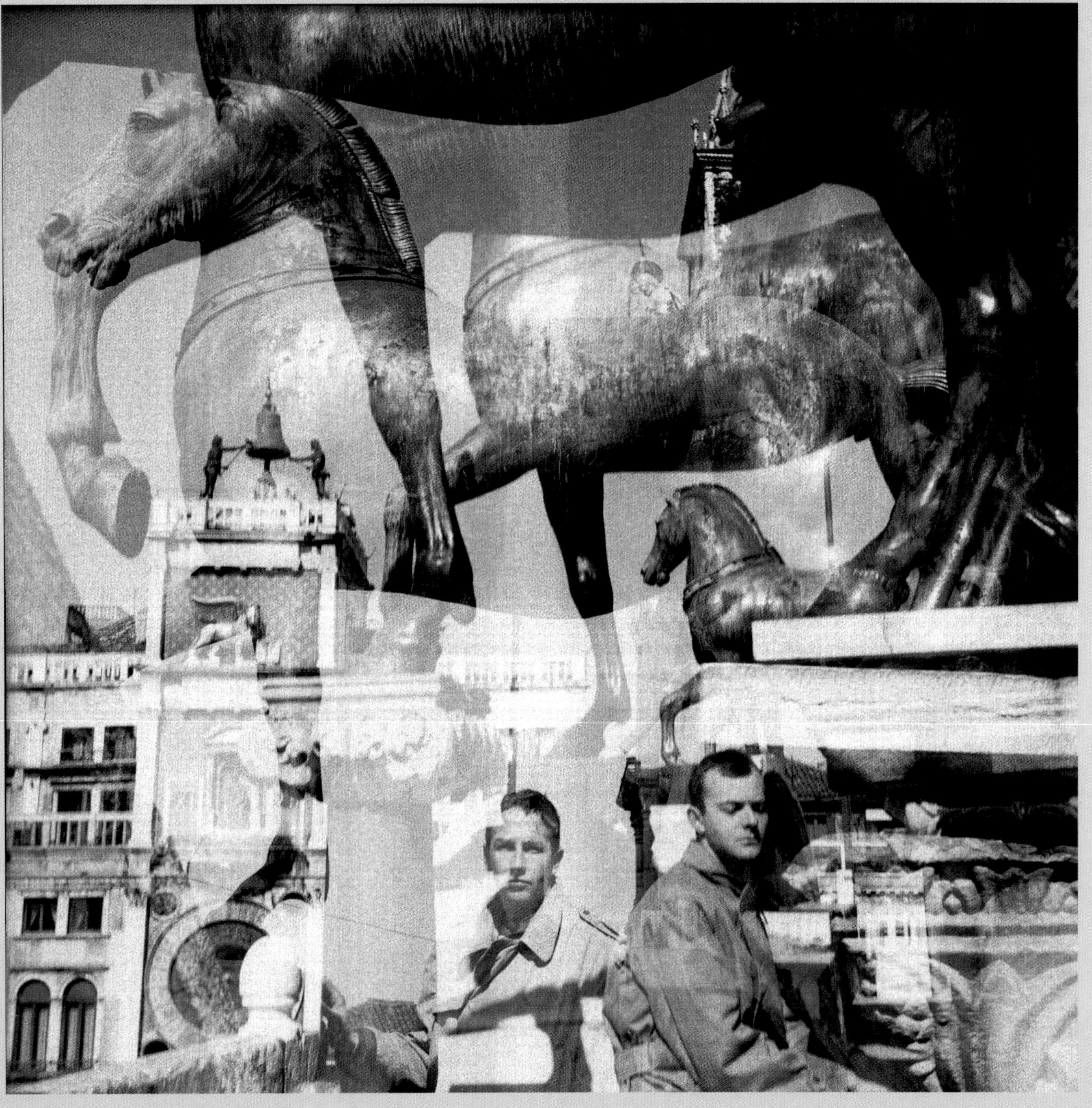

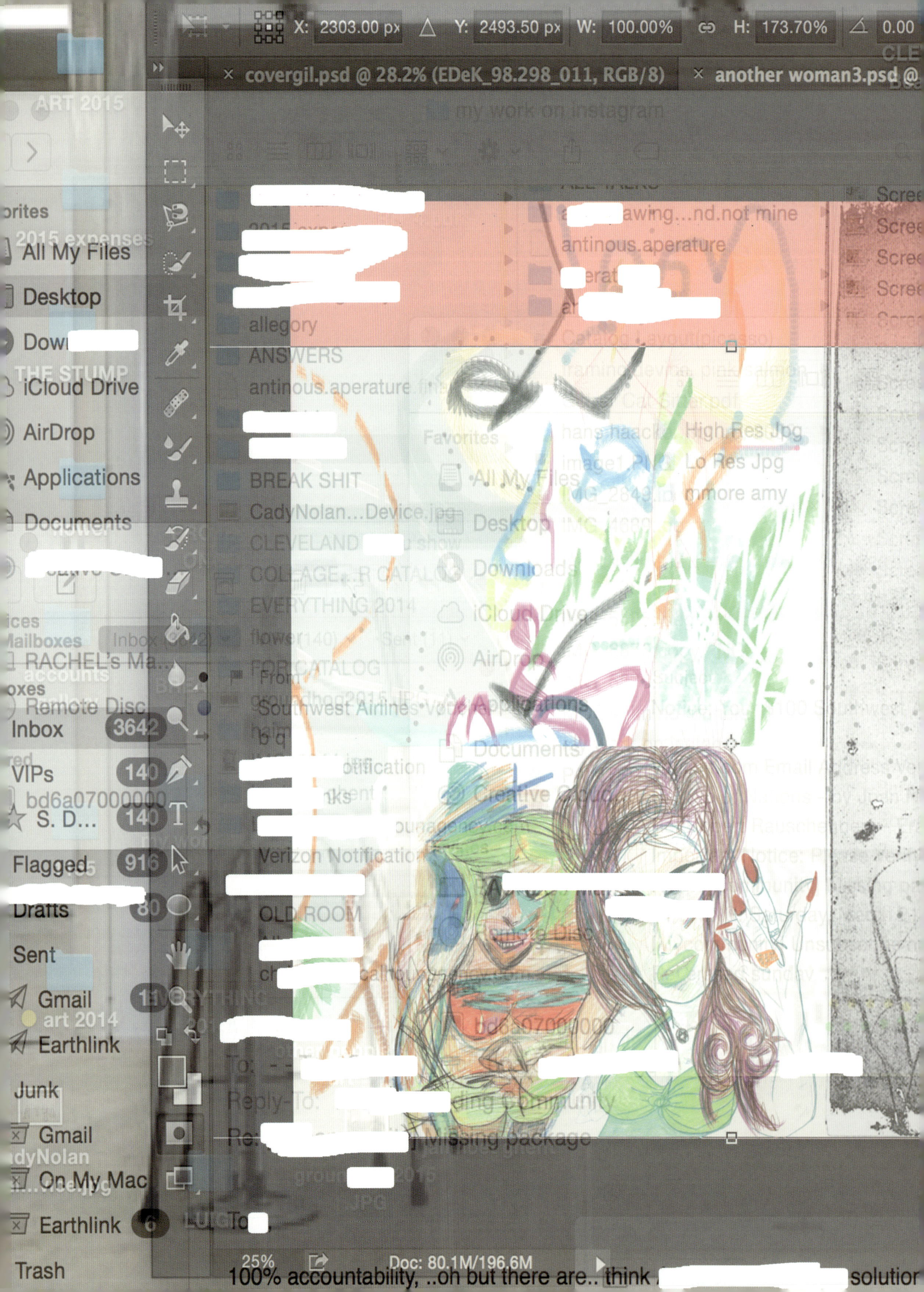
X: 2303.00 px
Y: 2493.50 px
W: 100.00%
H: 173.70%
0.00
covergil.psd @ 28.2% (EDeK_98.298_011, RGB/8)
another woman3.psd @
ART 2015
my work on instagram
orites
2015 expenses
All My Files
Desktop
Dow
THE STUMP
iCloud Drive
AirDrop
Applications
Documents
ices
ailboxes
RACHEL's Ma...
accounts
oxes
Remote Disc
Inbox 3642
VIPs 140
bd6a07000000
S. D... 140
Flagged 916
Drafts 80
Sent
Gmail
art 2014
Earthlink
Junk
Gmail
dyNolan
On My Mac
Earthlink 6
Trash
allegory
ANSWERS
antinous.aperature
BREAK SHIT
CadyNolan...Device.jpg
CLEVELAND
COLLAGE...R CATALOG
EVERYTHING 2014
flower
FOR CATALOG
From
Southwest Airlines
Verizon Notification
OLD ROOM
To:
Reply-To:
Re:
Missing package
awing...nd.not mine
antinous.aperature
Favorites
All My Files
Desktop
Downloads
iCloud Drive
AirDrop
Applications
Documents
Creative Cloud
hans haack
High Res Jpg
Lo Res Jpg
mmore amy
Scree
Scree
Scree
Scree
25%
Doc: 80.1M/196.6M
100% accountability, ..oh but there are.. think
solution

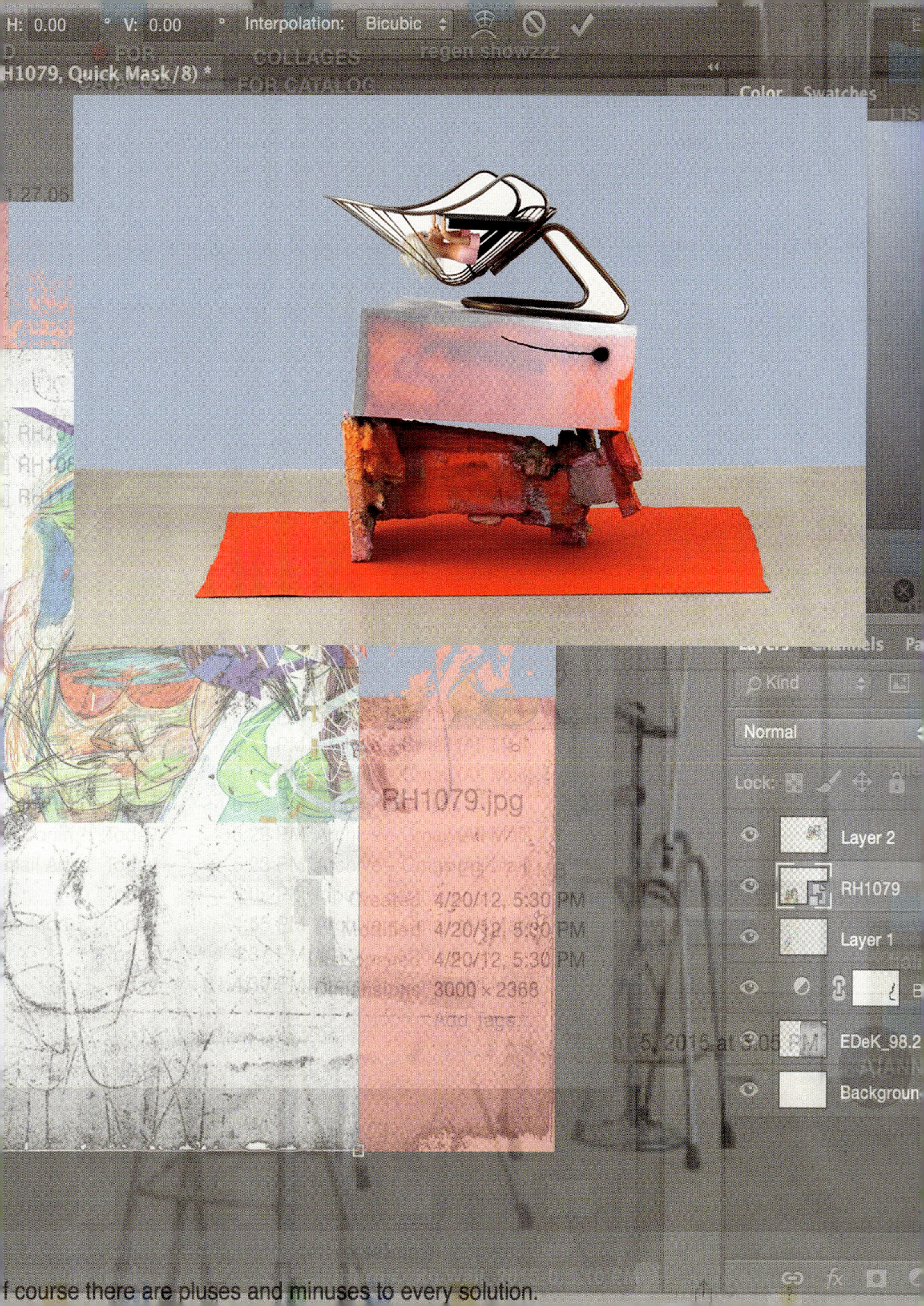
H: 0.00 ° V: 0.00 ° Interpolation: Bicubic
COLLAGES
FOR CATALOG
regen showzzz
H1079, Quick Mask/8) *
Color Swatches
1.27.05
RH1079.jpg
4/20/12, 5:30 PM
4/20/12, 5:30 PM
4/20/12, 5:30 PM
3000 × 2368
Add Tags...
Kind
Normal
Lock:
Layer 2
RH1079
Layer 1
EDeK_98.2
Backgroun
f course there are pluses and minuses to every solution.

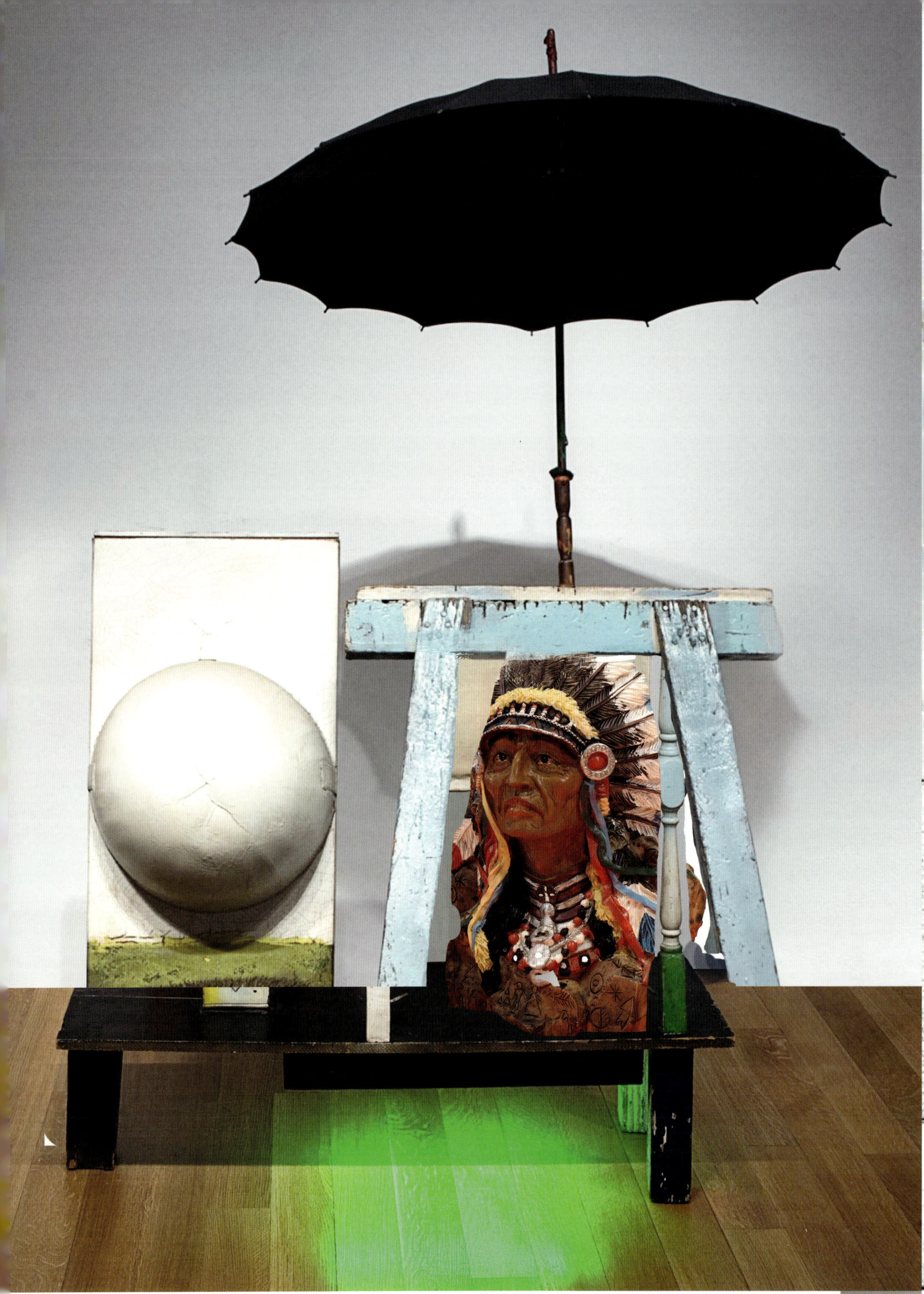

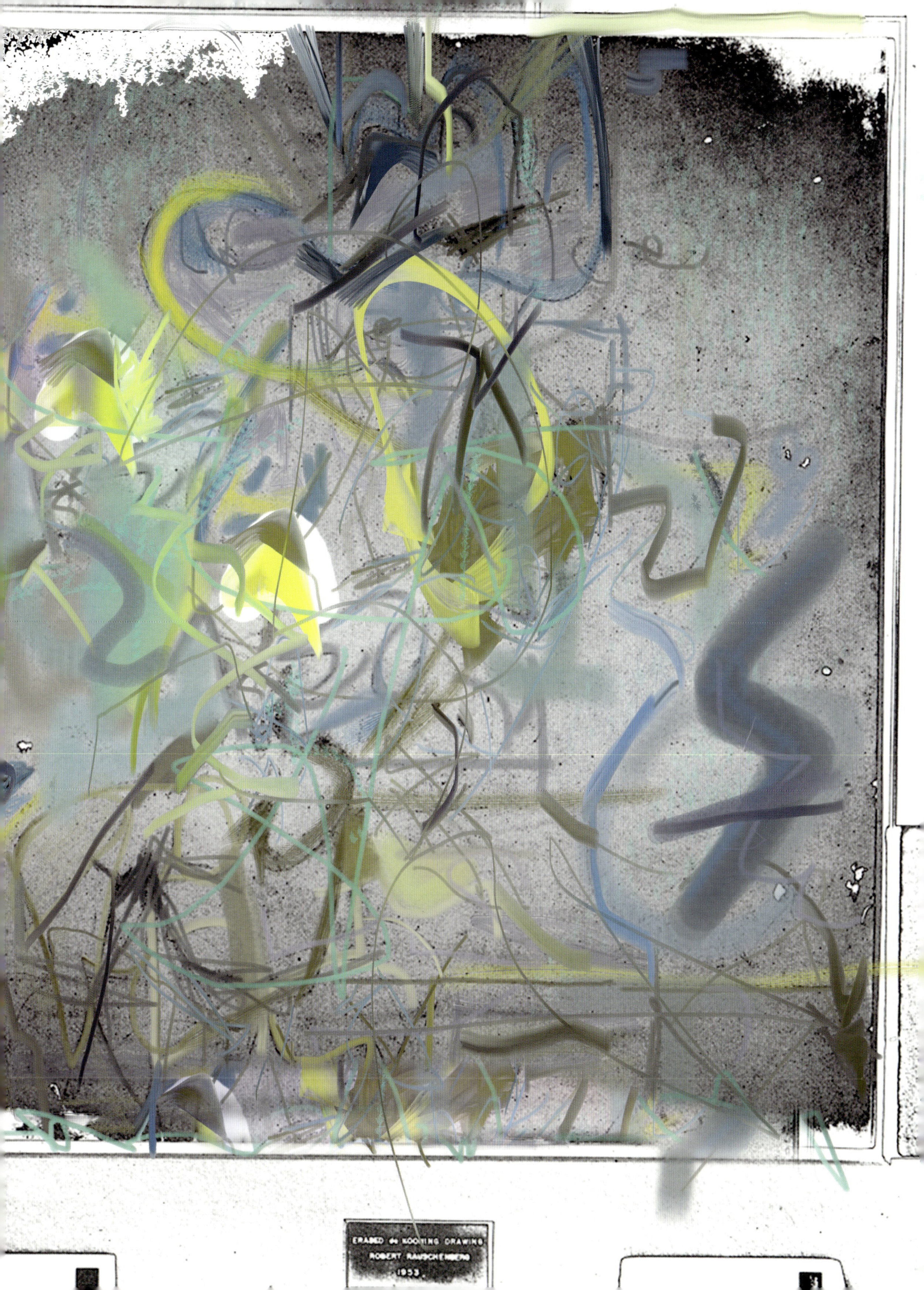
ERASED de KOONING DRAWING
ROBERT RAUSCHENBERG
1953

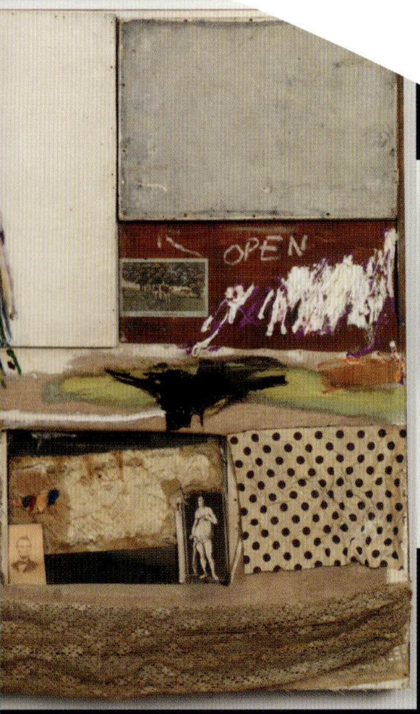
OPEN
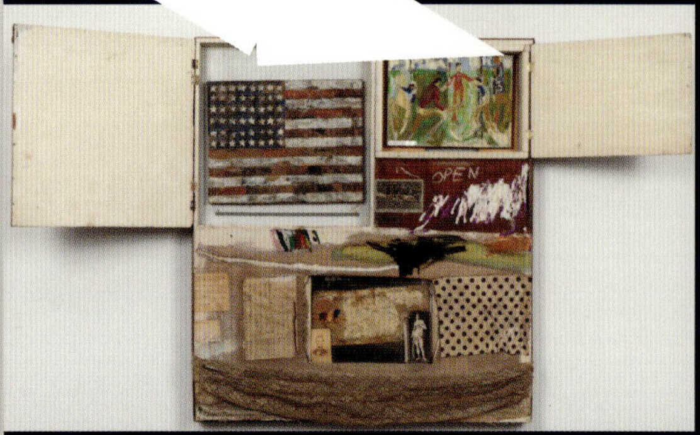
OPEN

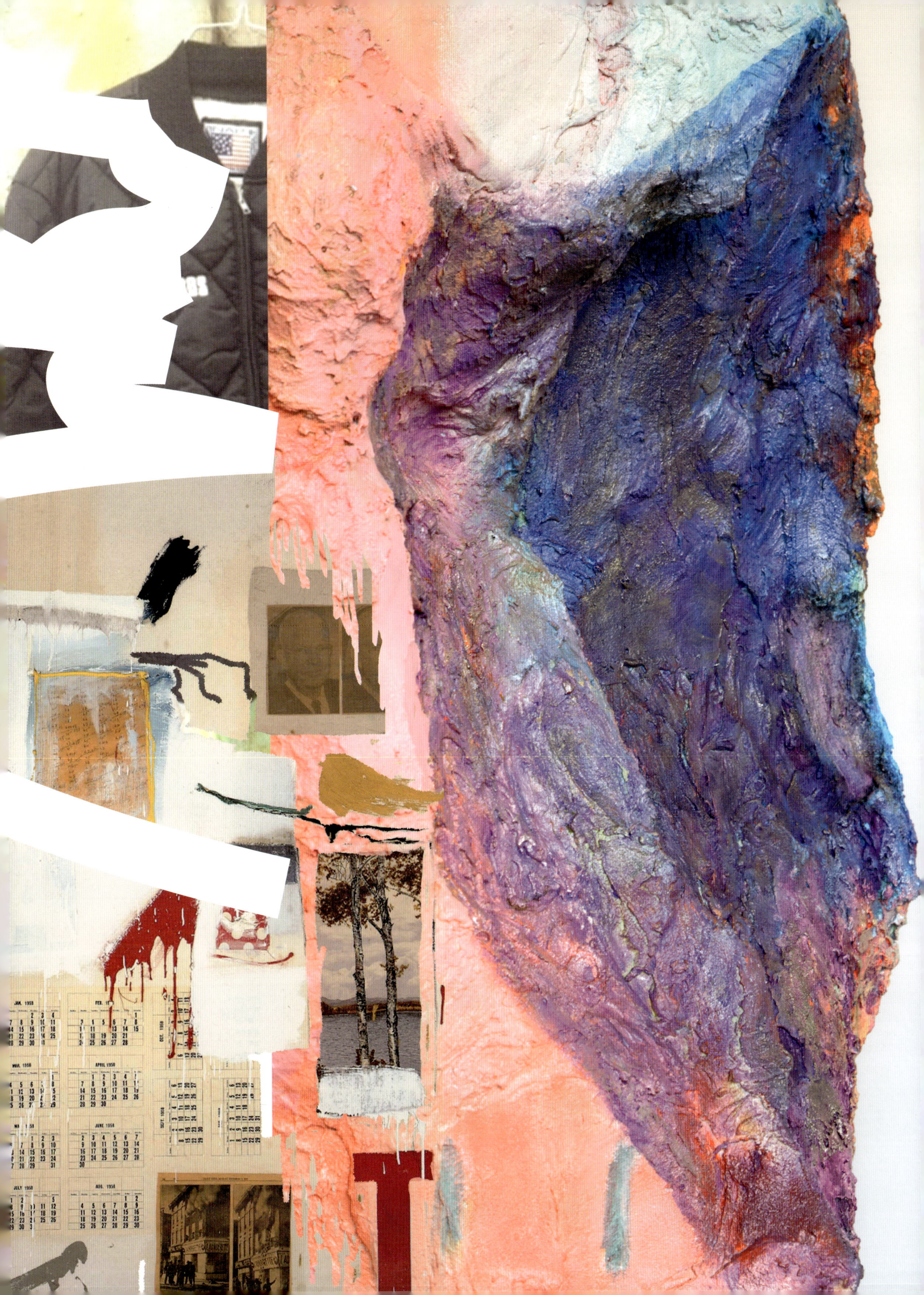

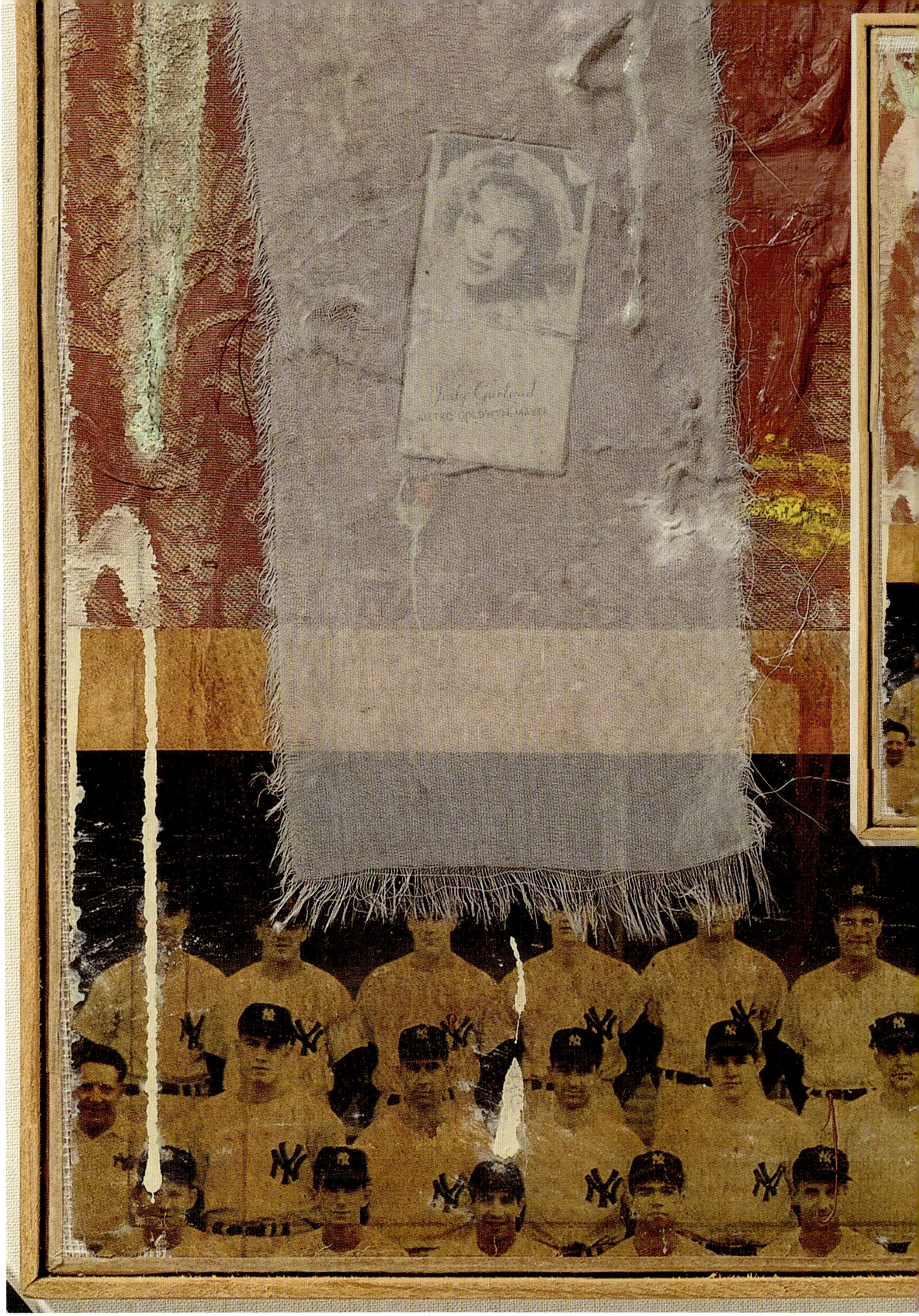

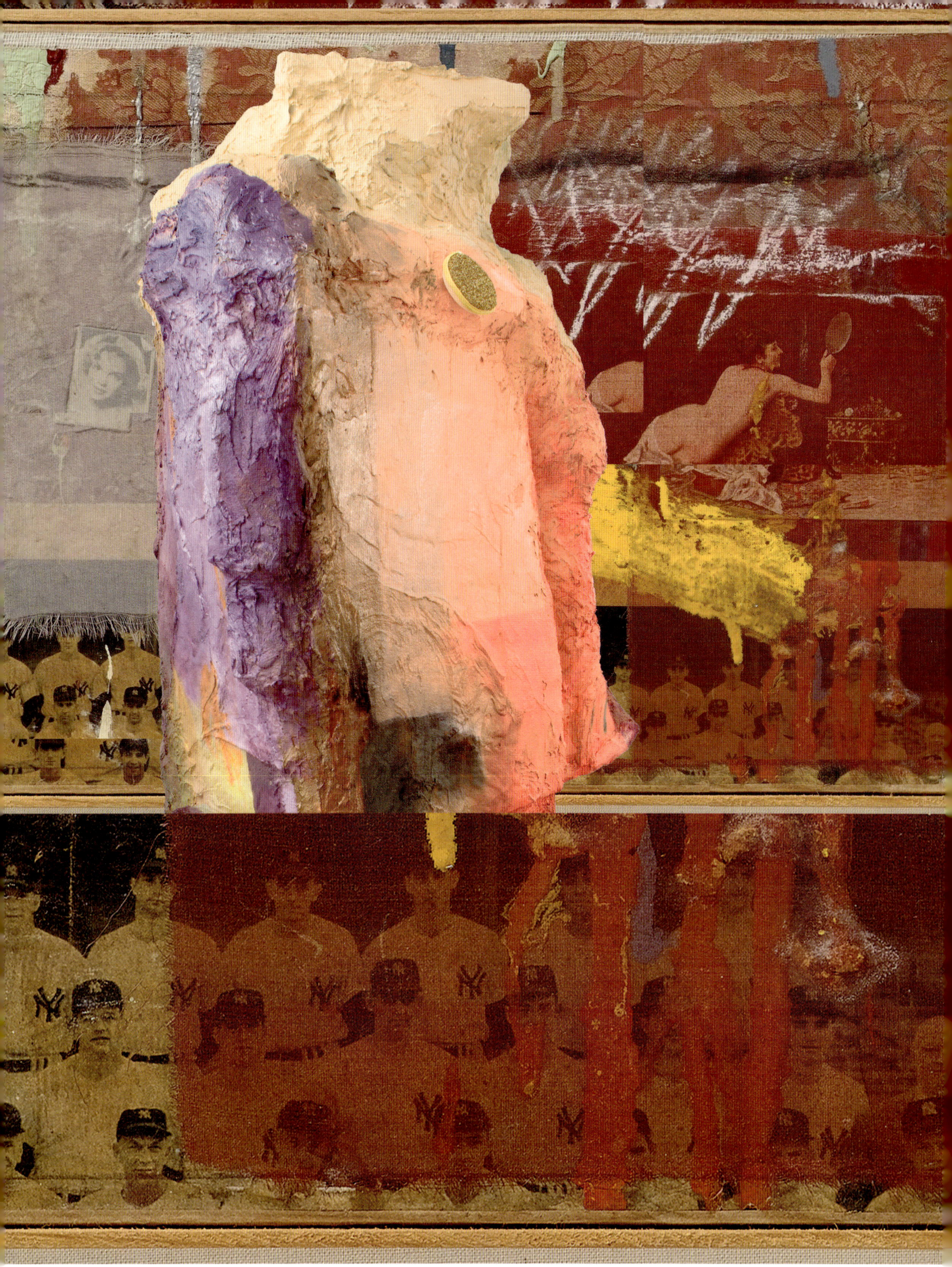

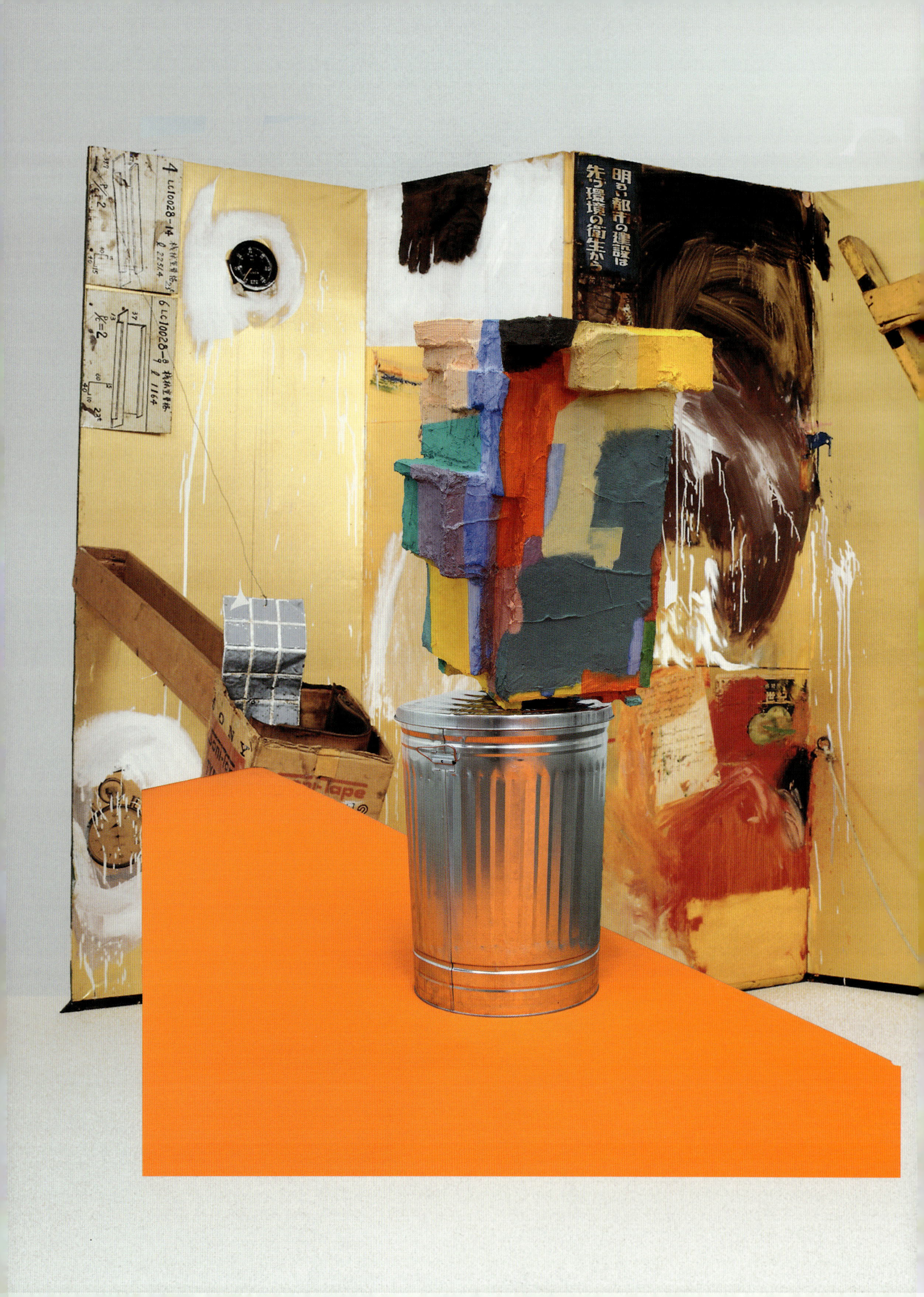
明るい都市の建設は
先ず環境の衛生から

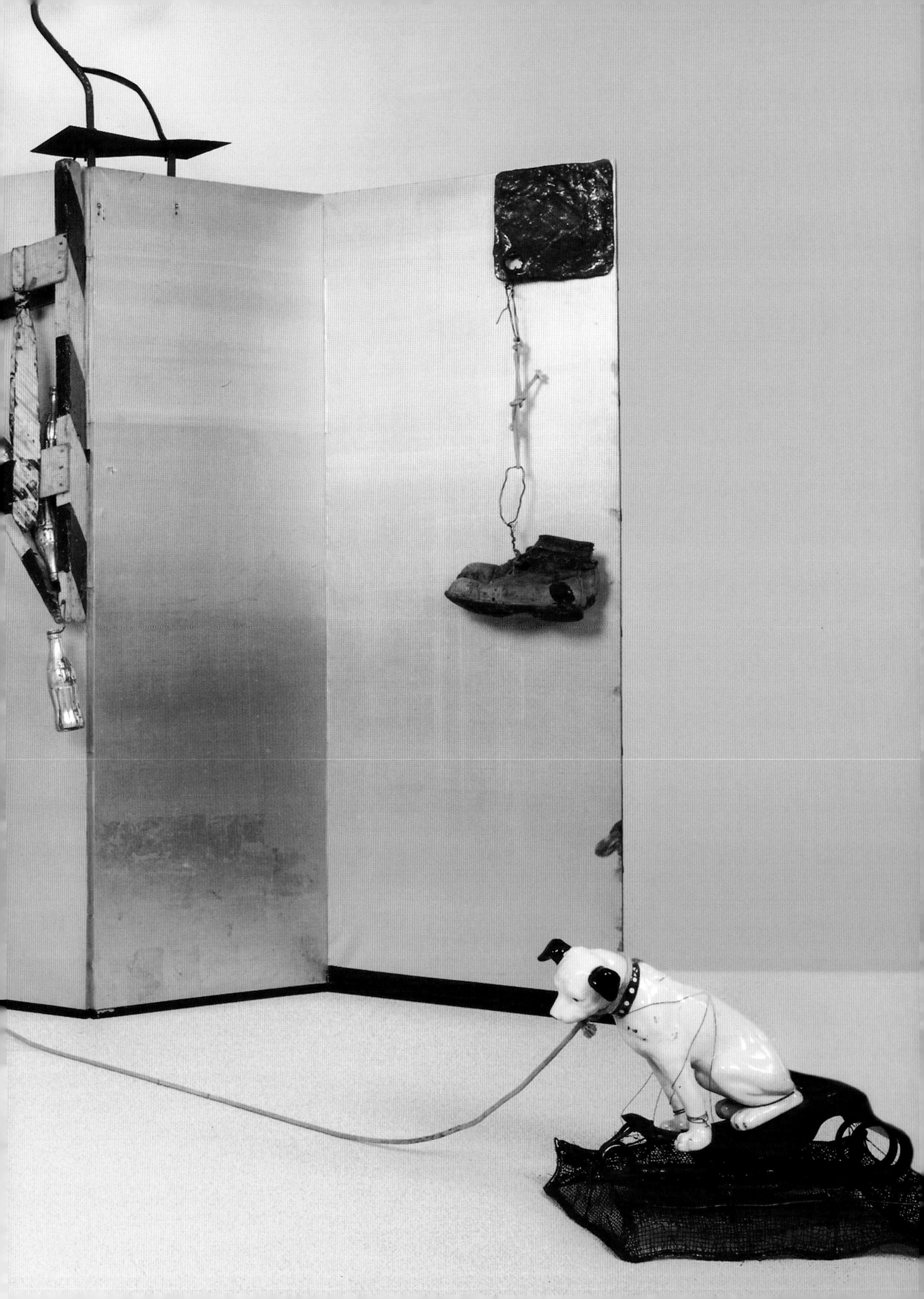

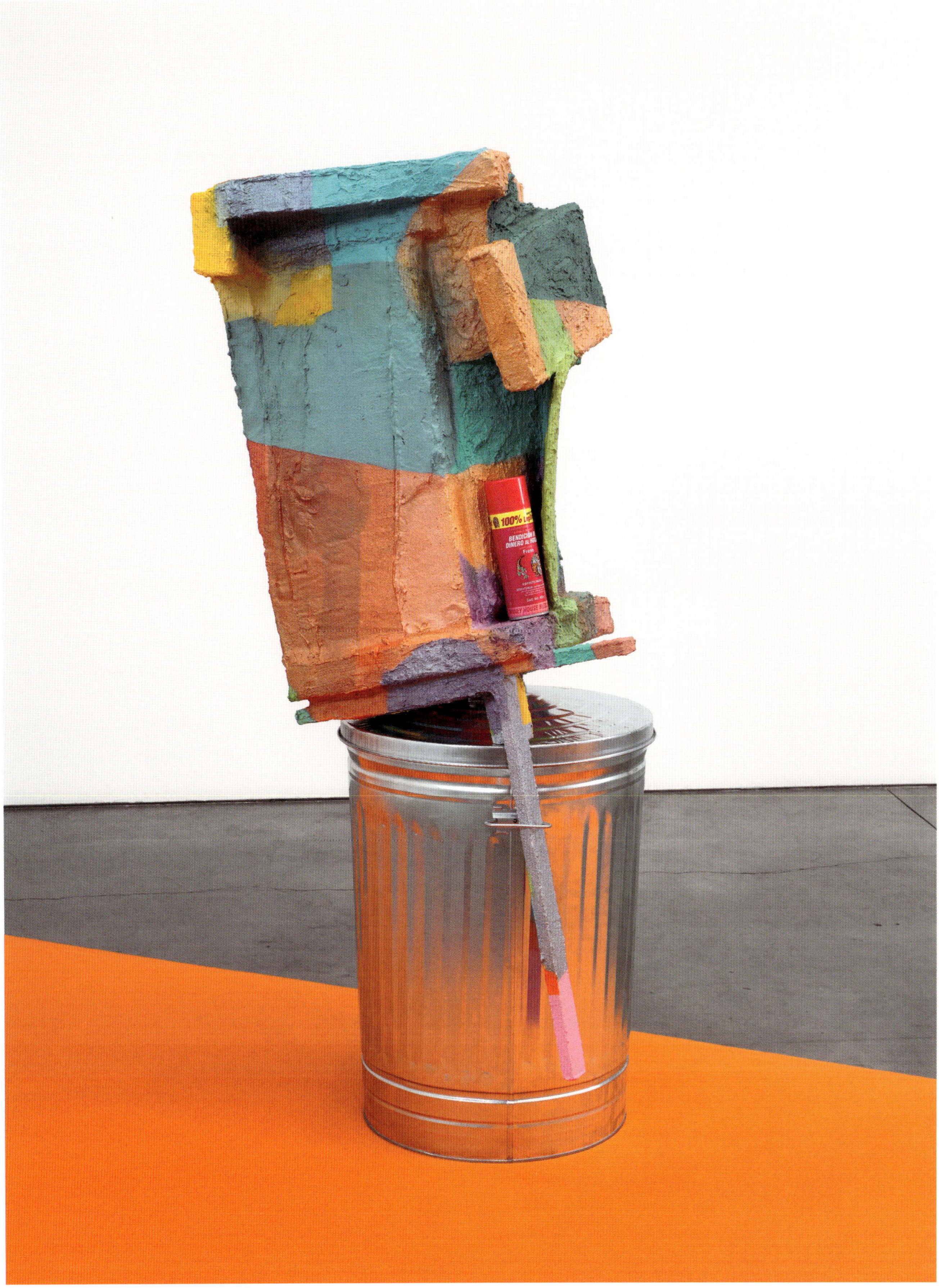

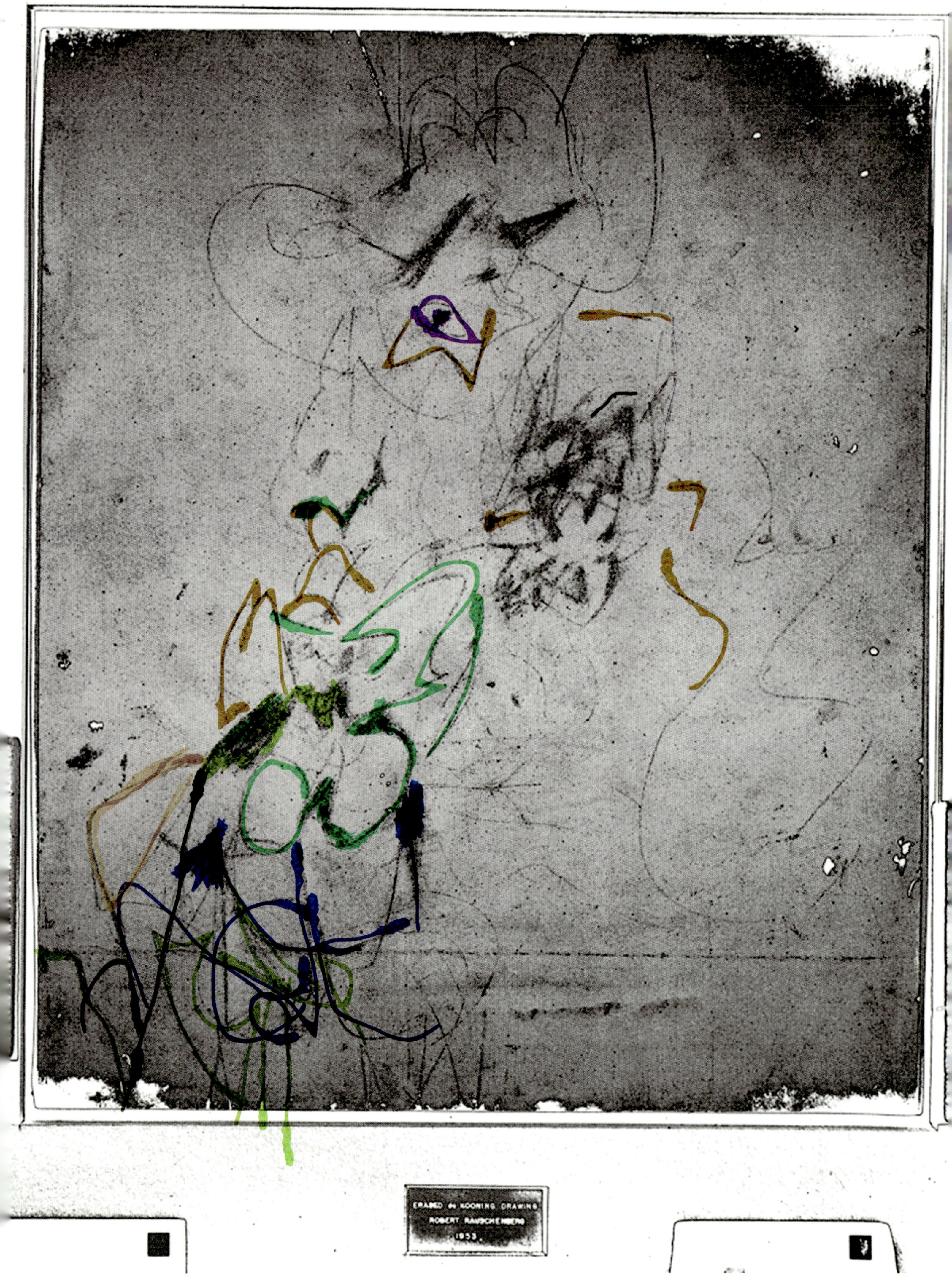
ERASED de KOONING DRAWING
ROBERT RAUSCHENBERG
1953

The Boys Jeered Her

When she was a little girl, Virginia Jaspers always drew a special measure of love and kindness. Her father William Jaspers, a New Haven railroad executive was most anxious that, in the home at least, his ungainly older daughter not suffer from "ugly duckling" comparisons with her lovely younger sister, Betty.

At school it was different. Virginia was slow and dull. Her boy classmates called her "horse," and "elephant," and mocked her strong ham hands. Such gibes she took with slow good nature, seemingly unhurt. Only rarely did she show flashes of a violent, sudden anger.

Virginia left high school at 19 to study pediatric nursing. "I've always loved children," she said later. "I've always wanted children of my own." She fussed over her charges extravagantly, and parents liked her.

Five years later, in 1948, one of "her" babies, Cynthia Hubbard, died suddenly at eleven weeks of a cerebral hemorrhage. Doctors in the case found suspicious signs of violence, as if the infant had been dropped or thrown. But the Hubbards trusted their nurse and asked her back to tend their second child.

"She handled the baby well," Mrs. Hubbard was to remember. "True, she was heavy-handed. When she burped the baby, she seemed a little strong. We kidded her about it a few times, but thought nothing serious about it."

A Bubble: Only three years later, another of Virginia's little girls died—3-month-old Jennifer Malkan. A doctor called by the nurse found the baby dead of asphyxiation—stifled by its own vomit. "It was a bubble," Virginia pleaded last week. "I picked her up and tried to get the bubble up. She began coughing. I saw her color wasn't good. I called a doctor. Honest to God, I didn't do anything violent to her. It was a bubble."

There were other incidents. One of her babies suffered serious head injuries, not definitely explained. Another, 3 weeks old, inexplicably broke a thigh bone, and the father was suspicious. "We sensed something was wrong with the nurse," he recalled last week. "We wondered about her emotional stability. One night we heard the baby cry out in pain while alone with her."

By this year, at least one New Haven pediatrician had long been searching for clear-cut grounds to bar Virginia Jaspers from nursing.

On Aug. 23, death took what certainly would be Virginia's last infant charge. That evening, Abbe Kapsinow, 11 days old, didn't want to take her formula. Exasperated, the nurse picked her up and gave her "a good shaking." At 2:30 a.m., Virginia awakened, heard the baby breathing too heavily, and called the parents. Two hours later, at New Haven Hospital, little Abbe died. The apparent cause of death, according to the medical examiner, was head and body injuries resulting from violent shaking.

Last week, after four days of preliminary investigation, police jailed Virginia Jaspers on a technical charge of "idleness," under $50,000 bond. She admitted maltreating five children, including the three who died in her care. As newspapers across the country carried the story, ten other parents recalled mishaps to children she had supervised and reported them to New Haven police.

"It was all uncontrollable," Virginia moaned to questioners. "I don't know why I did it. I ought to be put in the electric chair."

Newsweek

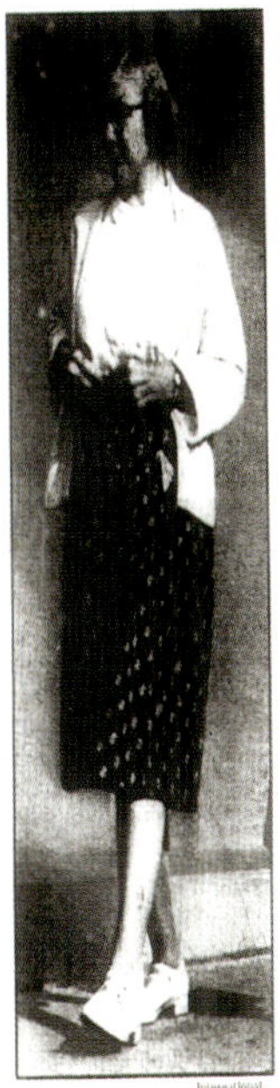

International

Size and Strength

The brutal and tragic career of nurse Virginia Jaspers is tied to her massive physical traits. Now 33, she is an ungainly 6 feet, weighs 220 pounds, has a 52-inch waist. Police concluded that she probably had no idea of the strength in her cruelly big arms and hands.

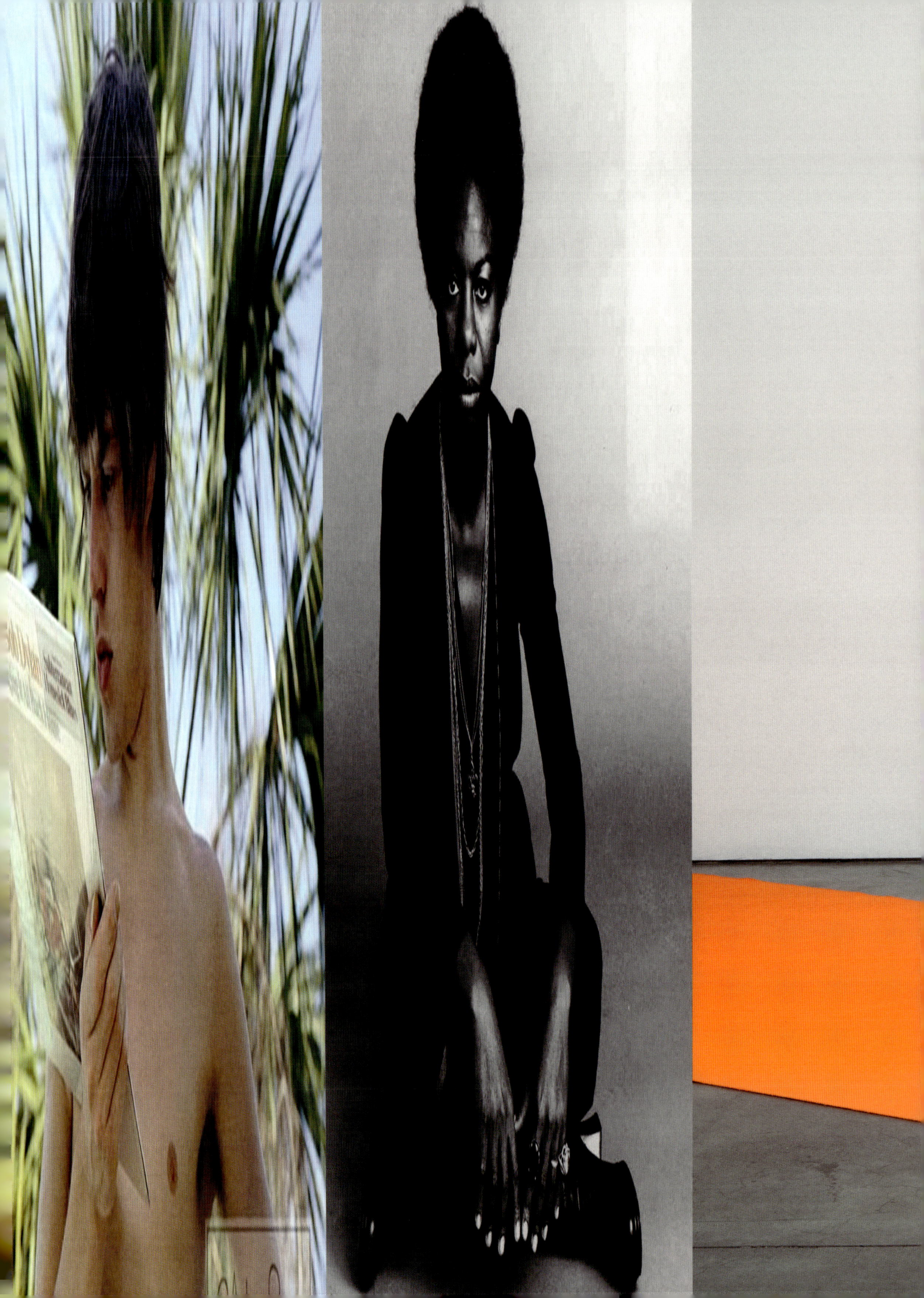

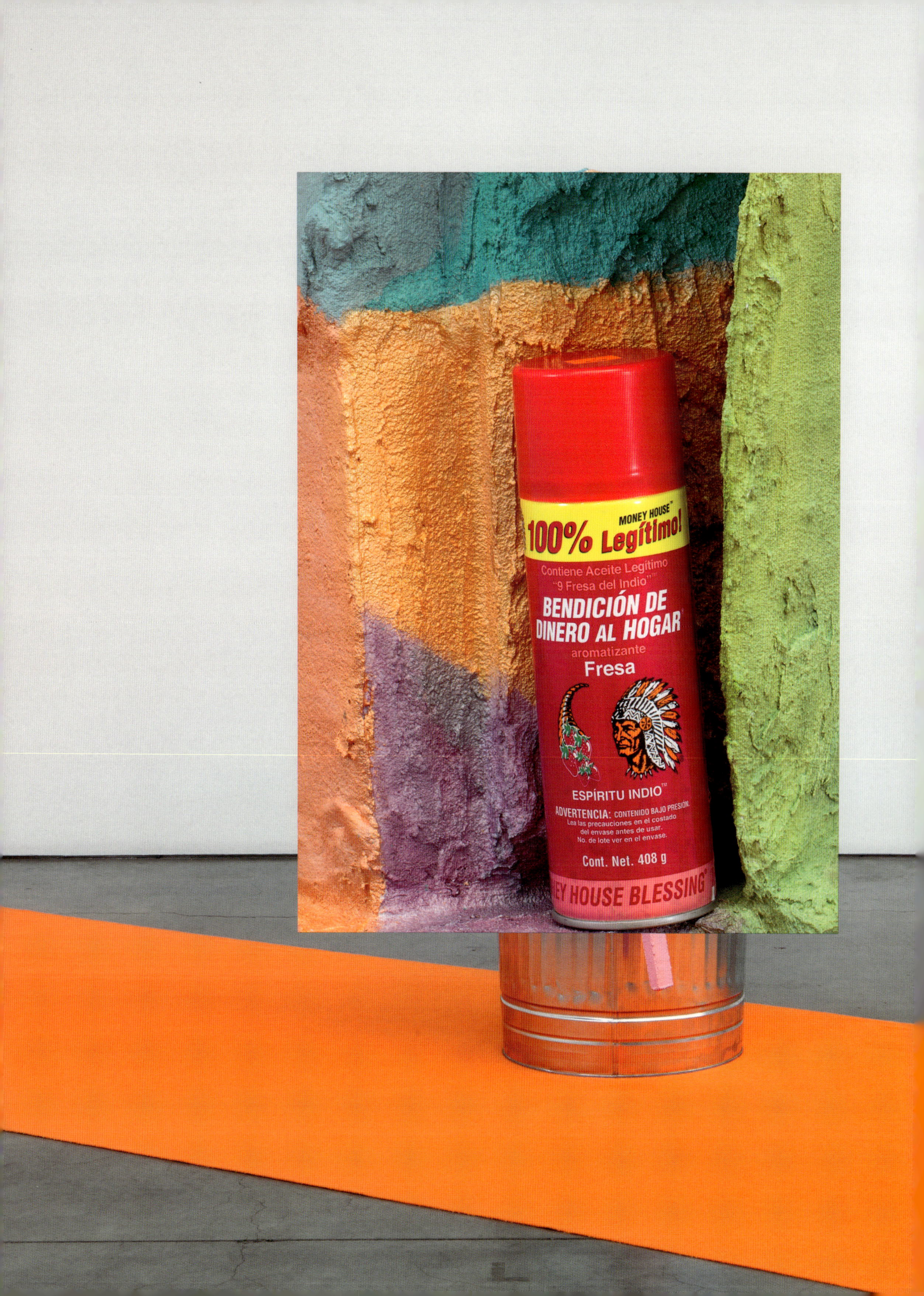
MONEY HOUSE™
100% Legítimo!
Contiene Aceite Legítimo
"9 Fresa del Indio"™
BENDICIÓN DE
DINERO AL HOGAR®
aromatizante
Fresa
ESPÍRITU INDIO™
ADVERTENCIA: CONTENIDO BAJO PRESIÓN.
Lea las precauciones en el costado
del envase antes de usar.
No. de lote ver en el envase.
Cont. Net. 408 g
EY HOUSE BLESSING™

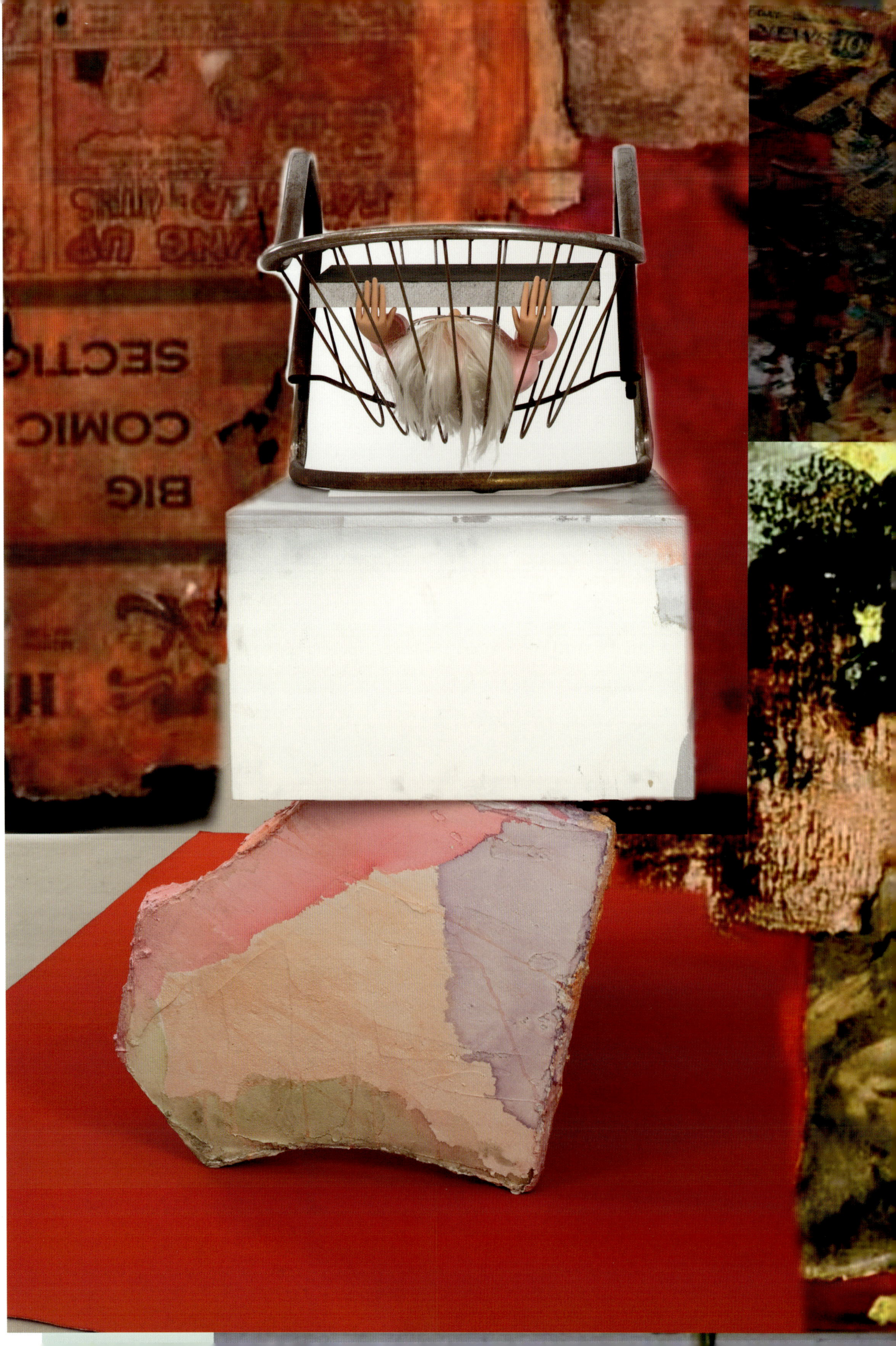
BIG
COMIC
SECTIO

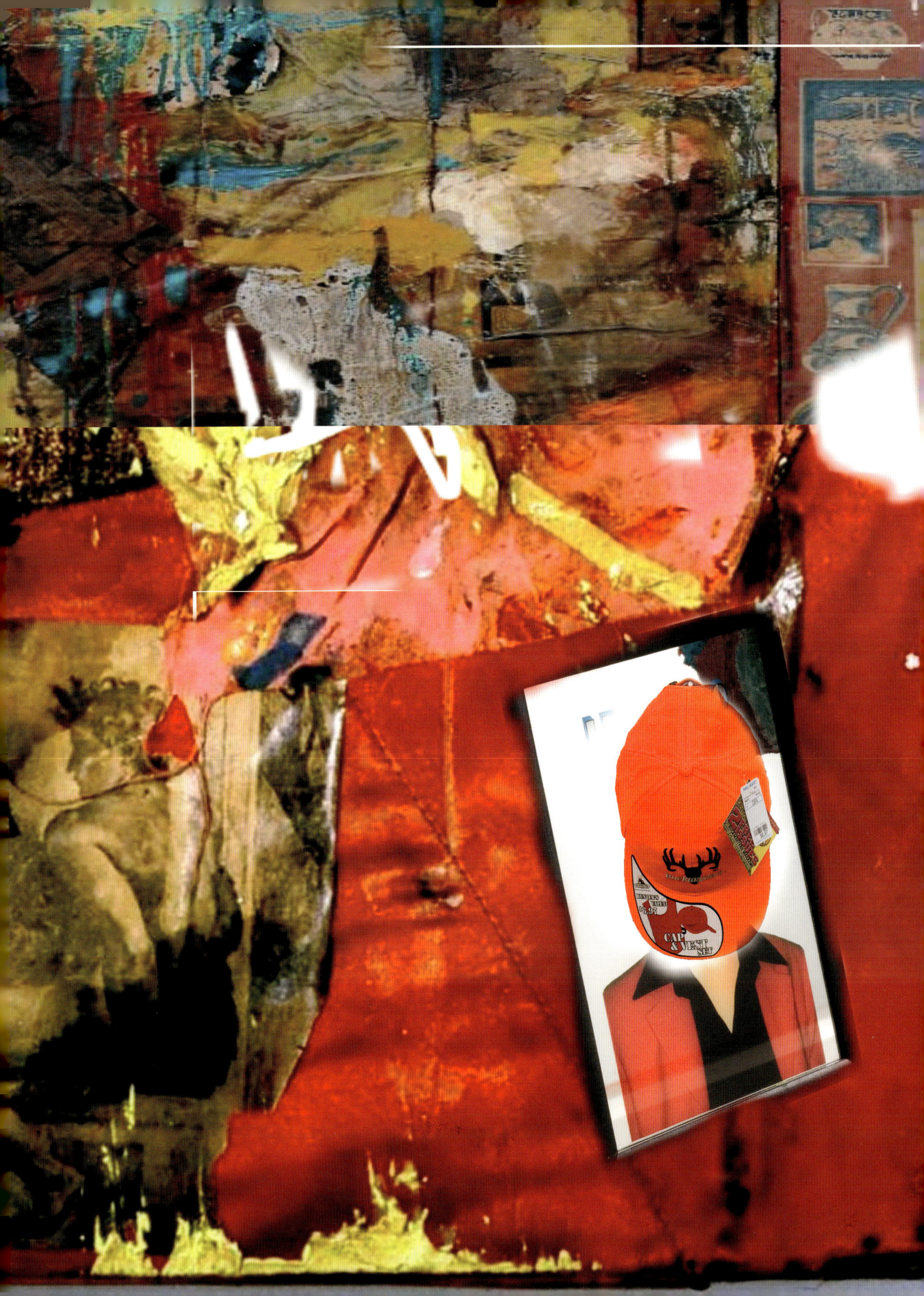
HUNTER'S VALUE
$6.97
CAP & VEST SET

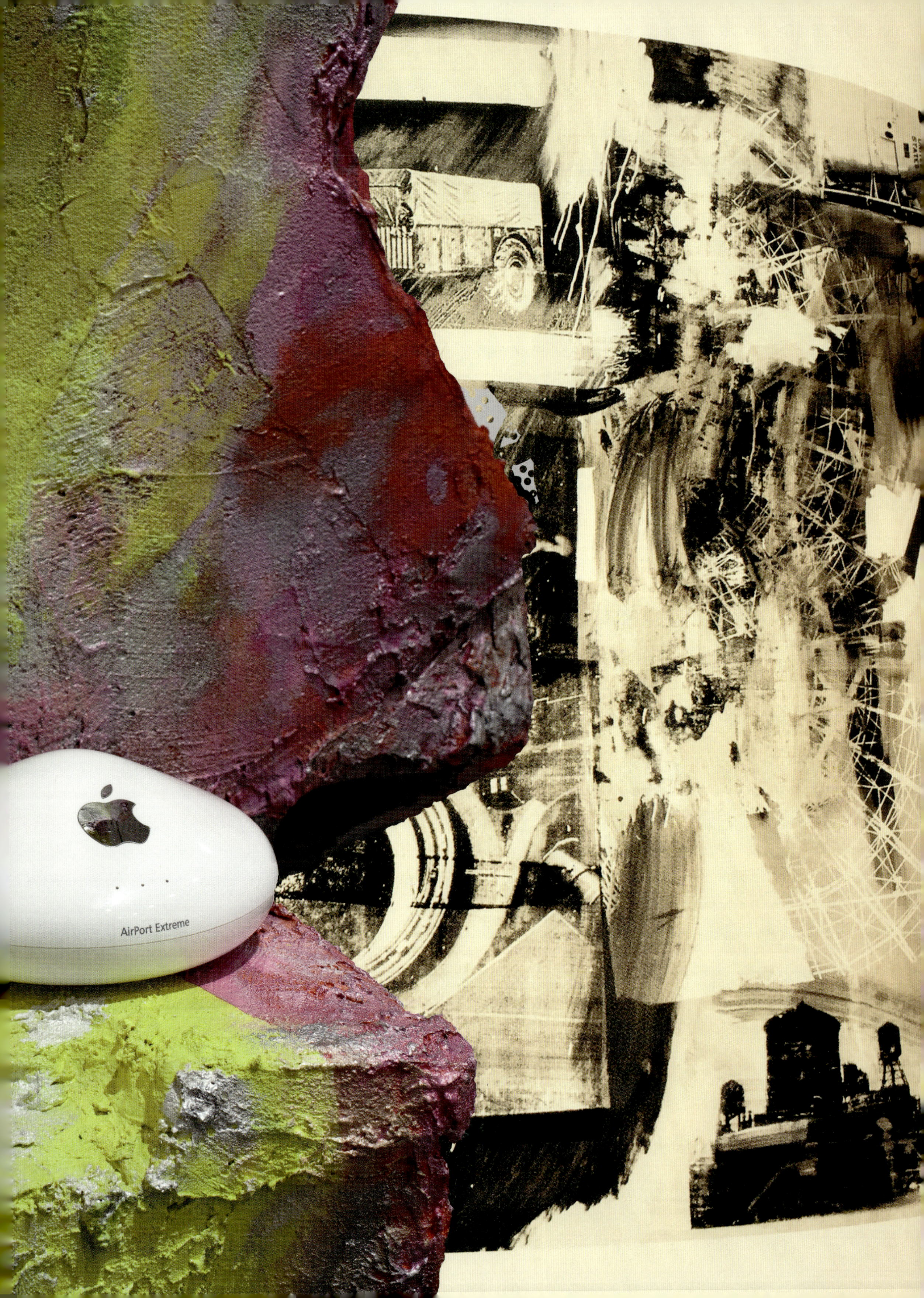
AirPort Extreme

Proposal for Nasher Xchange
Rachel Harrison
June 21, 2013

This proposal is for the fabrication of a large pink arrow for the plaza behind City Hall in downtown Dallas. This arrow would be placed next to Henry Moore's 1978 sculpture *The Dallas Piece* which is situated in the plaza on the back side of the building designed by I.M. Pei. The decision to build a new city hall was made by Dallas Mayor Erik Jonsson to reinvent the city's image after the tragic assassination of JFK in 1963. To create a modern city hall and municipal center was part of a larger plan to look to the city's future with bold civic planning. The up and coming architect I.M. Pei was chosen to design a modernist building and he in turn selected Henry Moore who was commissioned to create a new sculpture for the site.

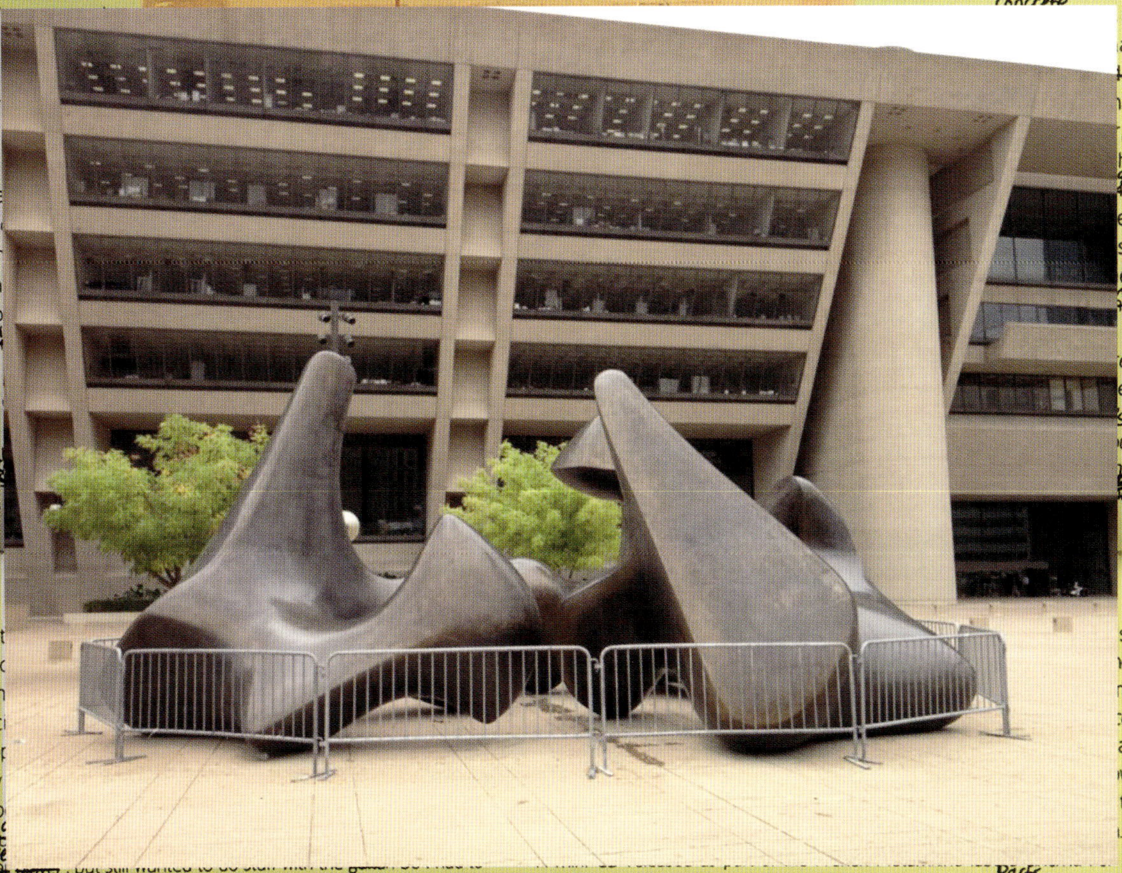

When I visited Dallas last year to learn more about the city and consider a public project I was struck by a set of police barricades positioned around the Moore while driving by in a car. It was quite a striking image. I asked if we could park to get out of the car in order to take a photograph. I immediately felt this site would be of interest to me for a project, not because of the Moore itself but because of the situation this artwork was in. I have been photographing for some time the variety of methods used by institutions to protect free standing sculptures. I sometimes find it depressing to see a great work of art surrounded by an ugly metal stanchion, sometimes you can't get close enough to really

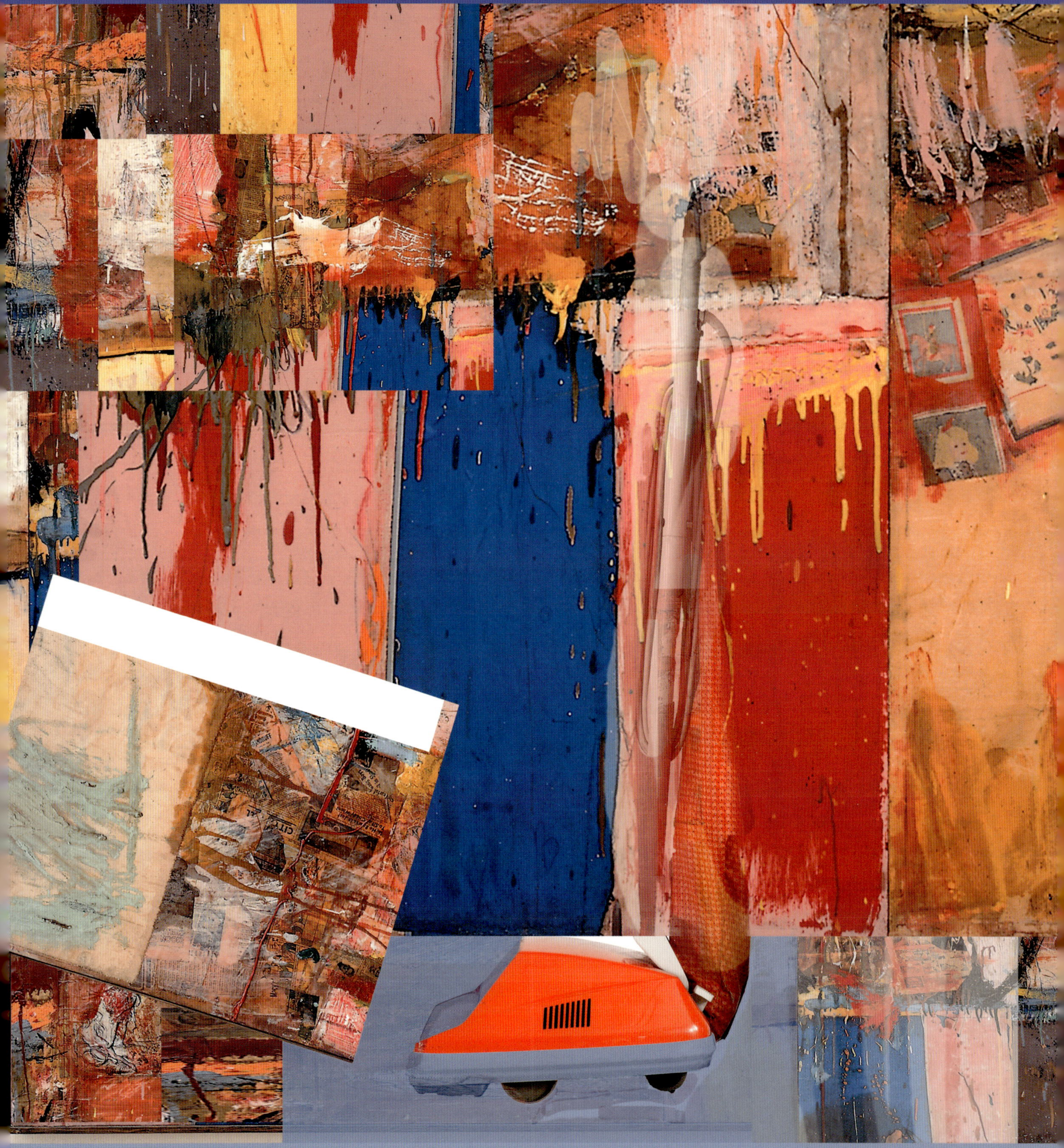

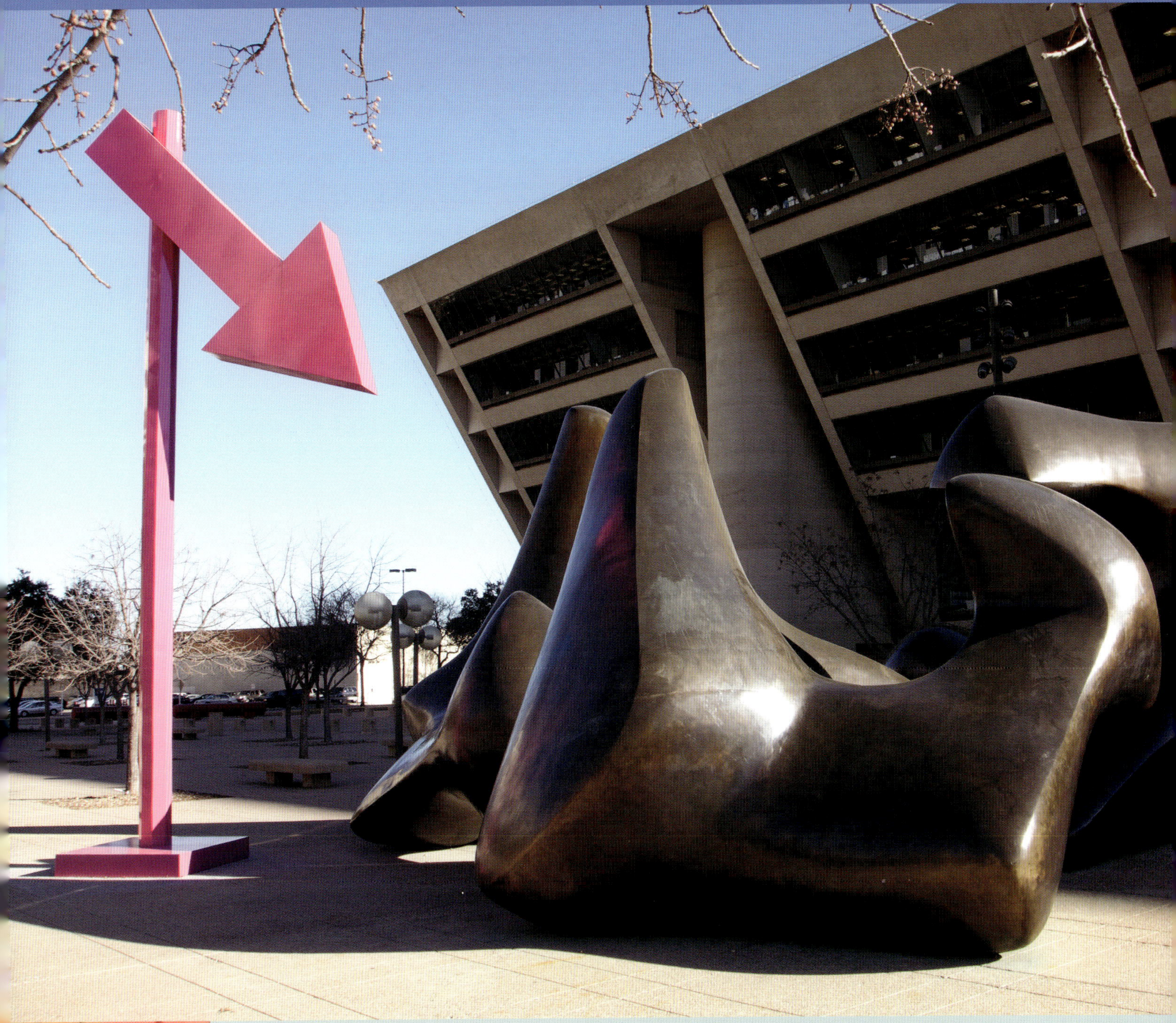

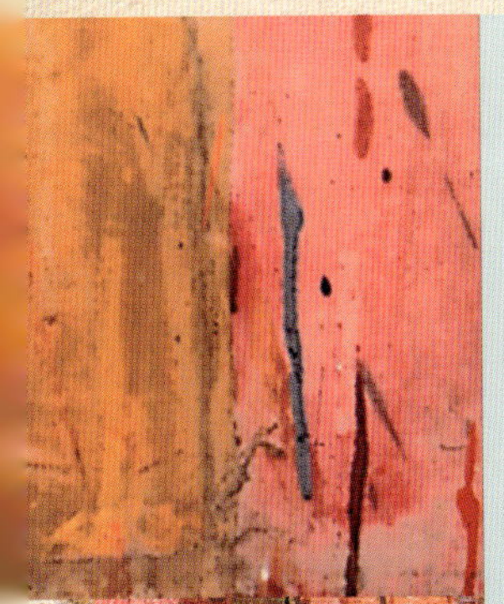

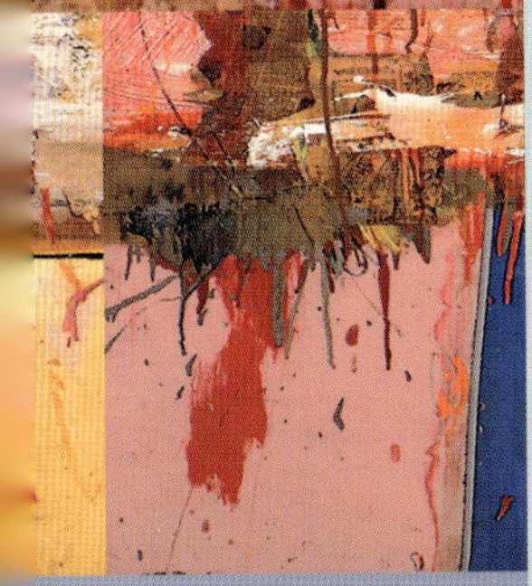

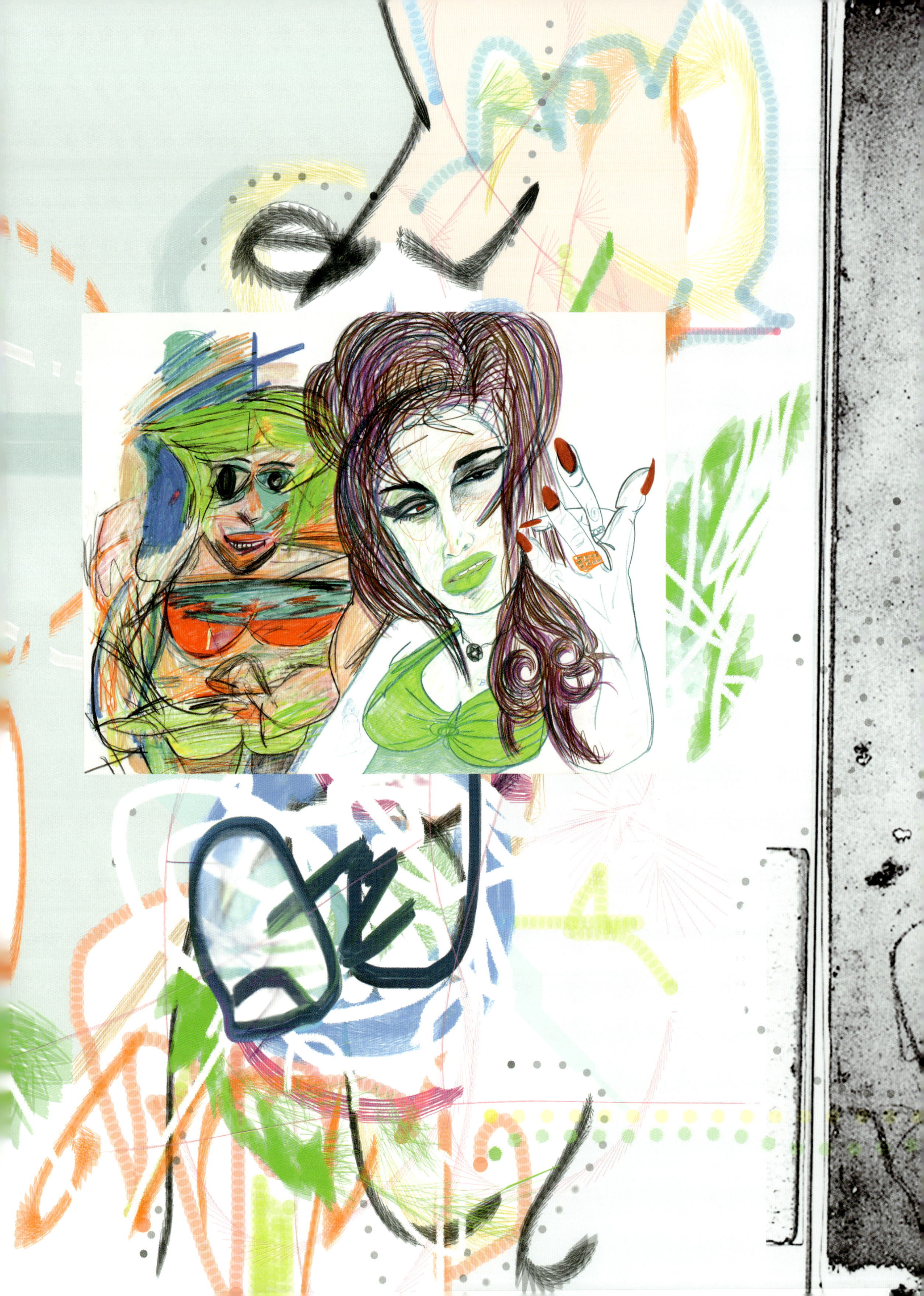

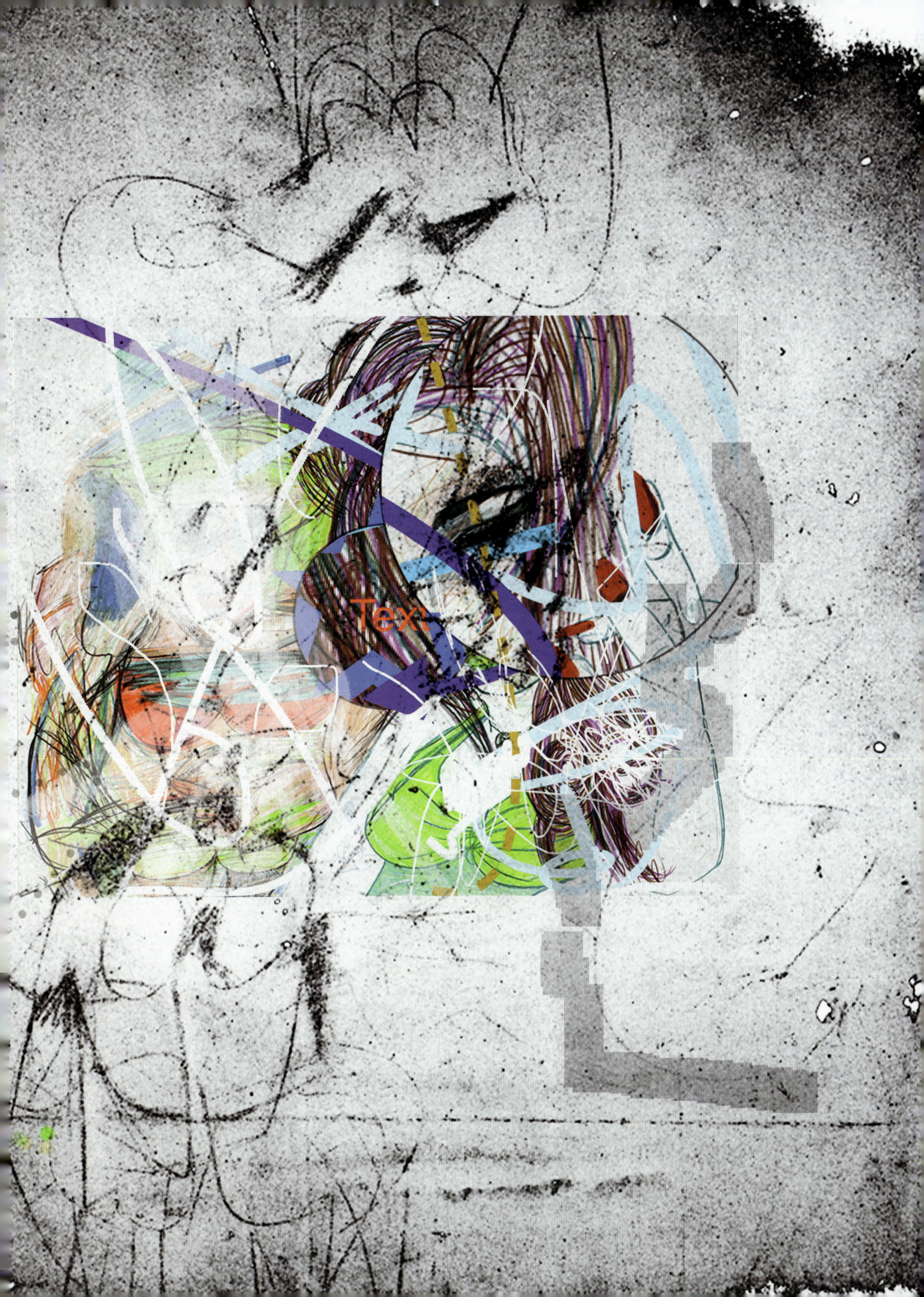
Tex

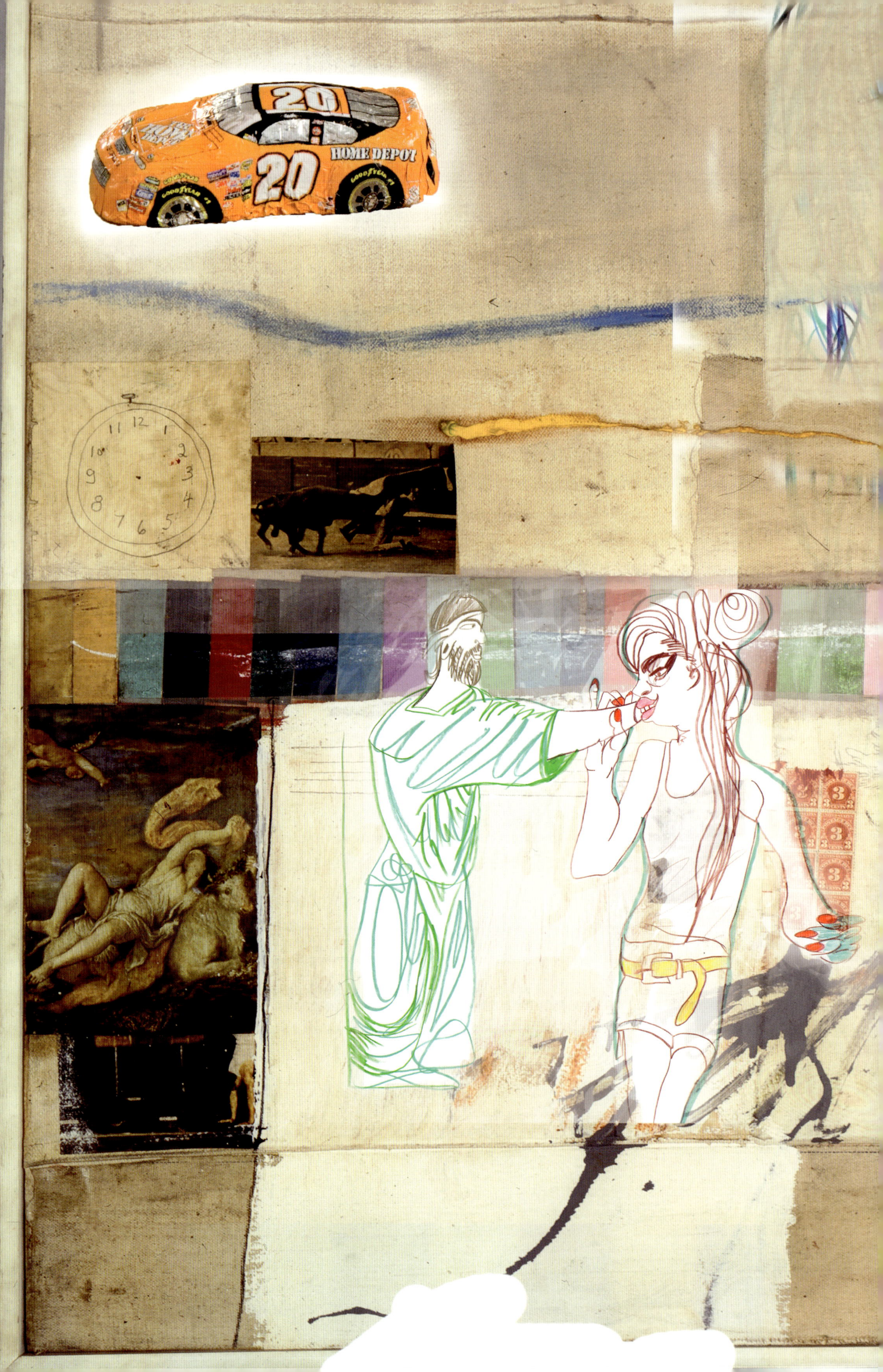
20
20
HOME DEPOT

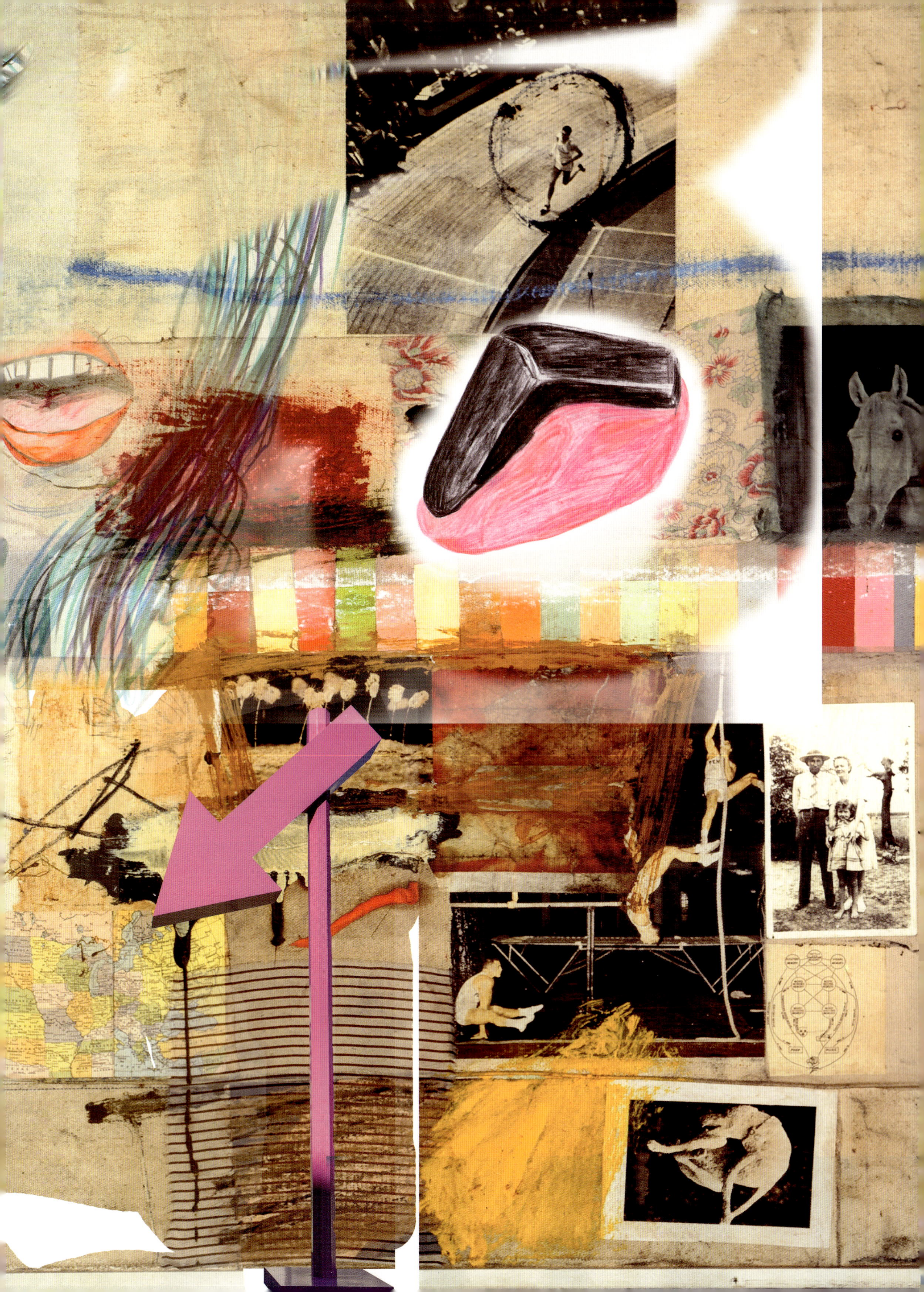

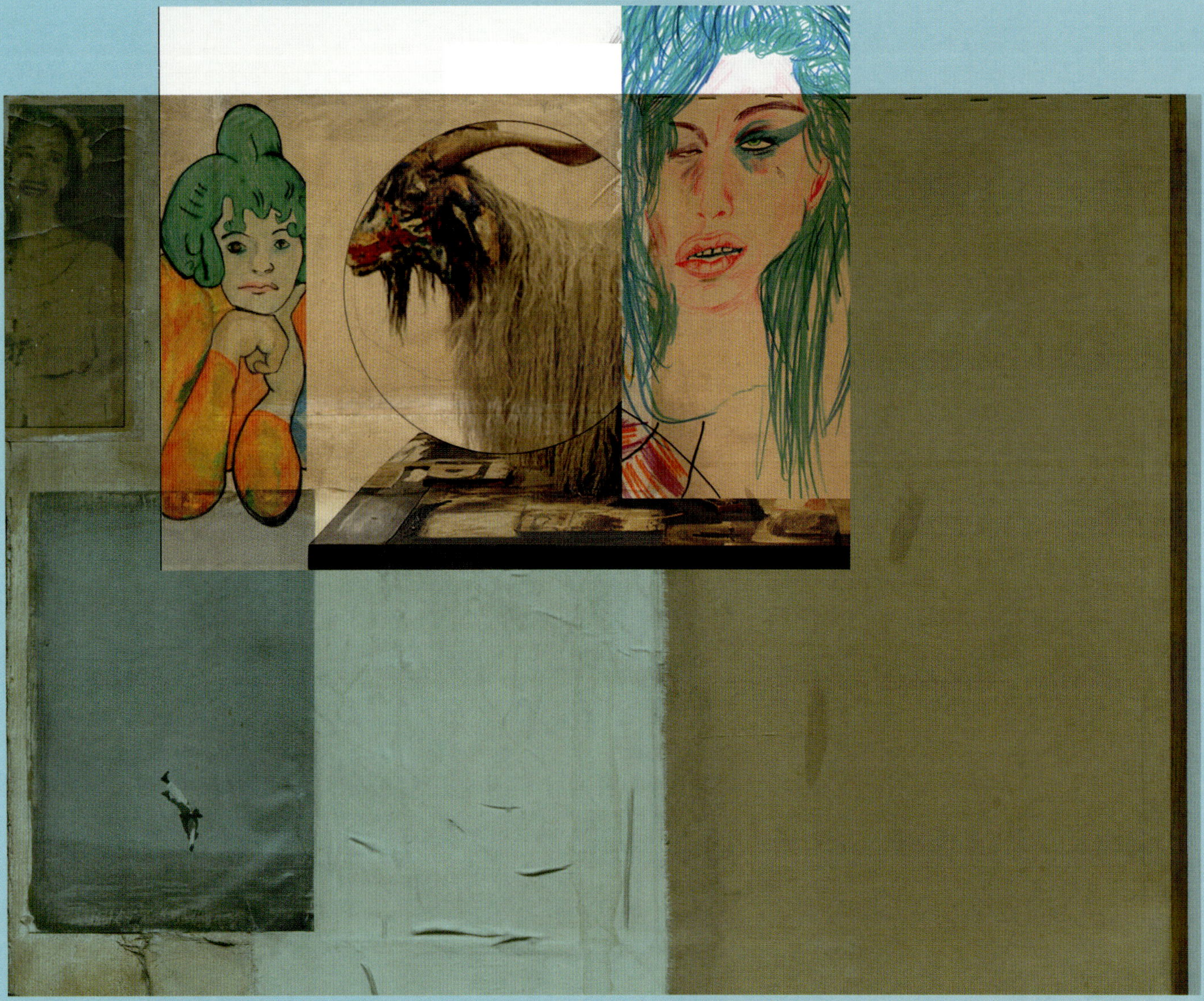

living it up. Click here to see what she had to say about her sex life.

Katy Perry's halftime show will feature a lion

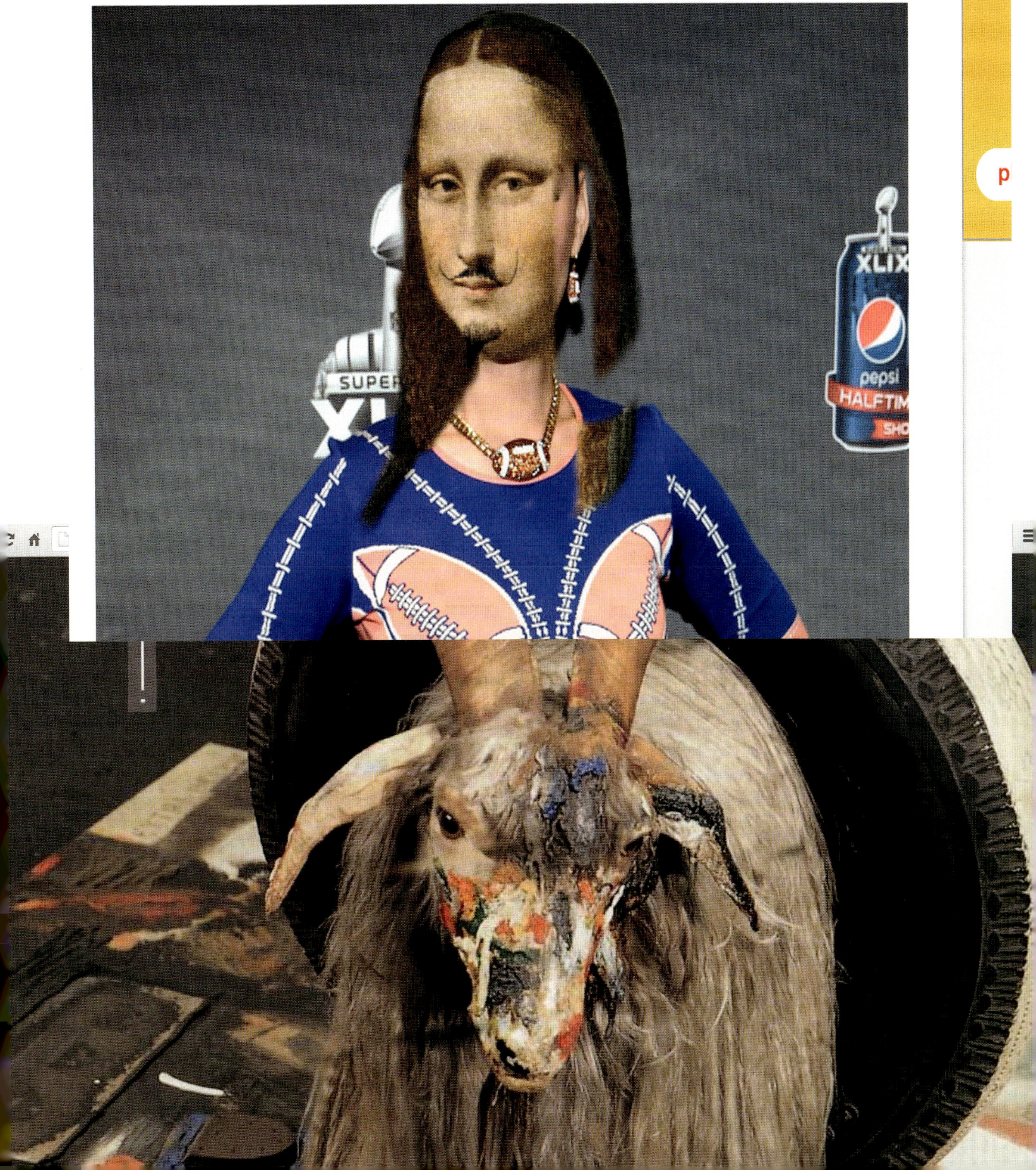

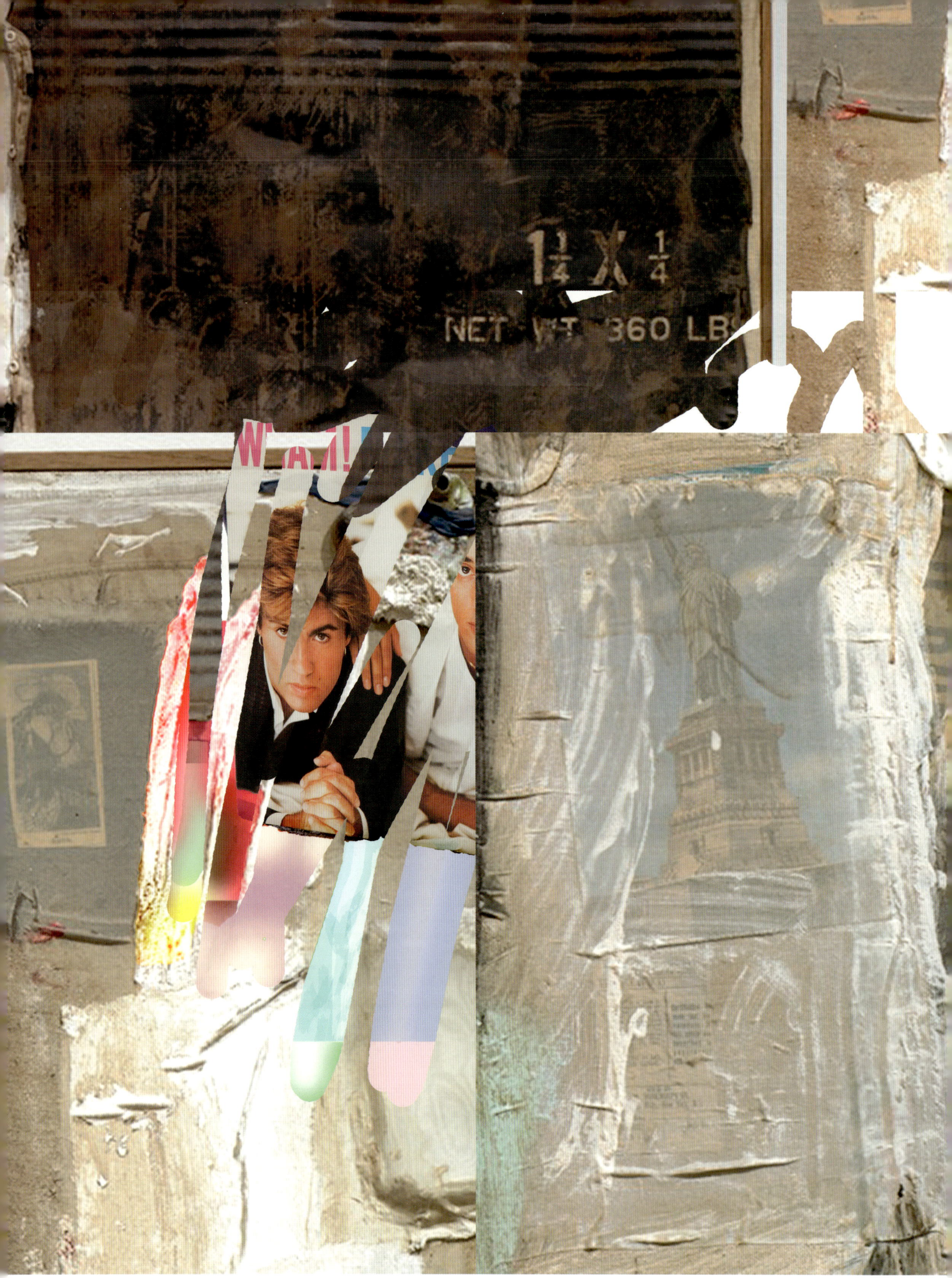
1¼ X ¼
NET WT 360 LB

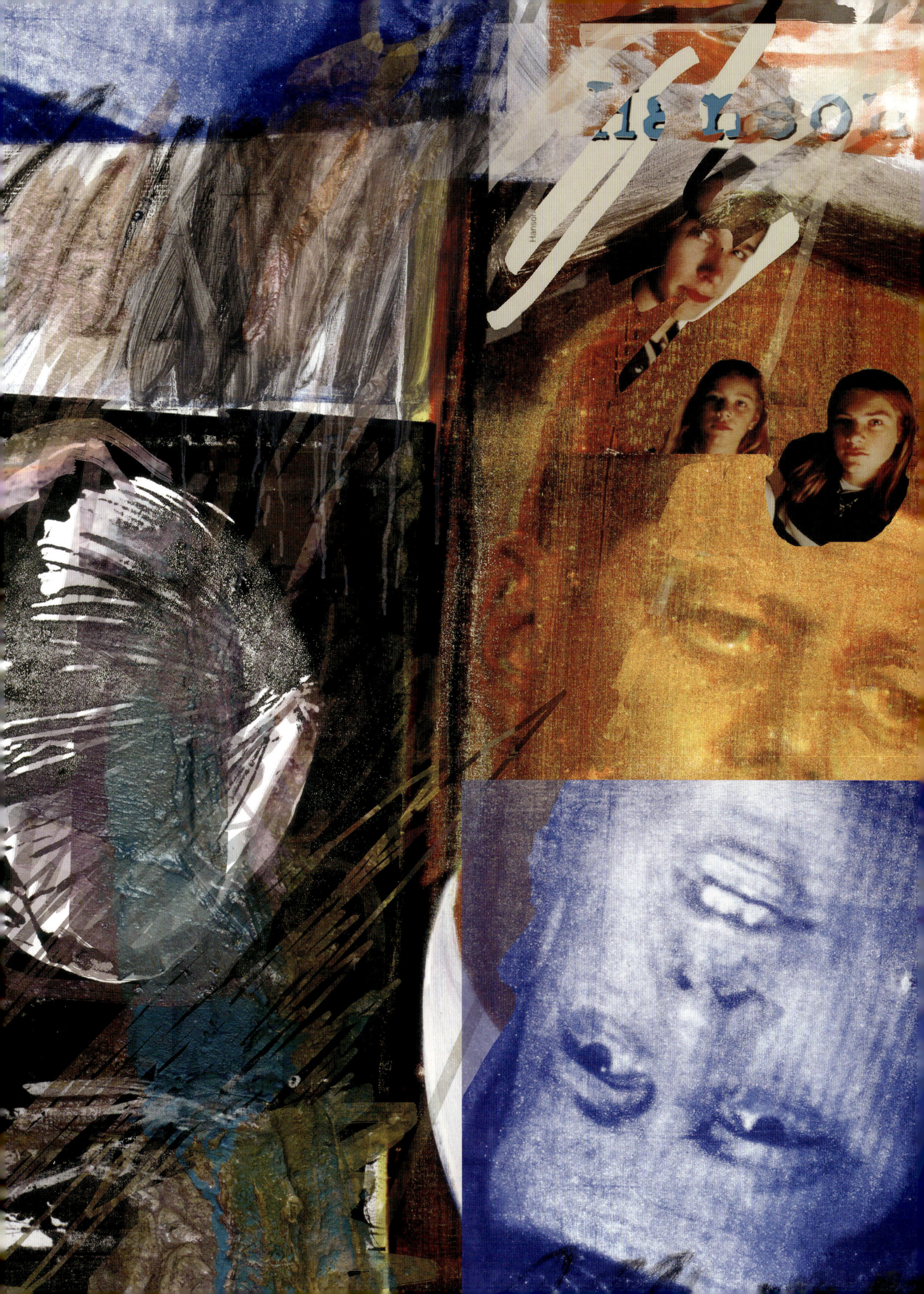
Hanson

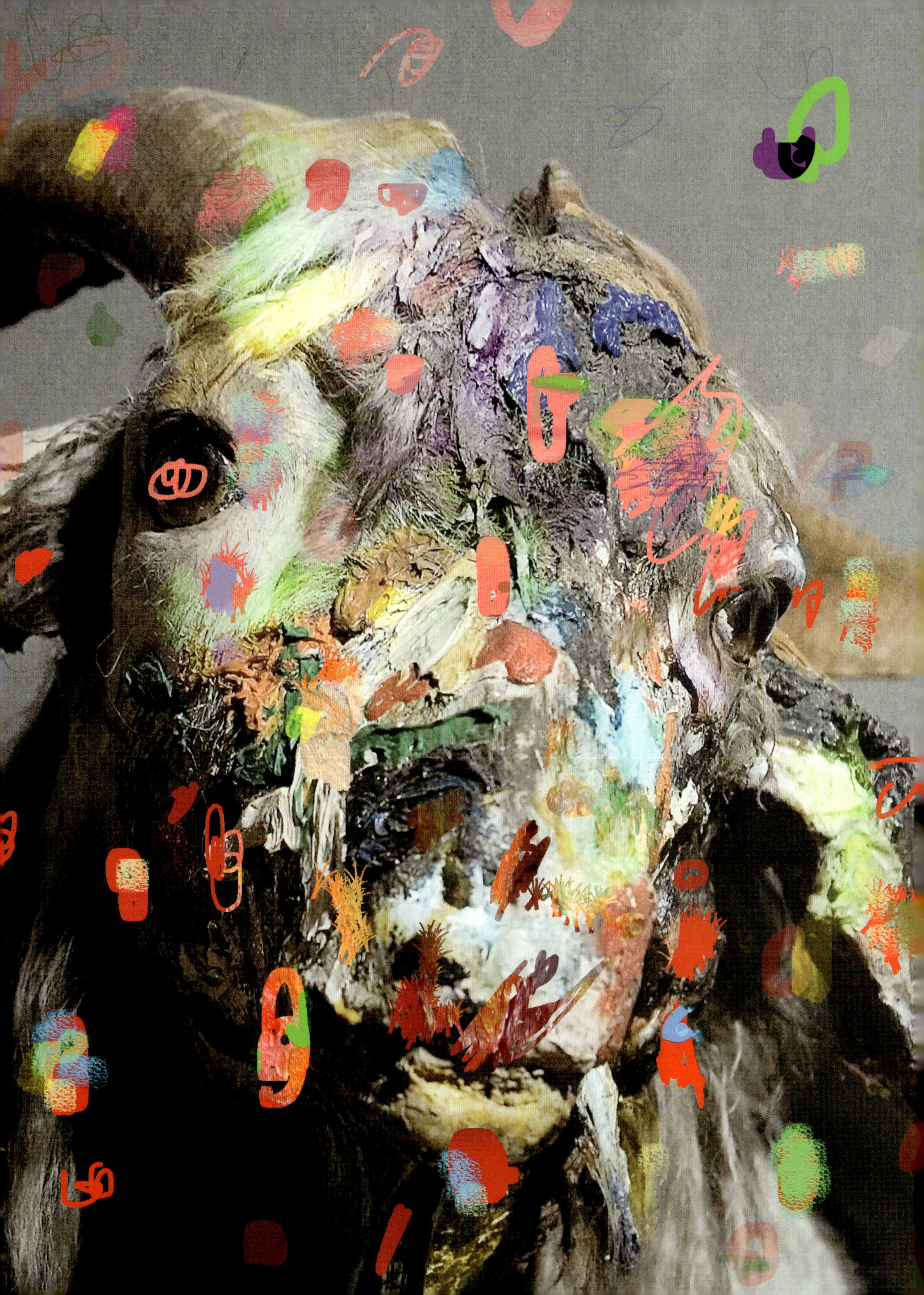

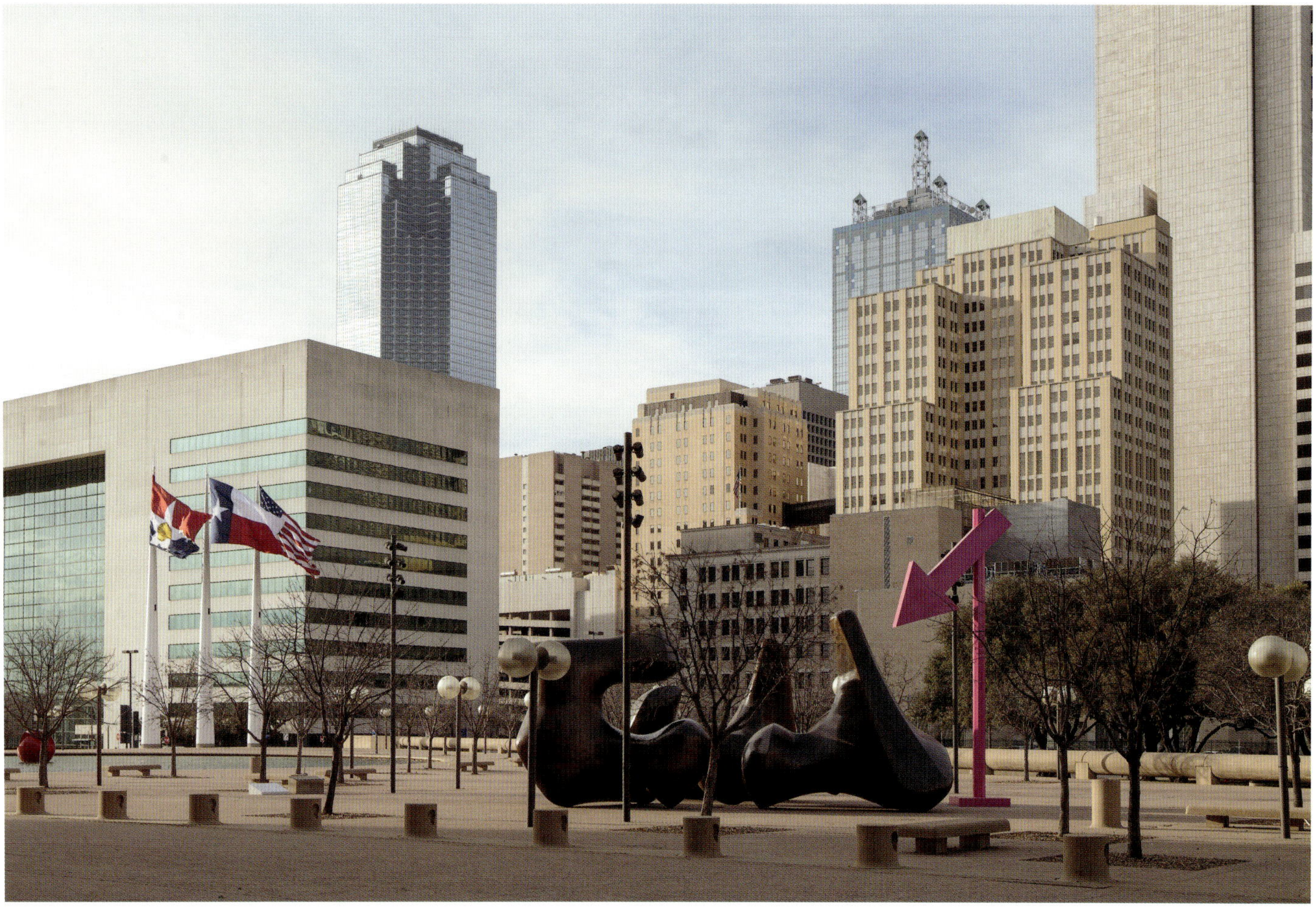

Rachel Harrison (American, b. 1966). *Moore to the Point*, 2013. Powder-coated steel; 731.5 x 298.1 x 127 cm. Installed at City Hall Plaza, Dallas. Courtesy of the artist and Greene Naftali, New York. Photo: Kevin Todora.

Say You Say Me

Johanna Burton

No Time Like the Present

In October of 2013, the Nasher Sculpture Center unveiled Nasher XChange, a project consisting of ten commissioned public artworks for the city of Dallas. Conceived as a platform to consider the "radically different approaches artists are taking to public work"—as well as the specificity of Dallas as a geographic and historic site—Nasher XChange was designed to fulfill the mandate of Raymond Nasher, who founded the center as a way of "making art accessible to all."[1] Such an articulated aim is hardly novel among advocates for public art, and yet debates around what such accessibility implies, to say nothing of how it is imparted, have raged on at least since Roosevelt's New Deal programs initiated the Federal Art Project and Percent-for-Art.[2] In this respect, Nasher XChange, which commemorated the center's tenth anniversary, is especially noteworthy given the particular legacy of Nasher himself, who is most remembered as the developer behind North Park Center—one of the largest commercial malls in the United States, and, as of 2007, one of the seven "retail wonders of the modern world."[3]

Nasher's way to place art publically, in other words, grew out of an implicit recognition that little in the world temporarily unites a large group of otherwise unrelated visitors so well as commerce. Indeed, North Park Center, which opened its doors in 1965, certainly can account for high numbers of both intentional and accidental encounters with art. As one of the first commercial arenas to implement an art program, it has shown, over the years, major works by Claes Oldenburg and Coosje van Bruggen, Frank Stella, and Andy Warhol, among many others. The mall, located at the crossroads of two major highways and today boasting 2 million feet of retail floor space, is arguably a continuing case study of the shifting relationship between avant-garde art and hyperbolic capitalism. But to say so is neither an indictment nor laudatory. Rather, it is to suggest we should reexamine the staid "making art accessible to all" paradigm for public art and see how its roots might well be mired in a kind of paradox—at least for the context of this essay, which considers the work of Rachel Harrison and, more precisely, the contrasting relationship it establishes for itself with the stuff of mass culture and, in turn, the very notion of a public. For while we can certainly find reason to critique the impulse of hanging priceless art within a frame born of H&M and Versace, it's no secret that that same frame has been seamlessly integrated into every museum with a corporate sponsor. The real difference is stark enough: MoMA has a $25 entrance fee; North Park Center is free unless you choose to shop there.

To best parse the relevance of such a paradox for Harrison's work, however, one must take into account the story of her 2012 invitation by Nasher XChange to scout locations for what would be her first public artwork. This visit brought her into contact with a 1978 outdoor sculpture by Henry Moore titled simply *The Dallas Piece*. Perhaps not unexpectedly, the setting for this work was conceived roughly contemporaneously with the mall's development. In 1964 Dallas mayor J. Erik Jonsson proposed a new city hall and municipal center, hoping to reinvigorate a city that was at an all-time low, shell-shocked by the assassination in November 1963 of John F. Kennedy and, in fact, dubbed "the City of Hate"—a symbol of all that was wrong in American politics as more attention was being paid to social justice due to the efforts of the civil rights, feminist, and antiwar movements. Designed by I. M. Pei in an intensely modern vein, the city hall was widely subjected to criticism upon its inauguration more than a decade later; intended to offset the building's severe lines was Moore's large-scale sculpture, whose three bronze parts were modeled on the soft geometry of individual sections of human vertebrae. Significantly, his piece was meant to encourage visitors to linger in the plaza rather than simply rush across its expanse. Indeed, images taken soon after the work was installed show families with young children playing and lounging on its contours, heedless of any symbolic connotation, intended or not, of bones scattered at the foot of city hall.

By the time Harrison encountered the work, *The Dallas Piece* had endured close to four decades of sitting on the plaza and in the process had undergone the strange kind of dual transformation inevitable to every such cultural object. On the one hand, its material self had borne the brunt of time and the elements, leading to an extensive renovation completed in 1998; on the other, its conceptual and aesthetic self had been framed and reframed as the decades rolled by. Moore's organic modernism—once understood as a postwar retreat to essential, universal forms—appears now, well after the turn of the millennium, as at once a period style and innocuously iconic of the artist's work. Put another way, it looks like what we know public art to look like. And so, as Harrison drove through Dallas, it wasn't Moore's sculpture that caught her eye but rather what had been done to it.

A tightly cinched ring constructed of police barricades encircled the sculpture, rendering it just off-limits to any visitor tempted to touch its surfaces, much less walk between or mount its forms. Though no sign of misconduct or vandalism was in evidence, the work's presence on the plaza became coded as the scene of a crime: whether past, present, or future was unclear, since the whole was suspended in a kind of indeterminacy. Indeed, when Harrison pulled her car over and got out to look more closely, there was nothing that explained why the barricades had been erected or when they would be taken down.

Returning to New York, she got in touch with the project manager for Nasher XChange and asked him to see if he could find out just what had prompted this situation. Though he asked around, nobody at the city level (or anywhere else) could tell him anything about the barricades—what their purpose was, when they would be removed, or even, surprisingly, when they had first been installed. It was as though, Harrison remarked in her proposal for Nasher XChange, someone had simply decided at some point that artworks should be protected from the very public they ostensibly address. The effect, of course, is that *The Dallas Piece* no longer worked publically: "Barriers," she wrote, "have the potential to create mental as well as physical barricades."[4]

But while Harrison's prodding yielded no information, it did yield results. One day, as mysteriously as they had appeared, the barricades were gone. On her next visit, she could see the Moore, which is to say, she saw it for the first time. In her proposal, she describes her thought process for moving forward with her own project: "I determined at that time that I had already created a work of art by getting the barricades removed, and that if this artwork was written about, it would then be historicized and considered a 'piece.' I decided I could still do something else, but that I didn't have to make an artwork, this had already been accomplished. It seems logical to continue to work with the site."[5]

For Nasher XChange, then, Harrison ultimately suggested—and then fabricated and installed—a large pink arrow, twenty-four feet tall, whose raison d'être was to point out Moore's sculpture, to mark its presence as an overlooked but worthwhile attraction. The barricades had been one kind of sign, easily readable as "stay away." Harrison's arrow, titled *Moore to the Point* (2013), was another kind of sign, calling attention to a form that had, over time, simultaneously persisted and disappeared—shifting in its most fundamental terms of accessibility—without moving an inch.

No Time Like the Past

If *Moore to the Point* isn't an artwork, though, we might ask, just what is it? We could consider its function—and friction—within Harrison's larger oeuvre and return to long-standing conversations about how to categorize her activities. She has been widely regarded as a sculptor for twenty years, and fans and detractors alike have used her as a case study to debate the vicissitudes of sculpture today. (Do her forms evoke presence or absence? Privilege color or mass? Do away with the pedestal or hyperbolize it? Continue legacies of the readymade or assemblage? Critique capitalism or reflect it? These are all questions, I think, that miss the forest for the trees.) Yet here it seems apposite, instead, to take Harrison at her word, if only because she has rarely, if ever, separated out any element of her practice as being distinct from "art," in all its expansive rubric today.

In his recent profile of Harrison in the *New Yorker*, Peter Schjeldahl conjectures, with respect to the artist's endeavors in Dallas (and wishing to underscore her engagement with objects in the world), that she is disappointed in the majority of public art, "for its obliviousness of the actualities of public life."[6] Notably in this brief discussion, the critic characterizes Harrison's interest in the site as driven by equal parts "scorn and praise" for Moore and the building his work accompanies, a summation meant less to comment on the older artist than to illuminate the texture of taking him up today. It's worth, in this vein, and as I've been arguing, returning then to an exploration of the actual events leading up to *Moore to the Point*—its publicness, one might say.[7] What's striking—and productive to reconsider—is also what reminds us that Harrison never wanted us to think of her pink Pop arrow as "the work," but rather as evidence that a distinct activity has taken place at and as its site.

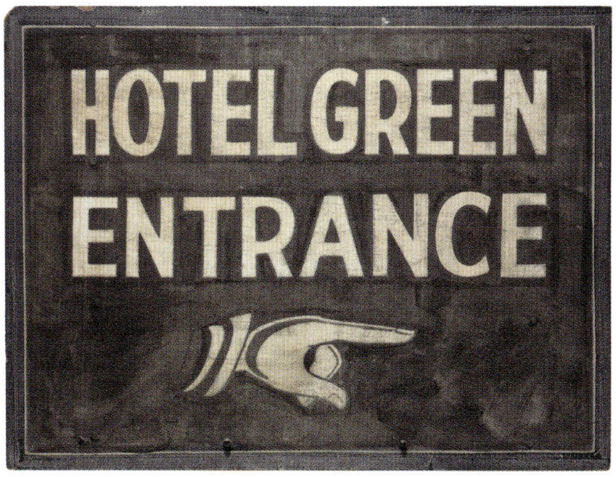

Marcel Duchamp (American, b. France, 1887–1968). *Signed Sign*, 1963. Signed, inscribed, and dated *Marcel Duchamp Pasadena 1963* (on the index finger). Oil on panel; 45.7 x 61 cm. Private Collection. © 2015 Succession Marcel Duchamp/ADAGP, Paris/ Artists Rights Society (ARS), New York. Image: © Christie's Images Limited.

Which is to say that Harrison is pointing at Moore neither in wonder nor derision, but to render him public in a sense easily overlooked—and which makes Harrison's anomaly, her one piece of public art, all the more significant both within her oeuvre and within the landscape of art making today.

By saying as much, I mean to expand the notion of what it means to "go public" and to consider Harrison's work—and not just the piece in Dallas—as enacting a particular kind of pointing in which any singular object is necessarily larger than its material footprint. Of course, acts of pointing are hardly new in art history. Duchamp pointed most famously in his *Tu m'* (1918; Yale University Art Gallery, New Haven), which he declared to be his final painting (and is often read in part as a manifesto against the tedium of such manually produced artworks). But his capacity to point only grew after he stopped making things; a particularly succinct example was a "signed sign" produced during his time staying at the Hotel Green in Pasadena as he prepared for his 1963 retrospective with Walter Hopps. Indeed, not many years later, the next generation of conceptual artists pointed, too—John Baldessari's Commissioned Paintings series was a kind of primer on the vernacular of advanced art. Paying a variety of Sunday painters to painstakingly replicate photographic images of hands pointing at everyday objects, Baldessari called attention to different kinds of artistic technique that, while impressive, had little currency in conceptual circles unless forcefully détourned. In some ways refuting Duchamp's decisive move away from connoisseurship, Baldessari's project nonetheless underlined its ultimate lesson. While each Commissioned Painting bore the name of its maker within the title, there was no question about who could ultimately claim—and be awarded—authorship of the work itself.

Harrison's work is ultimately distinct from these precedents, though there are clearly traces of some active dialogue with them. David Joselit has persuasively argued that, in her sculptures, the artist attempts to "keep ready-mades untransformed" or, put slightly differently, to "preserve their singularity by giving them new life in a new location."[8] He claims that rather than attempting to "redeem ordinary commodities or condemn them," her work possesses the particular capacity to "grasp" them. (The dual nature of that word is clearly in play, suggesting the sense of both holding and comprehending).[9] And to be sure, when one encounters such items as a pillowcase emblazoned with a picture of an eagle, a cheap mask with Dick Cheney's face, a rubber chicken, a picture of Mel Gibson, a pile of plastic potatoes, or a BMX bike, there is little frisson of auratic (or for that matter, desublimatory) transformation in the air around them.

That said, I would venture that in grasping these objects—and also ideas that are proffered in language, through her titles—Harrison is also pointing with them. Pointing at people, places, and things, but also at the ways in which we have learned to frame our interactions with those people, places, and things. This is what I would argue is the publicness of Harrison's work: there was much more to pointing at Moore than the fact that

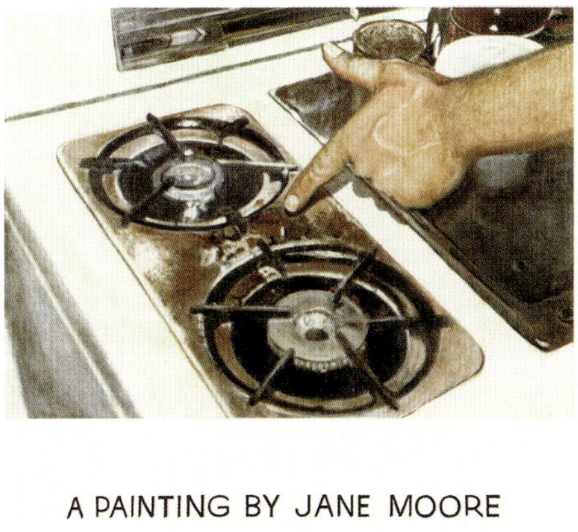

John Baldessari (American, b. 1931). *Commissioned Painting: A Painting by Jane Moore*, 1969. Oil and acrylic on canvas; 105.5 x 115.6 cm. Courtesy of the artist and Marian Goodman Gallery.

three large, anthropomorphic bronzes were forgotten on a plaza. The minihistory I gave of Dallas, from its shopping mall to Kennedy's assassination, literally figures in how we can understand Harrison's response to Moore, and how Moore, many years before, responded to his own context.

Etymologically, we are often told that *public* derives from "common," or "of the people," which is correct, but it is generally left out that this notion of ordinariness tends toward a thinly veiled concept of the vulgar. What is public is shared but often understood as representative of a lowest common denominator rather than a conscious construction for the larger good. Yet, as T. J. Clark reminds us—writing in 1994 about Abstract Expressionism, no less—it is vulgarity that allows objects, and perhaps art objects most of all, to remain present in culture well beyond their relevance.[10] (While Clark mainly addresses an apparently outmoded petit bourgeois context, it's worth asking whether the phenomenon of cross-class identification has reached new levels and taken entirely new forms.) Harrison's pointing, I would argue, is vulgar in the sense that what comes along with her—high art, boy band, or thrift-store junk propped up and placed in new configurations but never fully having sloughed off the patina of their travels— remains at the level of the common.

In his "Questions from an Abstraction Who Reads," Diedrich Diederichsen closely attends to the appearance of Amy Winehouse—particularly in drawings that also feature Gertrude Stein, Pablo Picasso, and Martin Kippenberger, among others—as a figure within Harrison's 2012 exhibition *The Help*.[11] The borrowed film title serves to remind that contemporary culture has produced a space that performs a kind of new transparency around issues of race, class, and gender—yet, as Diederichsen argues, the "ontological plane of the category of support, from physical support to living labor," has only made its proceedings increasingly difficult to picture.[12] Nevertheless, he contends that Harrison's work figures such support in two ways, as it attempts "to present the material orders behind symbolic production."[13]

"To present the material orders behind symbolic production." It's a phrase that reminds me of Sherrie Levine. In 2009 she made *After Courbet: 1-18*, a work consisting of eighteen identical postcards on mat board picturing Courbet's *L'Origine du Monde* (*The Origin of the World*) from 1866. Without going too far down the path of its history, it is worth pointing out that the painting, which now hangs in the Musée d'Orsay in Paris, has had a checkered past and is described on the museum's website as having finally "taken its proper place within the history of modern painting" despite the fact that it "still raises the troubling question of voyeurism."[14] That it was originally commissioned by a Turkish-Egyptian diplomat, lost for decades, then owned by Jacques Lacan before coming into the Orsay's collection is not inconsequential in this regard.[15] The social history of the painting as an object of gambling, obfuscation, and underground trading shows what happens to objects that confuse production and reproduction. Note: the words *public* and *pubic* derive from the same root.

Out of Time

Levine's treatment of Courbet renders him public. Once, and perhaps still, an image to be hidden or stolen away, *L'Origine du Monde* is nonetheless for sale in endless supply at the museum's gift shop, reproduced on postcards to be sent without even the need for an envelope. And by virtue of Levine making Courbet's image—but more so the everyday reproduction and dissemination of it—her own, we see it too, for the first time. (Harrison has, it bears mentioning here, also turned to Courbet's *L'Origine* in her own work, as an image of intense scopophilic and cultural interest, both imaginary and economic.)

Levine, we know, is most often categorized as appropriating her images. Harrison is almost never described this way. The distinction that is often made hews along the lines of intent: Levine leaves things as they are in order to examine the frames around them, while Harrison leaves

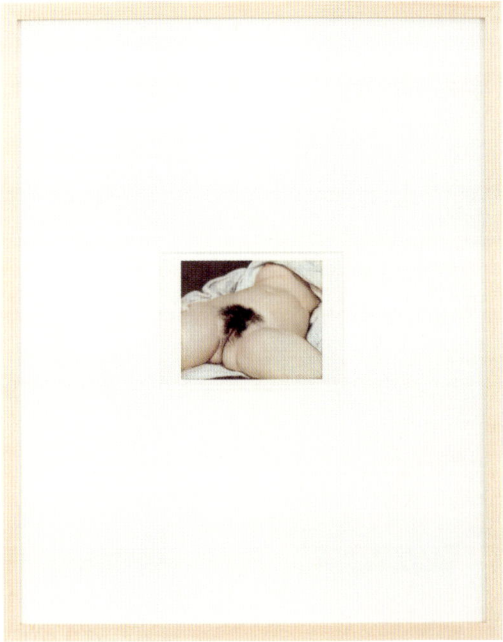

Sherrie Levine (American, b. 1947). *After Courbet: 1–18* (detail), 2009. 18 postcards on mat board; each 50.8 x 40.6 cm. Courtesy of Paula Cooper Gallery, New York. © Sherrie Levine.

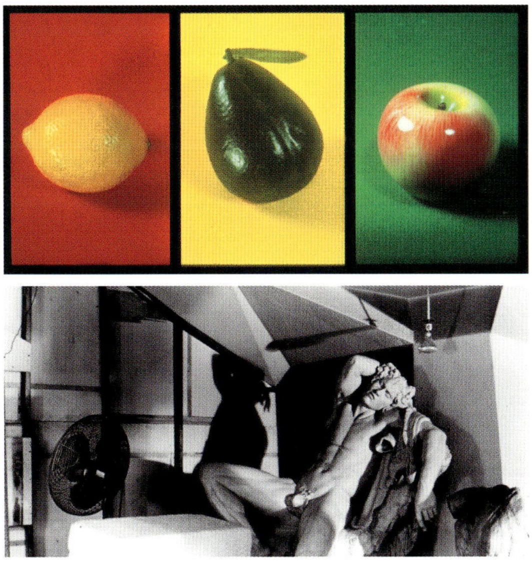

Louise Lawler (American, b. 1947). *Slides by Night: Now That We Have Your Attention What Are We Going to Say?*, 1985. Slide projection. Courtesy of the artist and Metro Pictures, New York. © Louise Lawler.

things as they are so we can actually look directly at them and understand them on their own terms.

But in the argument I am putting forward, these are both operations that deliver us back to the public, pointing us in the direction of understanding objects as they are handed down and over, and as they are valued, revalued, and unvalued. Art has a particular function here, of course. In 1985 Louise Lawler called it for what it is: she installed *Slides by Night: Now That We Have Your Attention What Are We Going to Say?* as a projection at the gallery Metro Pictures, then in Soho; the work was visible only from the street and only at night. Using the visual logic of a slot machine, Lawler's piece offered passersby the illusion of arbitrary configurations: fruits, baseballs, and bells appeared next to images of Lawler's own photographs. A jackpot comprised three matching classical sculptures, and the payoff was pictures we now think of as classic Lawler—artwork by other artists, in situ. Lawler wasn't only commenting on the gamble of playing the game of artist, art collector, museum curator, or gallery owner. She was, in offering this strange spectacle only to those who would be in Soho at night, after the shops and galleries had closed, asking that the support for such endeavors be rethought. Is an artwork an artwork if nobody sees it and nobody buys it?

In nature, there are animals who rely—indeed, survive—on symbiotic relationships with other animals. These relationships tend to be long and intimate. The most noted of these are amazing examples of creatures who otherwise would most certainly be at odds, with one destroying the other: small fish called wrasses cleaning the teeth of sharks or tiny birds known as oxpeckers removing ticks from massive rhinos. (In both cases, the smaller animal receives sustenance and protection in exchange for the grooming services it provides.) Yet in the spectrum of symbiosis, there is only one sort of arrangement that is beneficial to both (mutualism), while there are many cases in which just one partner benefits (commensalism) or one is actually harmed (parasitism).

Leaving aside the long debates around criticality vs. complicity, might it be useful to consider artists like Harrison, who point to cultural objects, people, and things—including other artists—through the lens of symbiosis? This is simply another way of getting back to where I started and repeating again that inherent to the work is a negotiation that moves away from any idea or ideal of autonomy and toward a function of publicness. Does Courbet benefit from Levine's treatment of his work in the here and now—and, in turn, does Levine herself profit? Do Harrison's gestures toward Duchamp, Picasso, Rauschenberg, and Stella mobilize these artists despite their already intensely high profiles (and dead bodies)?

When I last visited Harrison's studio, she was working toward her next show, tentatively titled *Lean In* at the time. A large, multicolored form stood in the space or rather tilted at a kind of awkward angle, its weight supported by a large wooden box tucked into what, if it was a person, might be its lower back. Sheryl Sandberg's face, adorning the cover of her infamous bestseller, grinned out from where the book sat tucked, temporarily, in another crevice of the sculpture. The piece wasn't done, the artist explained, but we looked at it together anyway. We also looked at a model for Regen Projects, the gallery in Los Angeles that represents Harrison and will house this next

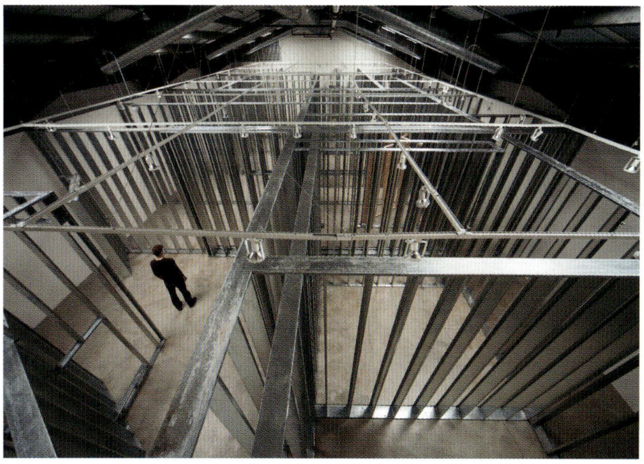

Michael Asher (American, 1943–2012). *Michael Asher* (installation view), Jan. 26–Apr. 12, 2008, Santa Monica Museum of Art. Photo © Grant Mudford.

endeavor, and discussed the layout she was considering. The artist planned to show sculpture but also to reorient viewers in the space using a tactic borrowed from Michael Asher's 2008 project at the Santa Monica Museum of Art, which consisted of the stud walls for all forty-four exhibitions that had been mounted in that space. The result was a labyrinthine construction that was barely navigable by viewers, who while not seeing the past shows, nonetheless experienced something of them. Harrison's evocation of Asher, however, will not address the prior life of art but something of its current state.

Hanging on the wall in her studio is a photograph of three young Asian women with a phone mounted on a long stick, huddled together to capture a group portrait. The picture is most notable for its placement online, where it illustrates the Wikipedia entry on the selfie stick. The caption reads, "Three tourists using a selfie stick to take a group portrait in Prague." One of the women holds her fingers out in a peace sign. Since I had not heard of selfie sticks until visiting Harrison's studio, I asked her what the connotation of the peace sign is. Harrison noted that the gesture is pervasive within tourist selfies and tantamount to a kind of empty sign of participation, reciprocating the camera's action of framing. In museums all over the world, selfie sticks are causing big problems as people back into artworks and each other. In L.A., Harrison's walls will frame a large space, within which her works will be placed. The Asher-inspired framework is then an artwork but also something other than that. It is a framing device that points beyond the footprint of the objects and asks viewers to consider their place in relation to them. It's worth noting, in this vein, that in 2014, at an exhibition with Liam Gillick at Galerie Meyer Kainer in Vienna, Harrison made her own interest in such framing explicit in yet another way, with five works. These were feats of sculptural ambivalence—heavy anchors that supported, or perhaps nailed down, barely-there sketches rendered in colored cord. Constitutionally at odds with his work, they nonetheless *rendered* something of Fred Sandback's legacy, placing it in the present while recognizing this as an impossible transplant.

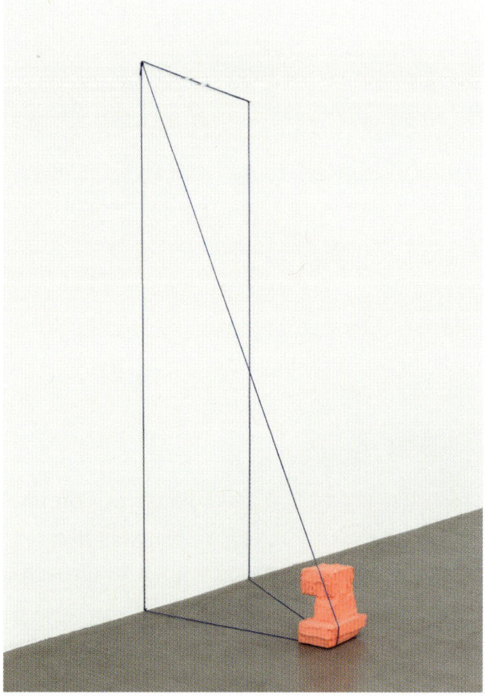

Rachel Harrison. *Framing Device (Pink)*, 2014. Wood, polystyrene, cement, acrylic, and parachute cord; 270 x 90 x 110 cm. Courtesy of the artist; Greene Naftali, New York; and Galerie Meyer Kainer, Vienna. Photo: Karl Kühn.

Fred Sandback (American, 1943–2003). *Untitled (Sculptural Study, Two-part Black Corner Construction)*, 1975/2008. Black acrylic yarn; 196.9 x 172.4 x 172.4 cm. Courtesy David Zwirner, New York/London. © 2015 Fred Sandback Archive.

In Andrea Fraser's 2005 essay "Why Does Fred Sandback's Work Make Me Cry?" she details her own affective relationship to the older artist's work. The text comprises both a formal reading of Sandback's work, which Fraser characterizes as "an art of absences, an art that's only just barely there to be seen," and an institutional one that places art, impossibly, both within and outside its own "field." In her conclusion, she considers her place alongside Sandback. "By removing himself to the extent he does," she writes of his barely-there sculpture, "he makes a place for me. It's not a place in front of his work, or next to his work, or inside his work (he once wrote that he aspired to make 'sculpture that didn't have an inside'). It makes a place for me inside the institution that the work is inside. It is a place that exists between fact and illusion, between reality and fantasy."[16]

Postscript

The title for this essay, "Say You Say Me," is not mine. It was first, and obviously, Lionel Richie's, in 1985.[17] Then it was put in as dummy text by Harrison and the designer of this book, Joseph Logan, because it was playing on the radio while they worked around an essay that was not yet written. When I saw the title, I knew what to write about: the negotiation of people and things pointing at other people and things across time and space and saying "you" in order to say "me." In other words, the content was delivered to me prior to my conceiving it. As Sherrie Levine once wrote, "I have the same relationship to van Gogh as Pierre Menard had to Miguel de Cervantes, that is to say, I have influenced him."[18]

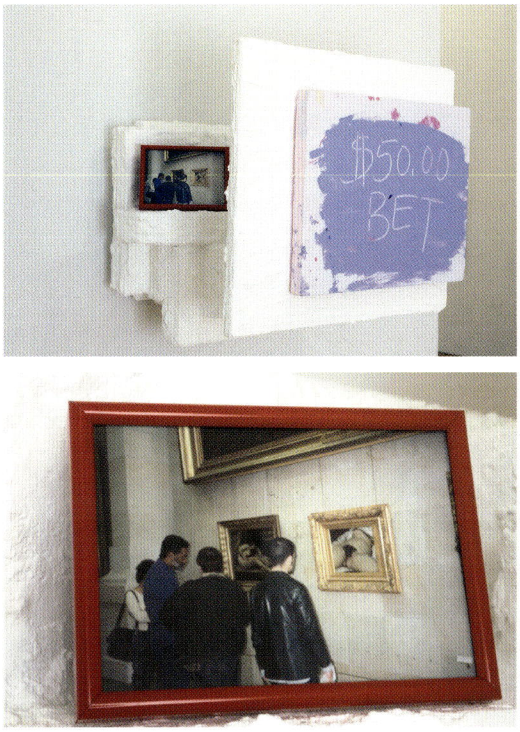

Rachel Harrison. *20 x 24" (for CDL)* (and detail), 1999. Wood, polystyrene, cement, acrylic, and chromogenic print; 55.9 x 48.3 x 45.7 cm. Courtesy of the artist and Greene Naftali, New York. Photo: Oren Slor.

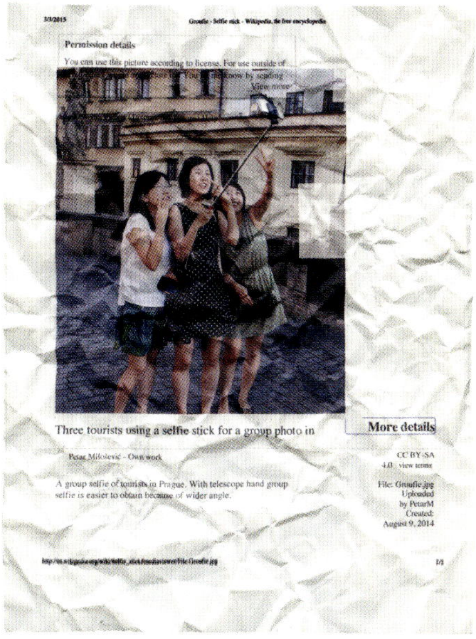

Rachel Harrison. Poster for an exhibition, 2015. Laser print on paper; 27.9 x 21.6 cm. Courtesy of the artist and Greene Naftali, New York. Photo: Rachel Harrison.

NOTES

1. See http://www.nashersculpturecenter.org/art/exhibitions/exhibition?id=28; accessed March 28, 2015. Nasher XChange included commissioned works by Lara Almarcegui, Rachel Harrison, Alfredo Jaar, Charles Long, Liz Larner, Rick Lowe, Vicki Meek, Ruben Ochoa, Ugo Rondinone, and Good/Bad Art Collective. Artists were encouraged to utilize all parts of the city in the hope that visitors would, in turn, experience areas they otherwise might not find themselves.

2. The most prevalent critique of Roosevelt's programs was that they were overtly propagandistic, designed to promote national pride at precisely a historical moment in which American citizens were being increasingly underserved by state and federal support.

3. See the mall's official website, http://www.northparkcenter.com/pages/northpark-photo-tour; accessed April 26, 2015.

4. Rachel Harrison, "Proposal for 'Nasher XChange,'" June 21, 2013.

5. Harrison, "Proposal."

6. Peter Schjeldahl, "The Shape We're In: The Timely Sculpture of Rachel Harrison," *New Yorker*, December 22/29, 2014, 70.

7. Schjeldahl, "The Shape We're In," 70.

8. David Joselit, "Touch to Begin…," in *Rachel Harrison: Museum with Walls*, ed. Eric Banks and Sarah Valdez, exh. cat. (Annandale-on-Hudson, NY: Center for Curatorial Studies, Bard College; London: Whitechapel Gallery; Frankfurt am Main: Portikus 2010), 188.

9. Joselit, "Touch to Begin…," 188.

10. See T. J. Clark, "In Defense of Abstract Expressionism," *October* 69 (Summer 1994): 22–48.

11. Diedrich Diederichsen, "Questions from an Abstraction Who Reads," in *Fake Titel: Rachel Harrison*, ed. Susanne Figner and Martin Germann, exh. cat. (Cologne: König, 2013), 74–78.

12. Diederichsen, "Questions from an Abstraction Who Reads," 78.

13. Diederichsen, "Questions from an Abstraction Who Reads," 78.

14. http://www.musee-orsay.fr/en/collections/works-in-focus/search/commentaire/commentaire_id/the-origin-of-the-world-3122.html; accessed April 26, 2015.

15. For a complete history of the painting, see Linda Nochlin, "Courbet's L'origine du monde: The Origin without an Origin," *October* 37 (Summer 1986): 76–86.

16. Andrea Fraser, "Why Does Fred Sandback's Work Make Me Cry?" *Grey Room* 22 (Winter 2005): 37–38, 45.

17. The title of Lionel Richie's song is "Say You, Say Me."

18. Sherrie Levine, 1998, unpublished statements given to the author. Also cited in Howard Singerman, "Sherrie Levine's Art History," *October* 101 (Summer 2002): 115. Singerman relays the quote as it was delivered during a Getty symposium held while Levine was a scholar in residence (2000–01).

Conversation

Amy Adler and Rachel Harrison

RACHEL HARRISON: You were asking me why I used an image of Hanson.

AMY ADLER: Yes.

RH: Other people like Hanson, and I'm interested in that fact. I'm interested in other people's interests.

AA: MMMBop.

RH: Can you sing a few bars?

AA: No, I can't sing.

RH: I was just as interested in the mirror as an object as who was on it, that mass-produced mirrors with boy bands exist. You look at them to look at yourself.

AA: I didn't realize it was a mirror. That's brilliant. I would really like to have that mirror in my house.

RH: I have a really good Donna Summer one, too. Do you like how the boys are leaning in, in the picture? Very Sheryl Sandberg.

AA: Very Carl Sandburg, especially with their long hair. I like how they're girl boys. Look at how pretty they are.

RH: I Googled them not long ago, to use them now in a collage, but they didn't turn out as pretty, and I felt bad for them.

AA: We should talk about Rauschenberg, and erasing, too, and regenerating.

RH: When I began to think about the show, I wanted to learn more about the work he made before *Gloria*, prior to the Combines. In addition to collages and assemblages, he made monochromes—black paintings, gold paintings, white paintings. He said the white paintings gave him the idea for *Erased de Kooning Drawing*. He wanted to create a void, to take everything out. And then after erasing he starts to make Combines, which is putting everything in. *Gloria* is an elegantly selective transition into complete excess. It's not as tidy a narrative as I'm making it, but that's the gist of it.

AA: There's a story about Jasper Johns, who said he destroyed all his work when he was still an unknown artist. And as soon as he did it, he had a dream in which he pictured himself painting the American flag; that's how the flags began. There's this idea of destroying stuff to create a space or a void that enables creativity—as you were saying about the Combines. Coming after the erasure, they're so crowded inside. It's everything. Getting rid of everything, Rauschenberg's now got everything in.

RH: *Erased de Kooning* was made in 1953; I recently read that 1954 is considered his breakthrough year. To me these timelines never make sense, since you are always working on your old and new work at the same time, but as with Johns, his erasure leads to a new sort of production. What he puts in can look arbitrary, but to me it always feels very personal, almost hidden because there's all this other stuff around it. Even in *Gloria*, you notice Gloria Vanderbilt, but you don't notice Virginia Jaspers right away. She's easy to miss.

AA: Or there's a risk of discounting the role of accident, too, which I'm sure was interesting to him.

RH: Yes, the paint feels like that, accidental. But if those two appeared on the same page and he used them, it's not an accident.

Anyway, for this book I wanted to use Photoshop—in a heavy-handed way—to further distance my own work from his Combines. Rauschenberg's use of materials is pure genius; I'm not interested in going there. These are simply files, they don't really exist.

Maybe the best way to explain it is I can't erase his *Bed* [1955; Museum of Modern Art, New York] in real space, but on the computer I can choose the eraser, set the size, and in one stroke it's gone, if that makes any sense.

AA: And the idea of making a mark against—in opposition to—something?

RH: Oh, it's not really for or against anything, and maybe that's what I mean: you can't make a grand single gesture today that has any real art-historical resonance. I think we're past that point. It could be because of the Internet or just that art has eaten its own tail. To make a singular gesture like *Erased de Kooning* wouldn't have the impact today that it did in the '50s.

AA: It's hard even to conceive of a work of art now that could both profoundly shock people as well as generate so much new work in the way that *Erased de Kooning* did.

RH: Well, I do wonder how much impact it had initially, outside a very small group of people. It wasn't exhibited until 1955 in a group drawing show that Johns was also part of. Wikipedia says it wasn't shown in public until 1963—that isn't true—but it is true its reputation grew after that time. Anyway, much later MoMA didn't want it. SFMOMA acquired it in 1998.

AA: Theodor Adorno said that art revolts against its essential concepts while at the same time being inconceivable without them. Is it possible this revolt has been too successful? Has the category of art become "inconceivable"? Maybe that self-questioning has reached a limit?

RH: We won't know until we see what comes next. Personally I'm interested in art that is in dialogue with other art, because I think that's really the only thing that defines it, that keeps it special and distinct from the rest of the world.

AA: What does that dialogue look like with the presence of those ghosts? It's kind of like Hanson in the mirror. There are the famous lines of Harold Bloom that weaker talents idealize, but strong poets wrestle with their strong precursors even to the death.

RH: You're always creating something in relationship to the past—you have to embrace it. Sometimes it works to show off the ghosts. [In *Hans Haacke with Sculpture*, p. 23] I scanned a picture of a Hans Haacke artwork with this idea in mind. It's two things at once: a picture of Ronald Reagan as well as *Oelgemaelde, Hommage à Marcel Broodthaers*. It's all embedded, the identifying gesture is itself a form of pointing.

AA: I like what Jorge Luis Borges said, that poets create their precursors.

RH: Johanna Burton told me this great thing Sherrie Levine said. I'm going to get it wrong, but basically it was that Rembrandt learned a lot from looking at her work.

AA: That's great. I don't know when she said it, but I assume it was in a pre-Internet moment.

RH: If she did, that's even more prophetic.

AA: I bet there will come a day when people are not going to know who came first or care, or at least that's the way the Internet feels. It's the way Google Images feels. I sense that disorientation when looking at your work. There are moments of that very contemporary feeling of the day on the screen.

RH: Oh, that's interesting, because I'm very material-based in my thinking. And I make stuff out of stuff.

AA: But here in this book you're creating works that exist just for the space of a book. Not objects. What does it mean for you as a sculptor?

RH: Something I got into was adjusting opacity. It was fun to think about it, like mixing records—you have to choose two great songs, but it's how it sounds that makes it work. Erasing an image of my work on top of a Rauschenberg and deciding how much visibility to retain. One bit of history comes forward or recedes, a bit like Rauschenberg sloshing paint all over a canvas. He's also adjusting the opacity in his own interest in the referent, because he's masking things, and he's painting over some things but leaving others revealed.

If you start looking at a lot of Combines, one of the things that Rauschenberg famously did is cross things out as well as circle stuff. Duchamp points, Rauschenberg circles, but he is also erasing additively by covering. Like that *Honeysuckle* painting we were looking at from 1956, I assume that the blue paint is covering something he doesn't want us to see.

AA: In looking at your own work, there's not a lot of closure for a viewer. It can be an uncomfortable space where meaning is in flux and things don't just settle down. There are many artists one can kind of sum up pretty quickly. I don't think that's easy to do with your work. And there's a sense of frustration, as with Rauschenberg. You're never fully satisfied as a viewer.

I thought it was really interesting that David Joselit talked about frustration, disconnection, and lack of meaning in your work. He said the objects seem always about to slip or fall. He also compared the experience of spectatorship in your work to a form of searching, like a search engine. Those weird juxtapositions seem somehow very familiar from our digital lives.

RH: Which to me is the opposite of the form of my work, which is primarily sculptural and therefore static.

AA: If you put in a search term for an image, the results can be surprising. There's a feeling of a loss of control, but it's not like you have no input. Aren't you a little stunned about what happens when you put in a term?

RH: Yeah, I typed "Rauschenberg black painting" into Google Images, and white paintings came up.

AA: So now not to lose the thread, one thing that came up for me in thinking about your work is your relationship to the readymade or appropriation. Joselit also identified that the objects in your work are not transformed. Transformation is forestalled, rejected. What's interesting is that "transformation" is the key word right now that courts insist on in evaluating whether art is original and worthy of being protected in the realm of copyright, when someone is working with the past. The way transformation is used by Joselit is exactly the opposite of what courts assume an artist is supposed to do to make it new. So I was curious what you thought about that.

RH: I'm not making cake batter. Here I turned a Rauschenberg into my sculpture by cutting and pasting, but I'm not really transforming anything. I'm showing all the parts. The geology, the strata are askew.

AA: Let's go back to *Erased de Kooning* and this question of how to deal with a dialogue that you're having not just with Rauschenberg but with art history. What are the different strategies to deal with that? I'm just thinking of erasing, reconstructing, appropriating, and layering, as you did, for example, with the elements on top of the red carpet in your sculpture *The Spoonbender* (2011).

RH: Not appropriation—I'm not thinking about those ideas directly, even though they are obviously there. I'm not sure I'm thinking strategically either, the way both artists did with *Erased de Kooning*. When he chose the work to give Rauschenberg, de Kooning said it had to be a good drawing, so it would have more meaning. That's strategy. He chose something that was hard to part with.

AA: And also hard to erase.

RH: Exactly. A lot of lines and different materials. He wanted to make it challenging for him. It's a very macho thing to do.

AA: The whole story is.

RH: Rauschenberg said he worked a month on it, so he also made a big deal of the labor involved. Knocking on the door with a bottle of Jack Daniel's, the whole thing. This isn't something I could do as a woman, certainly not then. Something else interesting is that neither artist documented the drawing before it got erased; that would never happen today. Today our world is over-documented, all part of that big data.

AA: Along those lines, a lot of people think that art should never be modified but should instead be preserved exactly as the artist intended it. This is the idea behind moral rights. It stems from two different principles. One is that there's some kind of transcendent connection between the artist and the work that can never be disrupted. The artist is always in his work (I use "his" advisedly because it's a very masculine concept). The artist should control his work to protect it from modification or destruction even after he's sold it.

But there's another idea that animates our instinct that art should never be modified, too, and that's this idea that art is like a precious resource for all of us. The public owns it, not just the artist, all of us. If we allowed the destruction of an artwork, it would be like losing the bald eagle or an endangered species. But as painful as it is, I think that misses the creative possibilities of destruction and loss, as Rauschenberg showed us with *Erased de Kooning*.

RH: That's interesting.

AA: So in your case, you're not hurting the actual image but reckoning with the past. Yet you're modifying it in a way that might be seen as irreverent to this legacy.

RH: I certainly don't mean it as irreverent. I think it's funny.

AA: There seems to be some level of chutzpah, for lack of a better term, to take your own past, as in the Photoshopped air freshener cans from your 2009 exhibition at Bard, and put it on top of *Canyon* (see pp. 20–21).

RH: That's part of your interest in moral rights?

AA: Yes, because it misses the ways in which we may want to create things by modifying or destroying the past. That key moment of creativity, that moment of erasure that Rauschenberg understands or that moment of you imposing yourself into the past. Preservation would miss the importance of destruction and modification as a means of creativity and could stifle us.

RH: I like that impulse, but I don't quite understand it. Don't we need the original for the copy to exist? We need to protect what artists make, maybe even more so if it is so easy to re-create artworks.

AA: But does the proliferation of copies make the original less important or more? How should we think about the possibility of infinite reproduction? Even *Canyon* can be scanned and re-created—maybe not now, but eventually, with the capacity of 3D printing.

RH: The replication of that object would be very difficult even with the best conservators and craftsmen in the world to re-create it. You're talking about the DNA of an animal, but also the fact that Rauschenberg used the bald eagle decades before it had become an endangered species: you can't fake that authenticity.

AA: Two different thoughts. One is that the historical specificity you're describing is also something that we're losing by the leveling of culture that we've been talking about—

RH: But we're not losing it entirely, not at all.

AA: We're not?

RH: Who's buried in Grant's Tomb? Historical specificity exists in real space, you are just talking about the Internet. We don't live there, yet.

AA: Right. There's something else though. It comes up in copyright law or disputes over authenticity or preservation or any other place where we have to think about the relationship between copies and the original in a world in which copying has become so easy and pervasive. I think there are two possibilities. One is the familiar view that copies would ultimately destroy the original or destroy its importance. But there might be another view, that this proliferation of copying actually increases our desire to worship at the altar of the real. That it makes the real even more desirable because it's so scarce, because we're losing our relationship to it, and because we know the difference.

RH: I vote for the altar of the real—that works for me.

AA: I'm also wondering about the ways in which we can think about you as a woman artist or not. There are many ways in which the fact that you're doing this work as a woman is really not legible necessarily in the work.

RH: It's not clearly visible?

AA: No. Once I think about it, I find gender is a really interesting story, but I don't think it's so clear how it figures in your artwork. I used to teach feminist jurisprudence and so I'm particularly curious about how your identity as a woman artist might enter your work.

RH: Was there a gender balance in the classroom?

AA: No. At some point I changed the title of the course from "Feminism" to "Gender Jurisprudence" because feminism in itself is in some ways a dated and insufficiently capacious term. I did get more men when I changed the title. But still, in terms of my reputation as an academic, either title identified me as being interested in a "soft" topic, right? A topic that wasn't where the boys were. Even if I was doing good work within it, I was still doing good work in a ghetto. And so I took a break from working in it.

RH: Was the class about gender discrimination?

AA: No, it was more theoretical. But it was an area of concern that I thought was marking me in a way that I didn't want to be marked. I wanted my work to be more than simply that. Yet it's inescapable that I'm working as a woman academic.

RH: I can relate to everything you've just said. You've seen it in my work because you identified it in yourself as well.

AA: It sucks because it's a constraint. You're already wondering about your place at the table, and then you have to worry about whether calling attention to the fact that you're worried about it is going to further marginalize you. It's a weird double bind.

RH: Yes, absolutely. And it's inescapable. It's our history. You know, it might be hard for younger artists today to comprehend that Jasper Johns and Rauschenberg could not really be out, even as artists. Maybe it's important for us to identify our time.

Checklist of the Exhibition

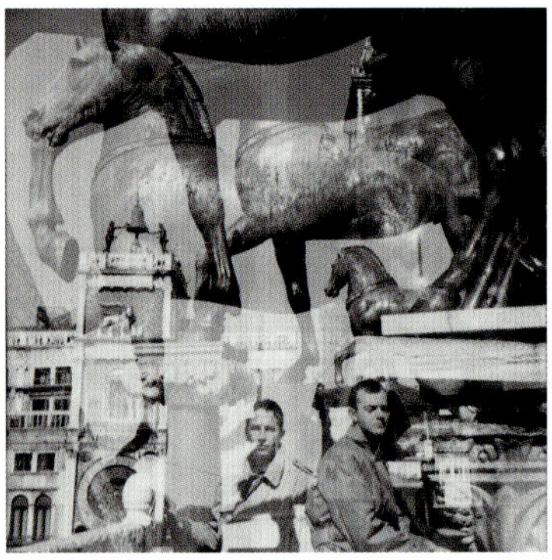

Robert Rauschenberg
Bob + Cy, Venice, 1952
Gelatin silver print
38.1 x 38.1 cm
Robert Rauschenberg Foundation
© Robert Rauschenberg Foundation/Licensed by VAGA, New York, NY
[p. 75]

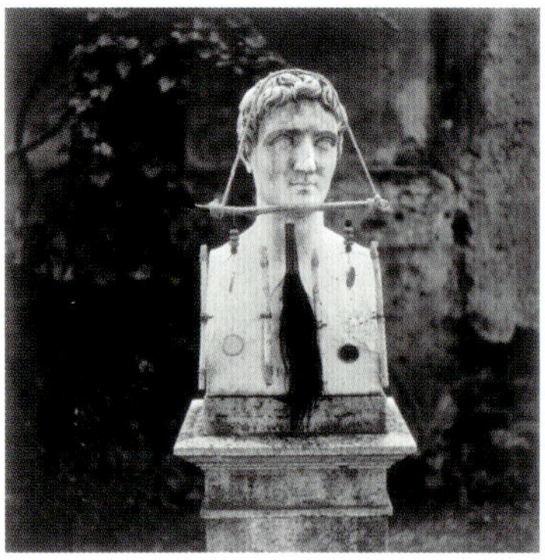

Robert Rauschenberg
Untitled [Feticcio Personale, Rome], 1953
Gelatin silver print
38.1 x 38.1 cm
Robert Rauschenberg Foundation
© Robert Rauschenberg Foundation/Licensed by VAGA, New York, NY
[p. 73]

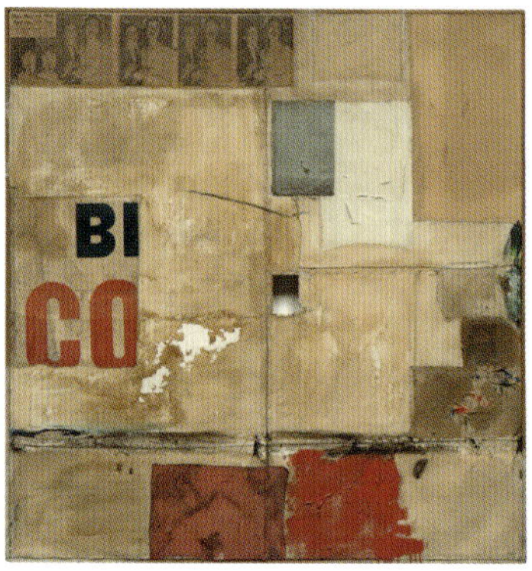

Robert Rauschenberg
Gloria, 1956
Oil, fabric, staples, newspaper, graphite on paper, printed paper, and printed reproduction on canvas
170.5 x 163.4 cm
The Cleveland Museum of Art, Gift of the Cleveland Society for Contemporary Art 1966.333
© Robert Rauschenberg Foundation/Licensed by VAGA, New York, NY
Image © The Cleveland Museum of Art
[pp. 2, 10, 44, 102]

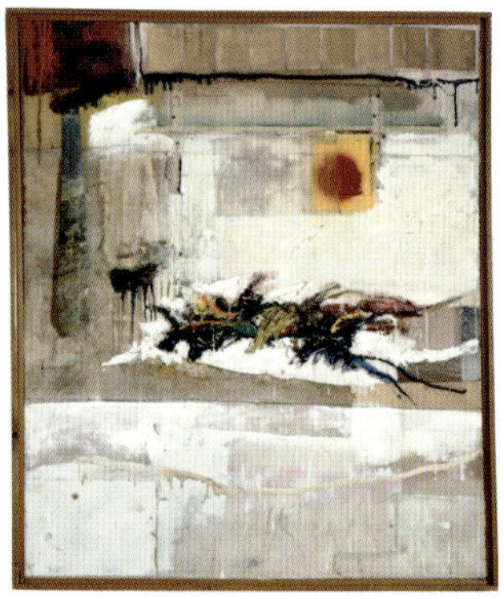

Robert Rauschenberg
Rhyme, 1956
Oil, fabric, paper, enamel, pencil, and synthetic polymer on canvas with necktie
122.5 x 104.5 cm
Fractional and promised gift of Agnes Gund in honor of Richard E. Oldenburg to the Museum of Modern Art, New York
© Robert Rauschenberg Foundation/Licensed by VAGA, New York, NY
Image © The Museum of Modern Art/Licensed by SCALA/Art Resource, New York
[pp. 4, 53, 55]

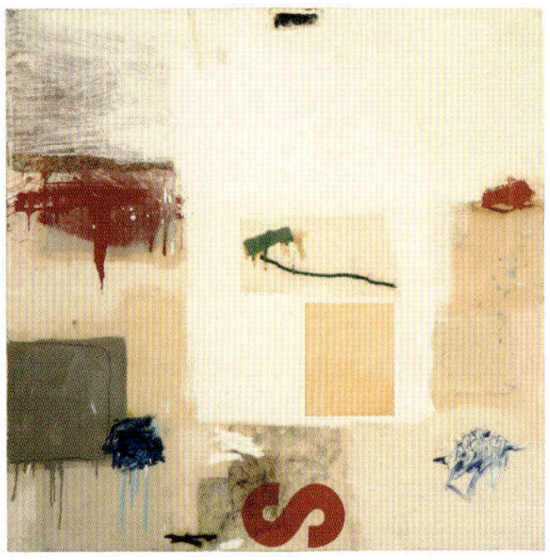

Robert Rauschenberg
Painting with Red Letter S, 1957
Oil, paper, printed paper, and fabric on canvas
128.3 x 132.1 cm
Collection of Albright-Knox Art Gallery, Buffalo, New York, Gift of Seymour H. Knox, Jr. 1959
© Robert Rauschenberg Foundation/Licensed by VAGA, New York, NY
[p. 45]

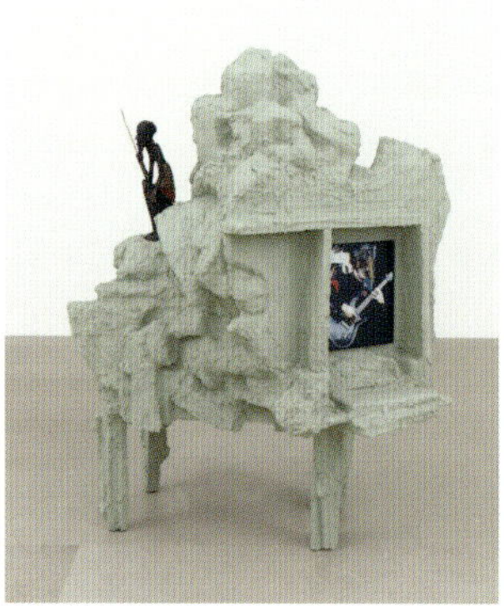

Rachel Harrison
Slipknot, 2002
Wood, chicken wire, polystyrene, cement, acrylic, chromogenic print, and wooden African figure
137.2 x 55.9 x 91.4 cm
Collection of Scott J. Lorinsky
Courtesy of the artist and Greene Naftali, New York
Photo: Elisabeth Bernstein
[pp. 32–33, 35, 37–38, 40–41, 65]

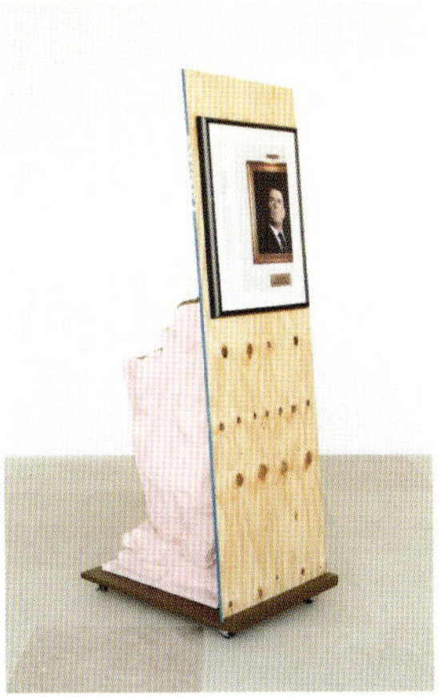

Rachel Harrison
Hans Haacke with Sculpture, 2005
Wood, chicken wire, polystyrene, cement, acrylic, wheels, and pigmented inkjet print of *Oelgemaelde, Hommage à Marcel Broodthaers* (1982) by Hans Haacke (German, act. U.S., b. 1936)
190.5 x 61 x 78.7 cm
Courtesy of the artist and Greene Naftali, New York
Photo: Elisabeth Bernstein
[pp. 23, 39, 48–52, 65]

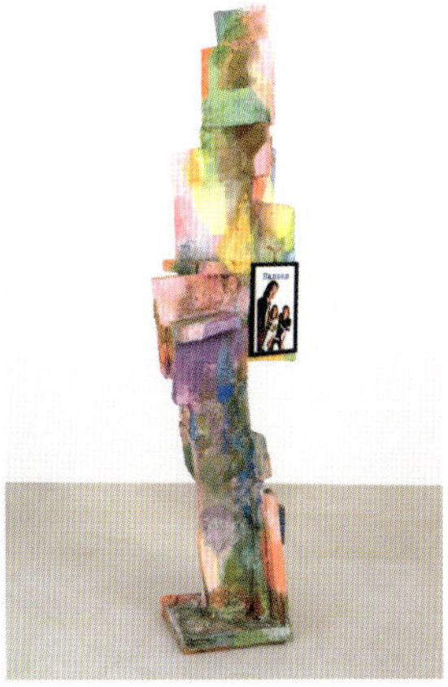

Rachel Harrison
Stella 1, 2006
Wood, polystyrene, cement, acrylic, and mirror
219.7 x 55.9 x 68.6 cm
Hort Family Collection
Courtesy of the artist and Greene Naftali, New York
Photo: Jean Vong
[pp. 22, 25, 105]

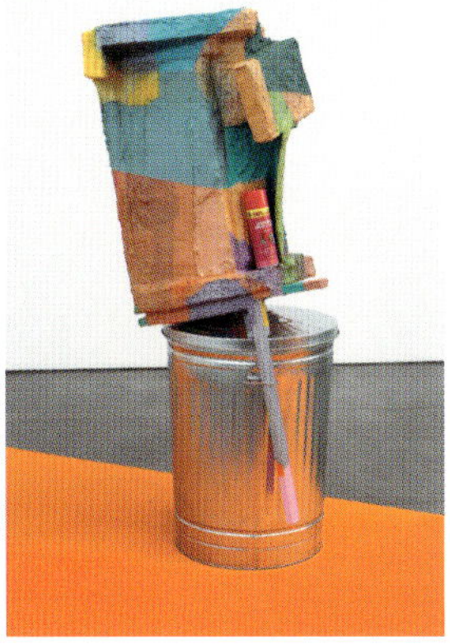

Rachel Harrison
Legitimo, 2012
Wood, polystyrene, cement, acrylic, metal can, aerosol can, and runway carpet
Sculpture: 166.4 x 74.9 x 63.5 cm; overall dimensions variable
Private collection
Courtesy of the artist and Greene Naftali, New York
Photo: John Berens
[pp. 84, 87, 91]

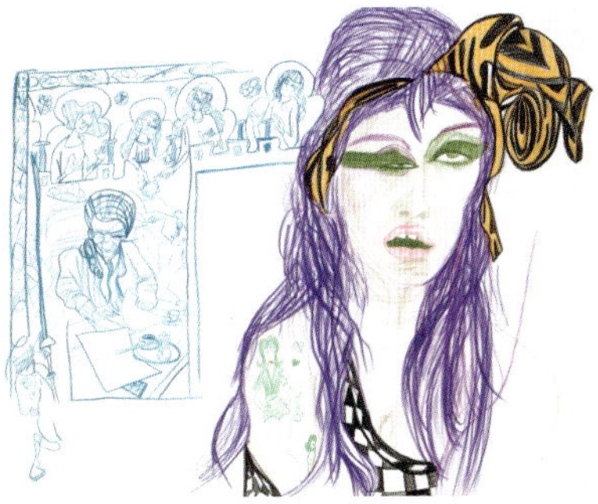

Rachel Harrison
Untitled, 2011
Colored pencil on paper; 56.8 x 70.8 cm
Collection of Sascha S. Bauer
Courtesy of the artist and Greene Naftali, New York
Photo: John Berens
[p. 27]

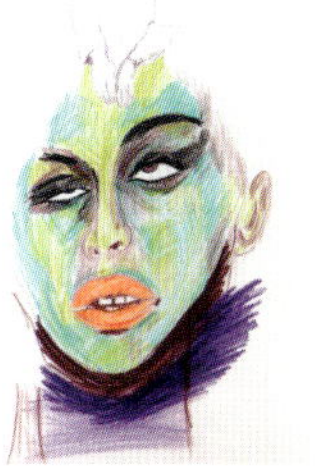

Rachel Harrison
Untitled, 2011
Colored pencil on paper; 56.8 x 70.8 cm
Private collection, New York
Courtesy of the artist and Greene Naftali, New York
Photo: Jason Mandella
[p. 19]

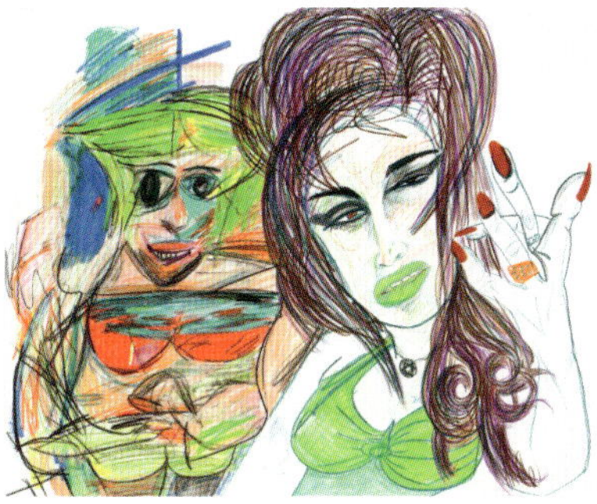

Rachel Harrison
Untitled, 2012
Colored pencil on paper; 56.8 x 70.8 cm
Private collection, New York
Courtesy of the artist and Greene Naftali, New York
Photo: John Berens
[pp. 76–77, 98–99]

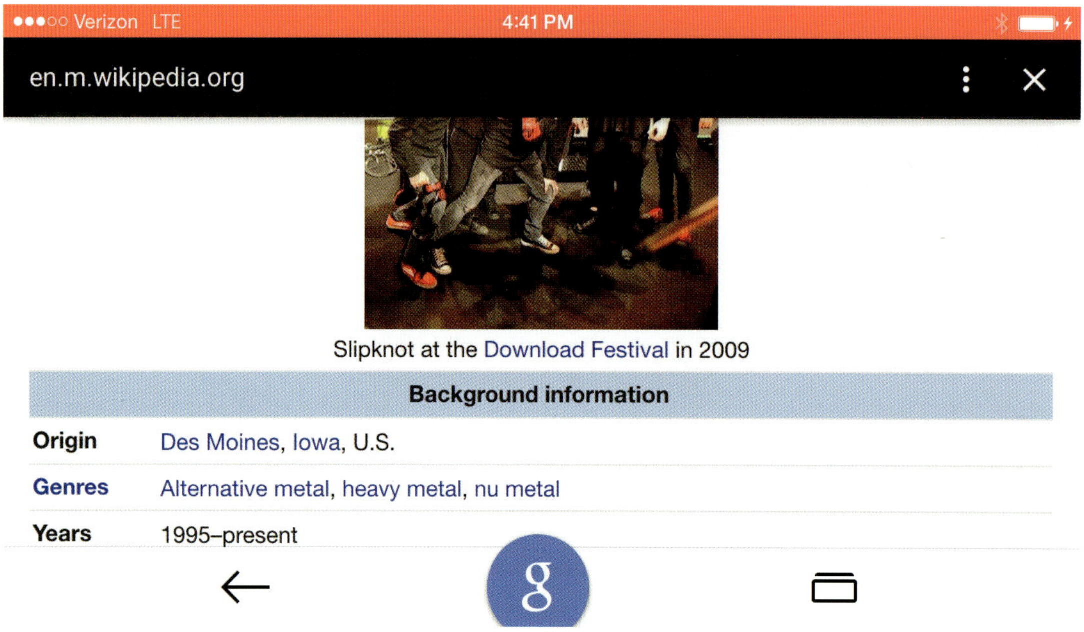

●●●○○ Verizon LTE
4:41 PM
en.m.wikipedia.org
Slipknot at the Download Festival in 2009
Background information
Origin Des Moines, Iowa, U.S.
Genres Alternative metal, heavy metal, nu metal
Years 1995–present
g

Contributors

Robert Rauschenberg

Robert Rauschenberg (1925–2008) was an artist whose practice encompassed media from painting and drawing to performance and printmaking. He studied under Josef Albers at Black Mountain College, where he met future collaborators John Cage and Merce Cunningham. His early work from the 1950s, especially the Combine series, is known for its engagement with the ethos of the early twentieth-century Dada movement while anticipating Pop Art. Rauschenberg's practice also veered into dance and technology; in 1966 he founded Experiments in Art and Technology with Billy Klüver. In 1984 he announced the Rauschenberg Overseas Culture Interchange, a seven-year tour of exhibitions and art making across ten countries. The artist's work, which resides in museums and private collections around the world, has been presented in numerous exhibitions, notably *Robert Rauschenberg: A Retrospective* (1997) and *Robert Rauschenberg: Combines* (2005), which traveled to venues throughout the United States and Europe.

Rachel Harrison

Rachel Harrison (b. 1966) lives and works in Brooklyn. Her art has been the subject of numerous recent solo exhibitions, including those at S.M.A.K. (Ghent, 2013); Kestnergesellschaft (Hannover, 2013); Whitechapel Gallery (London, 2010); Portikus (Frankfurt, 2009); and CCS Bard/Hessel Museum of Art (Annandale-on-Hudson, New York, 2009). Harrison's work was included in the 2003 and 2009 Venice Biennales and the 2002 and 2008 Whitney Biennials. It is represented in the collections of the Museum of Modern Art, New York; the Metropolitan Museum of Art, New York; the Solomon R. Guggenheim Museum, New York; the Whitney Museum of American Art, New York; the Art Institute of Chicago; the Philadelphia Museum of Art; the Museum of Contemporary Art, Los Angeles; the Walker Art Center, Minneapolis; Centre Georges Pompidou, Paris; Tate Modern, London; the Museum Ludwig, Cologne; and the Stedelijk Museum, Amsterdam, among many others. Harrison was the recipient of the 2011 Calder Prize and the 2010 Herb Alpert Award in Visual Arts.

Beau Rutland

Beau Rutland is Assistant Curator of Contemporary Art at the Cleveland Museum Art, where he curated *Anicka Yi: Death* (2014), the first solo museum exhibition of Yi's work, as well as a reinstallation of the permanent collection galleries devoted to contemporary art. He has also helped expand the institution's collection of contemporary art, acquiring pieces by Yi, Robert Morris, and Martin Wong, among others. Rutland, who has worked at the Whitney Museum of American Art, holds a masters degree from Columbia University in the history of modern art. He is a frequent contributor to *Artforum*, and his writing has also appeared in *Flash Art*, *Kaleidoscope*, and various exhibition catalogues.

Johanna Burton

Johanna Burton is Keith Haring Director and Curator of Education and Public Engagement at the New Museum in New York City. She is also an art historian, critic, and curator whose articles and reviews have appeared in numerous journals and publications such as *Artforum*, *Art Journal*, *October*, and *Texte zur Kunst* as well as in exhibition catalogues for institutions throughout the world.

Burton has curated or co-curated exhibitions including *Sherrie Levine: Mayhem* (2011); *Anti-Establishment* (2012); *Take It Or Leave It: Institution, Image, Ideology* (2013); and *XFR STN* (2013). She served as Director of the Graduate Program at the Center for Curatorial Studies at Bard College (2010–13) and Associate Director and Senior Faculty Member at the Whitney Independent Study Program (2008–10).

Amy Adler

Amy Adler is the Emily Kempin Professor of Law at New York University School of Law, where she specializes in the legal regulation of artistic expression. Her scholarship focuses on the intersection of law and culture, drawing on an array of fields, primarily from the arts and humanities. Adler's recent work has addressed issues including the moral rights of artists, the impact of postmodernism on obscenity law, and the hidden iconoclastic roots of the modern legal treatment of the visual. She has lectured about art and law to a wide variety of audiences, from attorneys general, to psychoanalysts, to the FBI. Adler has also acted as a consultant or expert witness in high-profile art cases, including the recent Richard Prince copyright litigation.

Acknowledgments

Many people put their time, thought, and energy into the exhibition *Gloria: Robert Rauschenberg & Rachel Harrison*, which has been in the works since I first started at the Cleveland Museum of Art in October 2013. Reto Thüring, Associate Curator of Contemporary Art and the most gracious boss I can imagine, was supportive from the start, and this project would not have been possible without him. The help and encouragement of the museum's leadership was also fundamental. Heidi Strean, Director of Exhibitions and Publications, was willing to give this exhibition and catalogue the support it needed; Deborah Gribbon, Interim Deputy Director of Collections, Education, and Performing Arts, was always quick to offer wise counsel; and William M. Griswold, Sarah S. and Alexander M. Cutler Director, gracefully shepherded this project into being soon after arriving at the museum. The unwavering support of the Robert Rauschenberg Foundation improved our work in infinite ways.

I am also indebted to many of my fellow staff members. First and foremost, Emily Mears, Exhibitions Specialist, deserves my deepest gratitude for her diplomacy and her willingness to make the never-happened-before happen. Jeffrey Strean, Director of Design and Architecture, offered helpful aesthetic guidance. Per Knutås, Eric and Jane Nord Chief Conservator, was crucial in bringing these fragile artworks into public view. I am also grateful to Barbara J. Bradley, Editor-in-Chief; Rachel Beamer, Image Acquisitions and Permissions Coordinator; Mark Cole, Curator of American Painting and Sculpture; Robin Koch, Curatorial Assistant; Amy Andersson, Assistant Registrar for Special Exhibitions; Mary Suzor, Director of Collections Management; Andrew Gutierrez, Exhibition Designer; and the museum's intrepid art handlers Barry Austin, Arthur Beukemann, Joseph Blaser, Tony Cisneros, Shawn Kerns, and Andrew Robinson. Thanks go as well to Matthew Gengler, Head of Access Services at the museum's Ingalls Library, and Alexander Penn, 2014 Warshawsky Fellow, for their invaluable research assistance.

This exhibition and publication are the result of closely collaborating with Rachel Harrison, and I am thankful to have had her as a partner in crime, thinking through the project, Rauschenberg's work, her work, and many other issues along the way. Johanna Burton, whose writing I have long admired, was eager to contribute to the catalogue and delivered a beautiful and insightful essay. Thanks also to Amy Adler for providing such an intriguing entryway into Harrison's work through their conversation. This book would not have been possible without the diligent effort and keen eye of designer Joseph Logan and editor Greg Nosan. Many heartfelt thanks to Carol Greene, who championed this show from the beginning. And thank you to Greene Naftali, New York, especially Linda Yun and Martha Fleming-Ives, for their insight and assistance in navigating Harrison's incredible output, as well as Eric Banks, Bob Monk, Christy MacLear, David White, David Joselit, Chris Calhoun, Shaun Caley Regen, Christian Meyer, and Renate Kainer.

I would also like to acknowledge those who helped shape this exhibition through support, inspiration, and wisdom of all kinds: Jenny Borland, Joe Coscarelli, Gaylen Gerber, Zara Golden, Camilla Hammer, Richard Hawkins, Tim and Debbie Hoelle, Branden Joseph, Cory Korkow, Michelle Kuo, Knight Landesman, Jane Rosenblum, Scott Rothkopf, Kristen and Melissa Rutland, Franziska Widmer, Zachary Woolfe, and Anicka Yi.

B. R.

The Cleveland Museum of Art
Board of Trustees

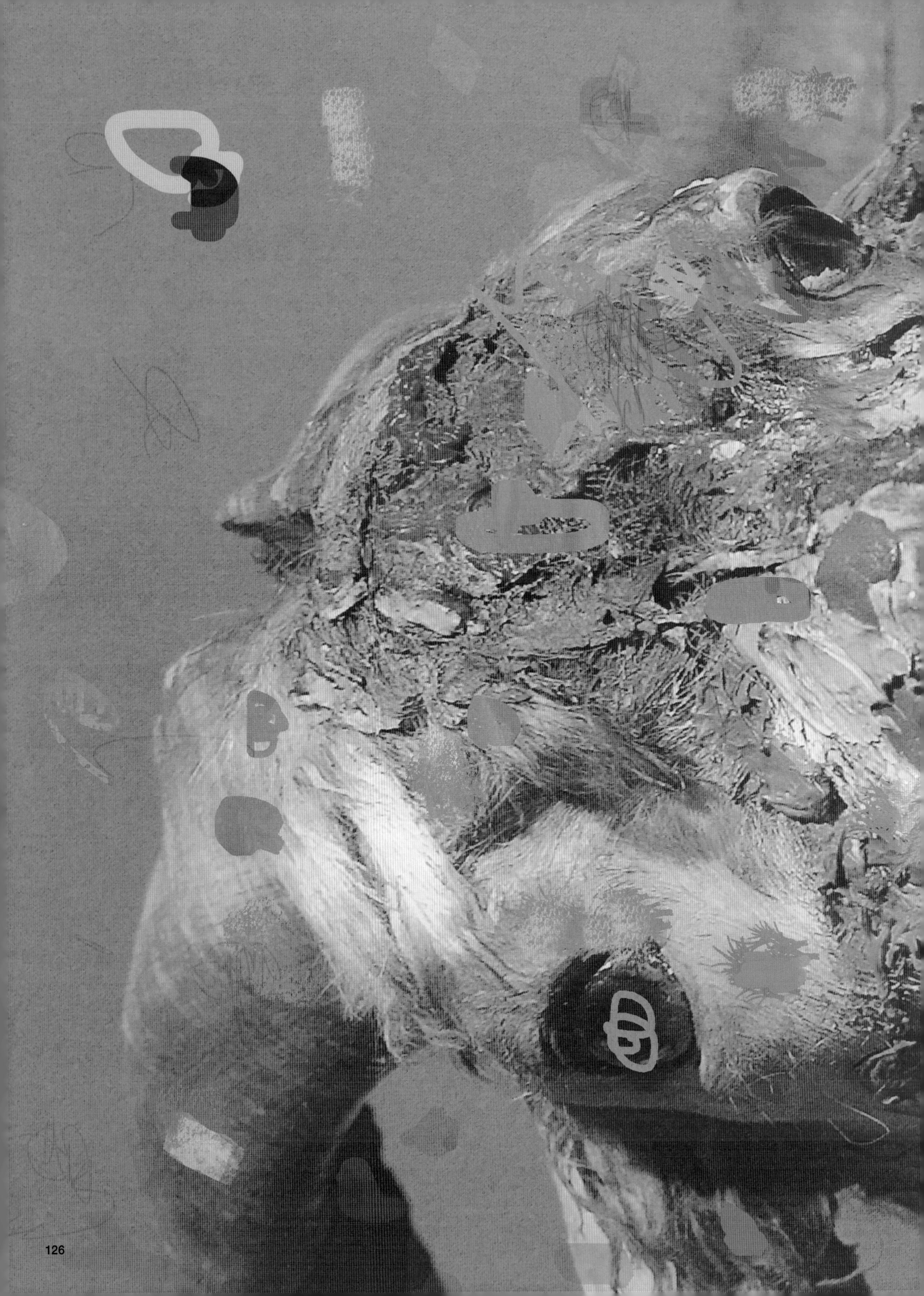

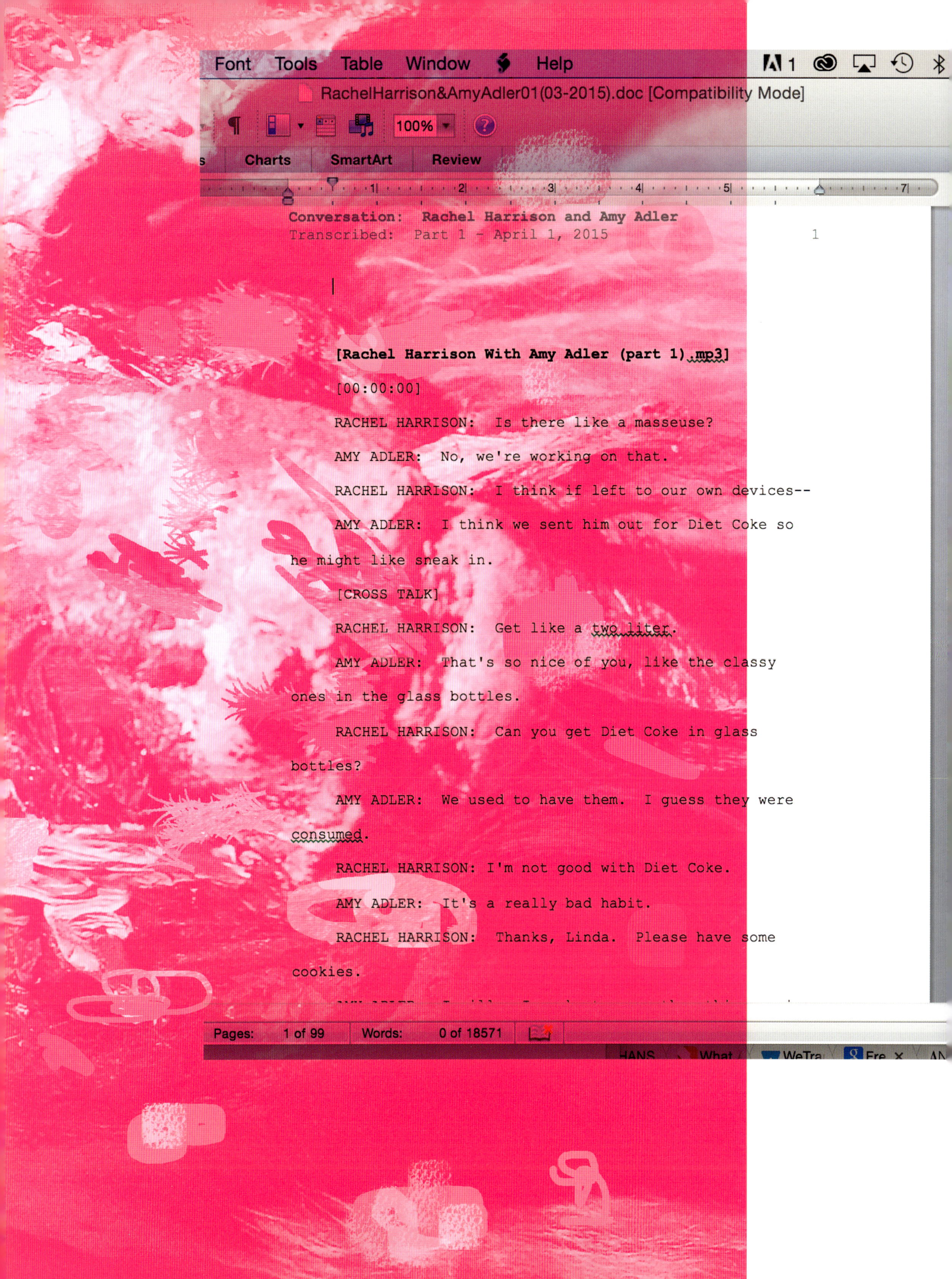

Conversation: Rachel Harrison and Amy Adler
Transcribed: Part 1 - April 1, 2015 1

[Rachel Harrison With Amy Adler (part 1).mp3]

[00:00:00]

RACHEL HARRISON: Is there like a masseuse?

AMY ADLER: No, we're working on that.

RACHEL HARRISON: I think if left to our own devices--

AMY ADLER: I think we sent him out for Diet Coke so he might like sneak in.

[CROSS TALK]

RACHEL HARRISON: Get like a two liter.

AMY ADLER: That's so nice of you, like the classy ones in the glass bottles.

RACHEL HARRISON: Can you get Diet Coke in glass bottles?

AMY ADLER: We used to have them. I guess they were consumed.

RACHEL HARRISON: I'm not good with Diet Coke.

AMY ADLER: It's a really bad habit.

RACHEL HARRISON: Thanks, Linda. Please have some cookies.

Published on the occasion of the exhibition
Gloria: Robert Rauschenberg & Rachel Harrison, July 1 to October 25, 2015,
organized by Beau Rutland at the Cleveland Museum of Art.

The Cleveland Museum of Art is generously funded by Cuyahoga County residents through Cuyahoga Arts and Culture. The Ohio Arts Council helps fund the museum with state dollars to encourage economic growth, educational excellence, and cultural enrichment for all Ohioans.

Support for this catalogue is provided by Greene Naftali, New York,
and the Andrew W. Mellon Foundation.

ISBN: 978-0-300-21596-0
Library of Congress Control Number: 2015938107

Cover: Digital collage by Rachel Harrison with works by Robert Rauschenberg including an image of *Canyon,* 1959 (original digital image © The Museum of Modern Art/Licensed by SCALA/Art Resource, NY).
Page 4: Curator's photo of the exhibition catalogue *Robert Rauschenberg: Combines* (Los Angeles: Museum of Contemporary Art, 2005). Original photograph by Shunk-Kender. The Getty Research Institute, Los Angeles (2014.R.20), Gift of the Roy Lichtenstein Foundation in memory of Harry Shunk and Janos Kender. Image © J. Paul Getty Trust.
Pages 19–107, 122, 126–27: *Heir Fresheners*, 2015. Rachel Harrison. Digital collages. © Rachel Harrison. Courtesy of the artist and Greene Natfali, New York.

Prepared by the Exhibitions and Publications department of the Cleveland Museum of Art, Heidi Strean, director, Emily Mears, exhibitions specialist, and Barbara J. Bradley, editor-in-chief
Edited by Greg Nosan
Designed by Joseph Logan and Rachel Harrison with the assistance of Rachel Hudson
Printed and bound by The Avery Group at Shapco Printing, Inc., Minneapolis

The Cleveland Museum of Art
11150 East Boulevard
Cleveland, OH 44106-1797
www.ClevelandArt.org

Distributed by Yale University Press
302 Temple Street
P.O. Box 209040
New Haven, CT 06520-9040
www.yalebooks.com/art

cuyahoga arts & culture

50 years 1965-2015 Ohio Arts Council